Legal Aspects of Death

Legal Aspects of Death

by

Bridgit Dimond

MA, LLB, DSA, AHSM, Barrister-at-law

Emeritus Professor of the University of Glamorgan

CBS

CBS PUBLISHERS & DISTRIBUTORS

NEW DELHI • BANGALORE • PUNE (INDIA)

CBS Publishers ISBN : 978-81-239-1757-3
Quay Books ISBN : 978-1-85642-333-5

First Indian Reprint : 2009

Authorised reprint from the English language edition published by Quay Books, a division of MA Healthcare, London

Published by Satish Kumar Jain and produced by Vinod K. Jain for
CBS Publishers & Distributors,
4819/XI Prahlad Street, 24 Ansari Road, Daryaganj, New Delhi - 110 002, India.
e-mail: cbspubs@vsnl.com, cbspubs@airtelmail.in
Website: www.cbspd.com

Branches:

- Seema House, 2975, 17th Cross, K.R. Road,
  Bansankari 2nd Stage, Bangalore - 560 070
  Fax: 080-26771680 • e-mail: cbsbng@dataone.in
- Shaan Brahmha Complex, Basement, Appa Balwant Chowk,
  Budhwar Peth, Next to Ratan Talkies, Pune - 411 002
  Fax: 020-24464059 • e-mail: pune@cbspd.com

Printed at :
Chaman Offset, Delhi (India)

Contents

Preface

Like the other books in this series, this monograph follows the publication of a series of articles in the *British Journal of Nursing* on the law relating to death. Those articles, revised and updated, form the basis of a concise publication covering the main concerns which arise in the law relating to deaths in the NHS and private sector.

This book, like the others in this series, is intended for all health professionals who are likely to be involved in caring for dying patients whether in hospitals or in the community. It should also be of assistance to others such as health service managers, to lecturers and clinical supervisors, patient groups and their representatives and individuals who need to understand the legal consequences of death. Each chapter uses a situation to illustrate the relevant laws so that the law can be explained in a practical jargon-free way. The basic facts of the legal system are briefly set out in the first chapter. The book does not pretend to be encyclopaedic in its coverage, rather it is intended to introduce readers to the basic principles which apply and the sources of law, so that they can, by following up the further reading and websites provided add to their knowledge. Changes in the statutory provisions and new cases will require some amendments over time. The recommendations from the Inquiry following the Shipman case are only gradually being introduced and this book covers the progress so far and the reforms that are still to be initiated. It is hoped that this book will provide a baseline upon which readers can develop their knowledge and understanding of the law relating to death.

It is the intention that the chapters will lay the foundation for an understanding of the legal implications of the many issues that can arise when a person dies. At that critical time, it is essential that health and social services professionals, managers, relatives and others have an understanding of the laws which apply and can carry out their duties with a sensitivity and awareness of the different facets of the situation. Inevitably there will be changes as the new coroner's legislation is brought into existence and implemented, as new cases set judicial precedents for the future and as new Department of Health and professional guidance is published. It is hoped that future editions of this book will be able to track such developments and that it will continue to be a resource for professionals and lay persons alike.

Glossary

Accusatorial:	a system of court proceedings where the two sides contest the issue (cf. *inquisitorial*)
Act:	of Parliament, *statute*
Action:	legal proceedings
Actionable *per se:*	a court action where the claimant does not have to show loss, damage or harm to obtain compensation, eg. an action for *trespass to the person*
Actus reus:	the essential element of a crime which must be proved to secure a conviction, as opposed to the mental state of the accused (*mens rea*)
Adversarial:	the approach adopted in an *accusatorial* system
Advocate:	a person who pleads for another: it could be paid and professional, such as a *barrister* or *solicitor*, or it could be a lay advocate either paid or unpaid; a witness is not an advocate
Affidavit	a statement given under oath
Alternative dispute:	methods to resolve a dispute without going to court such as dispute resolution
Altruistic donation:	a form of non-directed living donation, where a kidney is donated by a healthy person without that person being told who the recipient will be
Anatomical examination:	macroscopic examination by dissection for anatomical purposes
Anatomical specimen:	the body of a deceased person to be used for the purpose of anatomical examination, or the body of a deceased person in the course of being used for the purpose of anatomical examination (including separated parts of such a body). A former anatomical specimen is an organ or body part donated for anatomical examination which is retained once the examination of the rest of the body has been completed
Anatomist:	an expert in *anatomy*
Anatomy:	the science of the structure and organisation of the living body and its parts
Anonymised:	a procedure to ensure that if material is removed

	from a body, all necessary steps are taken to avoid identifying the person from whose body the material has come
Appellate court:	a court that hears appeals from lower courts, eg. Court of Appeal and House of Lords
Appropriate consent:	defined in the Human Tissue Act by reference to the person who may give consent, with a 'nominated representative' provided for, who may make decisions about regulated activities after a person's death
Autologous use:	cells or tissue removed from and transplanted into the same person
Autopsy:	a *post-mortem* examination
Barrister:	a lawyer qualified to take a case in court
Battery:	an unlawful touching (see *trespass to the person*)
Bench:	the magistrates, *Justice of the Peace*
Biopsy:	a procedure where tissue is removed from a living body for examination under a microscope.
Bolam Test:	the test laid down by Judge McNair in the case of *Bolam v. Friern HMC* on the standard of care expected of a professional in cases of alleged *negligence*
Bona fide:	in good faith
Breach:	breaking, usually of a legal duty
Burden of proof:	the duty of a party to litigation to establish the facts, or in criminal proceedings the duty of the prosecution to establish both the *actus reus* and the *mens rea*
Case citation:	the reference to an earlier reported case made possible because of the reference system, eg. *1981 1 All ER 267* means the first volume of the *All England Reports* for 1981 at page 267 which is the reference for the case of *Whitehouse v. Jordan*, where Whitehouse is the *plaintiff* (*claimant*), Jordan the defendant and 'v' stands for versus, ie. against. Other law reports include: *AC Appeals Court; QB Queens Bench Division; WLR Weekly Law Reports; EWCA England and Wales Court of Appeal*
Cause of action:	the facts that entitle a person to sue
Cells:	individual human cells or a collection of human cells when not bound by any form of connective tissue
Certiorari:	an action taken to challenge an administrative or judicial decision (literally: to make more certain)

Civil action: proceedings brought in the civil courts

Civil wrong: an act or omission which can be pursued in the civil courts by the person who has suffered the wrong (see *torts*)

Claimant: the person bringing a civil action (originally *plaintiff*)

Clinical: based on, or involving, direct examination and care of patients

Clinical audit: a quality improvement process that seeks to improve patient care and outcomes through systematic review of care against explicit criteria. Stored tissue previously needed for diagnosis, for example, may need to be reviewed as part of this process

Clinical diagnosis: process where a disease is identified from medical history taking, diagnostic tests and physical examination

CPA: Clinical Pathology Accreditation is an organisation which provides a service to accredit medical laboratories in the UK

Committal proceedings: hearings before the magistrates to decide if a person should be sent for trial in the crown court

Common law: law derived from the decisions of judges, case law, judge-made law

Criminal courts: courts such as magistrates and crown courts hearing criminal prosecutions

Constructive knowledge: knowledge obtained from the circumstances

Coroner: a person appointed to hold an inquiry (inquest) into a death in unexpected unusual circumstances

Criminal wrong: an act or omission which can be pursued in the criminal courts

Cross examination: questions asked of a witness by the lawyer for the opposing side: leading questions can be asked

Damage: harm which has occurred

Damages: a sum of money awarded by a court as compensation for a *tort* or breach of contract

Declaration: a ruling by the court, setting out the legal situation

Designated individual: the person responsible for activities carried out under the licence and for compliance with the licence. Under the EU Tissue and Cells Directive, Article 17, the Designated Individual (DI) is equivalent to the 'responsible person'

Diagnosis:	a process where a disease is identified by signs and symptoms, a history and laboratory tests
Directed donation:	a form of donation where a healthy person donates an organ (usually a kidney) or tissue to a specific recipient following a tissue typing exercise. The recipient could be known to the donor (in the case of genetically or emotionally related donation) or unknown to the donor (in the case of paired/pooled donation)
Disclosure:	documents made available to the other party
Dissenting judgment:	a judge who disagrees with the decision of the majority of judges
Distinguished:	(of cases) the rules of precedent require judges to follow decisions of judges in previous cases, where these are binding upon them. However in some circumstances it is possible to come to a different decision because the facts of the earlier case are not comparable to the case now being heard, and therefore the earlier decision can be 'distinguished'
DNA:	(deoxyribonucleic acid) the genetic material of humans. DNA is located in the cell nucleus and controls heredity
Domino donation:	donation from a living donor, where the organ or tissue is removed for the health benefit of the donor, but is suitable for use in transplantation. The common form is from a cystic fibrosis patient, who undergoes a heart and lung transplant. The heart is unaffected by cystic fibrosis and is therefore suitable for transplantation
Donation:	donating human tissue, cells or organs intended for human applications
Donor:	every human source, whether living or deceased, of human cells or tissue
Embryo:	a fertilised egg that has the potential to develop into a fetus
Ethics:	the science of morals, moral principles and rules of conduct
Euthanasia:	bringing about gentle and easy death, mercy killing
Examination in chief:	the witness is asked questions in court by the lawyer of the party who has asked the witness to attend; leading questions cannot be asked

Ex gratia: as a matter of favour, eg. without admission of liability, of payment offered to a claimant

Existing holdings: relevant material being held or stored prior to the commencement of the Human Tissue Act 2004

Ex parte: on one side only, where the other side is not a party to the action

Expert witness: evidence given by a person whose general opinion based on training or experience is relevant to some of the issues in dispute (contrast with *witness of fact*)

Gamete: a cell connected with sexual reproduction, which is either a male sperm or a female egg

'Gillick' competent: a test of competence and method of determining the ability of a young person under the age of 16 to make decisions regarding his/her own healthcare from *Gillick v West Norfolk and Wisbech Area Health Authority [1985] 3 All ER 402 (HL)*

Guardian ad litem: a person with a social work and child care background who is appointed to ensure that the court is fully informed of the relevant facts that relate to a child and that the wishes and feelings of the child are clearly established. The appointment is made from a panel set up by the local authority

Guilty: a finding in a criminal court of responsibility for a criminal offence

Hearsay: evidence which has been learnt from another person

Heart-beating donors: this refers to the circumstances where organs and tissue for transplantation are removed from donors fulfilling the nationally agreed and legally defined criteria of brainstem death. In such cases the surgeon will have obtained either the prior permission of the deceased person or, after his/her death, permission from the highest ranking person in a qualifying relationship. Such donor hearts beat up to the time of organ and tissue removal because of mechanical support mechanisms (ventilators)

Hepatic: relating to the liver

Hierarchy: the recognised status of courts which results in lower courts following the decisions of higher courts (see *precedent*). Thus decisions of the House of Lords must be followed by all lower courts unless they can

	be distinguished (see *distinguished* above)
HSC:	Health Service Circular issued by Department of Health
Human application:	the use of tissue or cells on or in a human recipient and applications outside the body
Indemnity:	security against loss or damage, compensation for loss incurred
Independent assessor:	a person who acts as a representative of the Human Tissue Authority (HTA), trained and accredited by the HTA, to consider for approval all living organ donations for transplantation
Indictable:	can be tried on an indictment (ie. before the crown court – some crimes are triable either way, ie. before the crown court and summarily before magistrates)
Indictment:	written accusation against a person, charging him with a serious crime, triable by jury
Informal:	of a patient who has entered hospital without any statutory requirements
Injunction:	an order of the court restraining a person
Inquisitorial:	a system of justice whereby the truth is revealed by an inquiry into the facts conducted by the judge, eg. coroner's court
Invitation to treat:	the early stages in negotiating a contract, eg. an advertisement, or letter expressing interest. An invitation to treat will often precede an offer which, when accepted leads to the formation of an agreement that, if there is consideration and an intention to create legal relations, will be binding
Judicial review:	an application to the High Court for a judicial or administrative decision to be reviewed and an appropriate order made, eg. *declaration*
Judiciary:	judges
Justice of the peace:	(JP) a lay *magistrate*, ie. not legally qualified who hears *summary* (minor) *offences* and sometimes *indictable* (serious) *offences* in the magistrates court in a group of three (bench)
Liable/liability:	responsible for the wrong doing or harm in civil proceedings
Licence holder:	the person who applies for and is granted a licence,

who can be, but is not necessarily the *designated individual*. The licence holder is responsible for the payment of any fees charged by the Human Tissue Authority (HTA). The licence holder can be a corporate body. This definition is subject to change pending further consideration by the HTA

Licensed premises: premises to which a licence applies. A licence can only be granted to a specific place, not multiple sites. This definition is subject to change pending further consideration by the Human Tissue Authority

Licensing: a number of activities can only be carried out where the establishment is licensed under the Human Tissue Act by the Human Tissue Authority for that purpose. The activities are:
- carrying out anatomical examinations and storing anatomical specimens
- public display of a body or material from a deceased person
- making of post mortem examinations
- removing tissue or organs from a deceased person other than for transplantation, post mortem or anatomical examination
- storing of tissue from a human body (except for diagnostic material)

Litigation: civil proceedings

Living donor: the person donating organs or tissue for transplantation. The most common forms are live kidney donation (where one kidney is removed), or live bone marrow donation

Magistrate: a person (see *JP* and *stipendiary*) who hears *summary* (minor) *offences* or *indictable offences* which can be heard in the *magistrates* court

Mens rea: the mental element in a crime (cf. *actus reus*)

Negligence: (1) a breach by the defendant of a legal duty to take reasonable care not to injure the plaintiff or cause him loss, or (2) the attitude of mind of a person committing a civil wrong as opposed to intentionally

Next friend: a person who brings a court action on behalf of a minor

NHS Organ Donor Register: a confidential, computerised database managed by UK Transplant, which holds details of people who have signed up to become organ donors in the event of their death. The register is used after a person has died to help establish whether he/she wanted to donate and if so, which organs

Non-directed donation: circumstances where donation occurs without a known recipient. Most commonly, this is deceased donation where the organ is allocated to the most suitable person on the transplant waiting list

Non-heartbeating donation: donation in circumstances where the deceased donor was not ventilated at the time of death. Donation therefore occurs once death is certified following cardiorespiratory arrest (ie. the donor's heart has stopped beating)

Ombudsman: a commissioner (eg. health, local government) appointed by the Government to hear complaints

Organ: a differentiated and vital part of the human body, formed by different tissue, that maintains its structure, vascularisation and capacity to develop physiological functions with an important level of autonomy

Paired donation: where a close relation, friend or partner is fit and able to donate an organ but is not well matched to the potential recipient, that couple can be matched to another couple in a similar situation, enabling both people in need of a transplant to receive a well-matched organ

Perfusion: a method of treating organs following the death of the donor to preserve them before transplantation

Plaintiff: term formerly used to describe one who brings an action in the civil courts. Now the term *claimant* is used

Pooled donation: where a close relation, friend or partner is fit and able to donate an organ but is not well matched to the potential recipient, that couple can be matched to other couples in a similar situation, so that all people in need of a transplant receive a well-matched organ

Post mortem: a hospital post mortem examination is carried out, with the consent of relatives/friends, to gain a fuller

	understanding of the deceased person's illness or the cause of death, and to enhance future medical care. Coroners' post mortem examinations are carried out under the authority of the coroner and without consent to assist coroners in carrying out their functions
Practice direction:	guidance issued by the head of the court to which they relate on the procedure to be followed
Pre-action protocol:	rules of the Supreme Court provide guidance on action to be taken before legal proceedings commence
Precedent:	a decision which may have to be followed in a subsequent court hearing (see *hierarchy*)
Preservation:	the use of chemical agents, alterations in environmental conditions or other means during processing to prevent or retard biological or physical deterioration of cells or tissue
Prima facie:	at first sight, or sufficient evidence brought by one party to require the other party to provide a defence
Privilege:	in relation to evidence, being able to refuse to disclose it to the court
Privity:	the relationship that exists between parties as the result of a legal agreement
Processing:	all operations involved in the preparation, manipulation, preservation and packaging of tissue or cells intended for human applications
Procurement:	a process by which tissue or cells are made available
Proof:	evidence which secures the establishment of a *claimant*'s, *prosecution*'s or defendant's case
Prosecution:	the pursuing of criminal offences in court
Public display:	includes organised displays and exhibitions held in museums, galleries, exhibition venues and educational establishments. This definition is subject to change pending further consideration by the Human Tissue Authority
Public health monitoring:	using population-based or epidemiological techniques to ascertain the prevalence, spread and pattern of an established disease or condition in the community and relating its occurrence to public health programmes and activities
Qualitative:	relating to characteristics that are based on quality
Quality assurance:	a programme for the systematic monitoring and evaluation of the various aspects of a project, service,

	or facility to ensure that standards of quality are being met
Quantitative:	relating to characteristics that are based on numbers
Quantum:	the amount of compensation, or the monetary value of a claim
Quarantine:	the status of retrieved tissue or cells, or tissue isolated physically or by other effective means, while awaiting a decision on their acceptance or rejection
Queen's Counsel (QC):	a senior barrister, also known as a 'silk'
Ratio:	the reasoning behind the decision in a court case
Re F ruling:	a professional who acts in the best interests of an incompetent person who is incapable of giving consent, does not act unlawfully if he or she follows the accepted standard of care according to the *Bolam Test*. This common law principle applied until it was replaced by the Mental Capacity Act 2005
Relevant material:	described by the Human Tissue Act as material other than gametes, which consists of or includes human cells. In the Human Tissue Act, references to relevant material from a human body do not include: • embryos outside the human body, or • hair and nail from the body of a living person
Research ethics committee:	defined under regulations made under Section 1(9) of the Human Tissue Act to mean a local or multi-centre research ethics committee established in accordance with Department of Health guidance on the Research Governance Framework
Res ipsa loquitur:	the thing speaks for itself
Residual tissue:	material left over from a diagnostic or therapeutic intervention. This definition is subject to change pending further consideration by the Human Tissue Authority
Sanctions:	penalties, remedies following civil or criminal wrong
Scheduled purposes:	the activities relating to the removal, storage and use of human organs and other tissue, listed in Schedule 1 of the Human Tissue Act that require consent (see *Box 16.2* in *Chapter 16)*
Solicitor:	a lawyer who is qualified on the register held by the Law Society

Standard of proof:	the level that the party who has the burden of proof must satisfy, eg. on a balance of probabilities (civil courts); beyond reasonable doubt (criminal courts)
Statute law (statutory):	law made by *Acts of Parliament*
Statutory instrument:	orders and regulations having binding force. They must usually be laid before Parliament and will usually become law if they are confirmed by a simple resolution of both Houses (affirmative resolution). Some become law after they have been laid for a prescribed period unless they are annulled by resolution of either House (negative resolution)
Stem cell:	a precursor cell that can develop into more than one kind of cell. For example, early bone marrow cells can develop into red blood cells, white blood cells or platelets
Stipendiary magistrate:	a legally qualified *magistrate* who is paid (ie. has a stipend)
Storage:	maintaining the tissue under appropriate controlled conditions until distribution
Strict liability:	liability for a criminal act where the mental element does not have to be proved; in civil proceedings liability without establishing negligence
Summary judgment:	a procedure whereby the claimant can obtain judgment without the defendant being permitted to defend the action
Summary offence:	a lesser offence which can only be heard by *magistrates*
Tissue:	any constituent part of the human body formed by cells
Tissue establishment:	a tissue bank or a unit of a hospital or another body where activities of processing, preservation, storage or distribution of human tissue and cells are undertaken. It may also be responsible for procurement or testing of tissue and cells
Tort:	a *civil wrong* excluding *breach* of contract. It includes: *negligence*, *trespass* (to the person, goods or land), nuisance, breach of statutory duty and defamation
Transplant:	an implant of an organ, tissue or cells either from and into the same body or from one person to another
Transplant coordinator:	a person who helps a potential transplant recipient to

understand the transplant process and also coordinates the transplant evaluation between the dialysis unit, transplant surgeon, and tissue typing laboratory. After a transplant, the nurse provides a communication link between the recipient and the transplant doctors for post-transplant care

Trespass to the person: a wrongful direct interference with another person. Harm does not have to be proved

Trial: a court hearing before a judge

Ultra vires: Outside the powers given by law (eg. of a statutory body or company)

Vicarious liability: the liability of an employer for the wrongful acts of an employee committed while in the course of employment

Void: invalid or not legally binding

Voidable: Can be made *void*

Volenti non fit injuria: 'to the willing there is no wrong'; ie. the voluntary assumption of risk

Ward of court: a minor placed under the protection of the High Court, which assumes responsibility for him or her and all decisions relating to his or her care must be made in accordance with the directions of the court

Wednesbury principle: the court will intervene to prevent or remedy abuses of power by public authorities if there is evidence of unreasonableness or perversity. Principle laid down by the Court of Appeal in the case of *Associated Provincial Picture House Ltd v. Wednesbury Corporation [1948] 1 KB 233*

Without prejudice: without detracting from or without disadvantage to. The use of the phrase prevents the other party using the information to the prejudice of the one providing it

Witness of fact: a person who gives evidence of what they saw, heard, did or failed to do (contrast with *expert witness*)

Writ: a form of written command, eg. the document which used to commence civil proceedings. Now a claim form is served

Useful websites

Audit Commission: www.audit-commission.gov.uk
Bristol Inquiry (Kennedy Report): www.bristol-inquiry.org.uk
British Humanist Association: www.humanism.org.uk
British National Formulary: www.bnf.org/
British Transplantation Society: www.bts.org.uk/standards.htm
Civil Procedure Rules: www.open.gov.uk/lcd/civil/procrules_fin/crules.htm
Commission for Racial Equality: www.cre.gov.uk/
Department for Constitutional Affairs: www.dca.gov.uk
Department of Health: www.dh.gov.uk
Department of Trade and Industry now the Department for Business, Enterprise and Regulatory Reform: www.berr.gov.uk/
Department for Work and Pensions: www.dwp.gov.uk
Domestic Violence: www.domesticviolence.gov.uk
General Medical Council: www.gmc-uk.org/standards
Health and Safety Commission: www.hsc.gov.uk
Health and Safety Executive: www.hse.gov.uk
Health Professions Council: www.hc-uk.org
Help the Aged: www.helptheaged.org.uk/
Hinduism Today: www.hinduismtoday.com
Human Fertilisation and Embryology Authority: www.hfea.gov.uk/
Human Rights: www.humanrights.gov.uk
Islamic Law: www.al-islam.org/laws/
Judaism: www.jewfaq.org/death.htm
Medicines and Healthcare Products Regulatory Agency: www.mhra.gov.uk
Ministry of Justice: www.justice.gov.uk/
National Audit Office: www.nao.gov.uk
National Patient Safety Agency: www.npsa.org.uk
National Service Framework: www.doh.gov.uk/NSF/National Treatment Agency: www.nta.nhs.uk/
Natural Death Organisation: www.naturaldeath.org.uk
NHS: www.nhs.uk
NHS Direct: www.nhsdirect.nhs.uk
NHS Professionals: www.nhsprofessionals.nhs.uk
NICE: www.nice.org.uk
Nursing and Midwifery Council: www.nmc-uk.org/
Open Government: www.open.gov.uk
Pain: www.pain-talk.co.uk
Pro-choice living will: www.livingwill.org.uk.

Royal College of Midwives: www.rcm.org.uk
Royal College of Nursing: www.rcn.org.uk
Royal Pharmaceutical Society of Great Britain: www.rpsgb.org.uk
Shipman Inquiry: www.the-shipman-inquiry.org.uk/reports.asp
Sikh faith: www.sikhismhomepage
Stationery Office: www.hmso.gov.uk
Stillbirth and Neonatal Death Society :www.uk-sands.org/
UK Government: www.direct.gov.uk
UK Parliament: www.parliament.uk
Victoria Climbie Inquiry: www.victoria-climbie.org.uk
Voluntary Euthansia Society: www.ves.org.uk

CHAPTER 1

Definition of death

Box 1.1. Definition of death

John, Kathy's son was injured in a road traffic accident and Kathy was rushed to intensive care to see him. He appeared to be sleeping very peacefully assisted by a ventilator. The doctors told her that John was dead. She could not accept that he was dead since he was clearly breathing, his heart was beating and he did not look dead. The doctors said that they intended to switch off the ventilator and Kathy protested that that would be to kill him. What is the law?

The traditional way of identifying that death had occurred was in recognising that breathing had ceased, there was no pulse and the heart had stopped beating. Holding a mirror to the mouth and nose could show that life had ended. However this traditional definition is not appropriate: it may be possible for the patient to be revived, for example following a drowning, and if the patient is ventilated, all these functions can continue. In addition it is possible for these functions to appear to be absent, and yet death has not occurred. In an amazing story reported in February 2007 (Bannerman, 2007) a two-week-old baby was pronounced dead, and resuscitation attempts were abandoned. Half an hour later, his parents heard him give a small cough and the medical staff recommended resuscitation and he survived. It was subsequently discovered that he had a blocked aorta that was successfully treated with surgery.

Brain death or brainstem death

In 1976 the Medical Royal Colleges published guidelines for determining if brainstem death had occurred (Conference of Medical Colleges and Their Faculties, 1976). These were updated in 1995 (Working Party of the Royal College of Physicians, 1995) and subsequently adopted by the Department of Health (1998) in its *Code of Practice for the Diagnosis of Brain Stem Death*. The details are shown in *Box 1.2*.

The medical Royal Colleges recommend that the possibility of brain death should be considered where the patient is deeply comatose (but where depressant drugs, primary hypothermia, and metabolic and endocrine disturbances can be excluded), or where the patient is being

Box 1.2. Definition of brainstem death

The diagnosis of brain death should be made by two medical practitioners who have expertise in this field. One should be the consultant who is in charge of the case and one other doctor (or in the absence of the consultant, his deputy who should have been registered for 5 years or more with adequate previous experience in the care of such cases, and one other doctor). The two doctors may carry out their tests separately or together. If the tests confirm brain death they should still be repeated. It is for the doctors to decide how long the interval between the tests should be. It may not be appropriate for the doctors to carry out all the recommended tests. The criteria are guidelines, not rigid rules.

These criteria are as follows:

- All brainstem reflexes are absent.
- The pupils are fixed in diameter and do not respond to sharp changes in the intensity of incident light.
- There is no corneal reflex.
- The vestibular-ocular reflexes are absent.
- No motor responses within the cranial nerve distribution can be elicited by adequate stimulation of any somatic area.
- There is no gag reflex or reflex response to bronchial stimulation by a suction catheter passed down the trachea.
- No respiratory movements occur when the patient is disconnected from the mechanical ventilator for long enough to ensure that the arterial carbon dioxide tension rises above the threshold for stimulation of respiration.

Additional recommendations are made as to how some of these tests should be undertaken.

maintained on a ventilator because spontaneous respiration had previously been inadequate or had ceased (relaxants or other drugs should be ruled out as a cause of respiratory failure), or where there is no doubt that the patient's condition is due to irremediable structural brain damage (the diagnosis of a disorder which can lead to brain death should have been fully established).

Cases recognising brainstem death

The guidelines shown in *Box 1.2* have not been incorporated in legislation, but they have been recognised as valid in several court cases. For example, in the case of *Re A,* a 19-month-old child who suffered serious head injuries from an accident at home. He was placed on a ventilator but showed no signs of recovery. The doctors applied the diagnostic tests for brain death and concluded that he was dead. An application was made to court to allow him to be removed from the ventilator. The judge held that in the light of the tests carried out by the consultant in accordance with the MRC guidelines, 'It is now Monday 27 January. I have no hesitation at all in holding that A has been dead since Tuesday of last week, 21 January.'

The House of Lords also recognised the validity of the use of brainstem death as a definition of death in the case involving Tony Bland (*Airedale NHS Trust v. Bland*). The House of Lords stated that although Tony Bland was in a persistent vegetative state he was not brain dead, since his brainstem was still functioning.

Removal from the ventilator

It follows from what has been said that where the recommended tests show that brain death has occurred, to switch off the ventilator is not an act of killing the patient: the patient has already died. In such a situation a claim under the Human Rights Act 1998 Article 2 (right to life) would fail. Article 2 states that:

> *Everyone's right to life shall be protected by law. No one shall be deprived of his life intentionally save in the execution of a sentence of a court following his conviction of a crime for which this penalty is provided by law.*

Removing a brain dead patient from a ventilator would not therefore be depriving a person of his or her life, since that person is already dead.

Brain scans

Further controversy into the situation of vegetative patients arose following the report of a brain scan on a person who had been in a vegetative state for over 10 months. The brain scan suggested that even though the patient was in a vegetative state she may have been able to hear and understand instructions given to her, since the scan showed activity in the brain similar to that in a healthy volunteer (Hawkes, 2006).

Significance of the time of death

In certain situations the actual time of death can be crucial. For example the rules of inheritance depend upon the order in which people die. If, therefore, there are incidents leading to multiple deaths, which victim died first can be very significant for inheritance. There are certain presumptions in law relating to the order of deaths in such circumstances, ie. the oldest died first. However, if one of the victims is supported on a life support machine and kept 'alive' longer the presumption would no longer operate. Some insurance policies may require that where death follows an accident it must be established that the death occurred within a fixed time limit in order to claim under the policy. In one case (*Mail Newspapers Plc v. Express Newspapers plc)* a dispute hinged upon whether one of the alleged copyright holders was dead. Mrs B had suffered a brain haemorrhage while 24 weeks pregnant and was kept on a life support system in the hope that the baby could be born alive. A dispute which arose over the husband's right to grant exclusive rights to photographs of himself and the baby within 24 hours of the birth, rested on whether Mrs B was alive, in which case she was a copyright holder, or whether she was dead. The judge held that the evidence suggested that she was probably clinically and legally dead.

Chain of causation in a criminal action

There have been several cases where people accused of murder have attempted to argue that it was the doctor who caused the death of the patient by removing the patient from the ventilator and that they were not therefore guilty of murder. For example, in one case Malcherek was convicted of the murder of a victim of assault who had been connected to a life support machine which had been disconnected by medical practitioners. He was sentenced to life imprisonment and appealed against this decision. In a similar case, Steel was also convicted and sentenced to life imprisonment. He applied for leave to put in further medical evidence as to the sufficiency and adequacy of tests by the doctors to determine brain death. Both Malcherek and Steel were challenging that there was a causal link between the assaults and the deaths of the victims. They were placing responsibility for the deaths on the doctors. In the trials, the two judges had withdrawn the issue of causation from the jury (*R v. Malcherek*).

The Court of Appeal heard both appeals together and held that in each case it was clear that the initial assault was the cause of the grave head injuries in the one case and of the massive abdominal haemorrhage in the other. In each case, the initial assault was the reason for the medical treatment being necessary and in each case, the medical treatment given was normal and conventional. The court looked in detail at the tests carried out by the doctors and stated:

> *It is not part of the task of this court to inquire whether the criteria, the Royal Colleges' confirmatory tests, are a satisfactory code of practice. It*

is not part of the task of this court to decide whether the doctors were, in either of these two cases, justified in omitting one or more of the so called 'confirmatory tests'. The doctors are not on trial: the applicant and the appellant were.

The Court of Appeal concluded that all the evidence suggested that at the time of death the original wound or injury was a continuing, operating and, indeed, substantial cause of death. The fact that the victim's life support treatment had been discontinued did not break the chain of causation between the initial injury and death. The actions of the defendants continued to be an operating cause of death. The issue of causation had therefore properly been withdrawn from the jury. The convictions were confirmed.

Before 1996 to constitute the offence of murder, there was a time limit within which the victim must have died, ie. within a year and a day of the act which led to the death. In 1996, this time limit requirement was removed. A murder charge could now be brought many years after the assault that led to the eventual death. An extreme example of a long period between the cause and the death is seen in the news report (Rose, 2007) that a cancer woman was killed by radiation 34 years after being exposed to 4500 rads, which was the standard dose at that time. The family stated that they did not blame anyone for what happened since the dose gave her 34 years of life, whereas others did not last that long. Had a criminal offence been committed, charges could still have been brought

Preservation of body for purposes of donation

Section 47 of the Human Tissue Act 2004 states that where part of a body (ie. of a deceased person) lying in a hospital, nursing home or other institution is or may be suitable for use for transplantation, it shall be lawful for the person having the control and management of the institution:

- to take steps for the purpose of preserving the part for use for transplantation, and
- to retain the body for that purpose.

However the authority given under this section only extends to the taking of the minimum steps necessary for the purpose mentioned in that provision, and to the use of the least invasive procedure.

Once it has been established that consent, making removal of the part for transplantation lawful, has not been, and will not be, given, then the authority under this section ceases to apply. Organ donation is discussed in *Chapter 16.*

Applying the law to the scenario in *Box 1.1*

The introduction of technology in medicine means that the traditional signs of death are no longer always appropriate. Holding a mirror to a patient on a ventilator in the intensive care unit will not provide the answer. The use of the brain dead test for death is nowadays more meaningful. However this can cause distress to relatives who may see the switching off of the ventilator as an action that causes death. In John's case, it is clear that Kathy needs to understand the fact that John's body is being ventilated, but in practice he has died as a result of the road traffic accident. Where a patient is brain dead, switching off the ventilator is not killing the patient. However an explanation will take time and sensitivity. In addition staff may wish to raise with her the possibility of John being a donor.

Conclusion

The tests for determining the end of life are crucial to the general public's confidence in the expertise of health professionals. More sophisticated tests are necessary in certain circumstances. Where the verification that death has occurred is delegated to non-medical staff many concerns arise and these are addressed in *Chapter 2*.

References

Airedale NHS Trust v. Bland [1993] 1 All ER 821

Bannerman L (2007) The boy who came back to life. *The Times* **28 Feb**

Conference of Medical Colleges and Their Faculties (1976) Diagnosis of Brain Death. *Brit Med J* **ii**: 1187–8

Department of Health (1998) *Code of Practice for the Diagnosis of Brain Stem Death*. HSC 1998/035. London: Department of Health

Hawkes N (2006) Brain scan records tennis thoughts of vegetative patient. *The Times* **8 Sept**

Mail Newspapers Plc v. Express Newspapers plc [1987] FSR 90 Chancery Division

Re A [1992] 3 Med LR 303 Fam Div

R v. Malcherek; R v. Steel CA [1981] 2 All ER 422

Rose D (2007) Cancer woman killed by radiation 34 years later. *The Times* **23 Feb**

Working Party of the Royal College of Physicians (1995) Criteria for the diagnosis for brain stem death. *J Roy Coll Phys* **29**: 381

CHAPTER 2

Certification, verification and registration of death

> **Box 2.1. An expanded role?**
>
> Daisy was a registered nurse who worked in a community hospital. One night Gwen, 85 years old, died and Daisy phoned the GP who was responsible for providing a service to the hospital. She was told that the GP did not come out at night for a death but would come in the morning. Daisy wanted the patient moved from the four-bedded ward to the mortuary, but was told that ward procedures did not permit that until a doctor had certified the death. Daisy felt that it was unsettling to the other patients who knew that Gwen had died. What is the law?

At present the law requires that where a death has occurred, the medical practitioner who attended that person during his or her last illness must sign a certificate in the prescribed form, stating to the best of his or her knowledge and belief the cause of death (Births and Deaths Registration Act 1953 S22).

Only a registered medical practitioner can undertake the activity of certification of death. It cannot be delegated to a nurse or any other health professional. The doctor will usually issue a medical certificate giving the cause of death. This is generally put in a sealed envelope addressed to the registrar for the next of kin to take for registration of the death. The doctor will also issue a formal notice which states that the doctor has signed the medical certificate and which provides information on how the death should be registered by the Registrar of Births, Marriages and Deaths. (Those circumstances where the doctor is unable to sign a medical certificate are considered in *Chapter 12*. The third Shipman Report has made significant recommendations on certification of death which are considered in *Chapter 14*.)

The informant

The informant is a term used to describe the person whose duty it is to notify the registrar of the death. Where a person dies in a house (house in this context has a much extended meaning and includes public institutions such as prisons or hospitals or other public or charitable institutions) the following are qualified to give information concerning the death (ibid S16):

1. Any relative of the deceased present at the death or in attendance during his or her last illness.
2. Any other relative of the deceased residing or being in the sub-district where the death occurred.
3. Any person present at the death.
4. The occupier of the house if he or she knew of the happening of the death.
5. Any inmate of the house who knew of the happening of the death.
6. The person causing the disposal of the body.

Where a person dies at home, a community nurse or other health professional becomes qualified to inform the registrar of the death under point 3 above if there are no persons covered by points 1 or 2. Where a person dies in hospital and there are no relatives then the manager of the hospital would qualify as an informant.

Where a person dies elsewhere than in a house (with the extended meaning) or where a dead body is found then the following persons are qualified to give information concerning the death:

1. Any relative of the deceased who has knowledge of any of the particulars required to be registered concerning the death (this could include a civil partner).
2. Any person present at the death.
3. Any person finding or taking charge of the body.
4. Any person causing the disposal of the body.

Whether the person died at home or elsewhere, any relatives who fail to give the information to the registrar, where the information is not given by anyone else, could be charged with an offence (ibid S17(3)).

Procedures for registering a death

The medical certificate should be taken by the informant to the Registrar for Births, Marriages and Deaths within 5 days of the death. The registrar will require the following information: the full name of the deceased, the last known address, date of birth, occupation, and whether the deceased was in receipt of a pension. The registrar will give the person registering the death a certificate of disposal form which can be handed to the undertaker (unless the death is to be reported to the coroner). If a cremation is intended, then certification by two doctors will be required. If the death has been referred to the coroner, then the relatives should be notified that they will not receive the certificate from the hospital. The coroner will issue his or her own disposal certificate. (The reporting of deaths to the coroner is considered in *Chapter 12*.) The registrar is required to notify the relevant registration body of the death of a doctor, dentist, pharmaceutical chemist, veterinary surgeon or ophthalmic or dispensing optician.

The relatives will receive from the registrar, in addition to the certificate of disposal form, a certificate of registration of death. This may be required by the Department for Work and Pensions (formerly the Department of Social Security) in order to claim any entitlements. (The death grant is no longer payable but other benefits are available to those who are eligible.) This certificate may also be required to obtain transfer of any bank accounts, etc., and further copies are available from the registrar on payment of a fee.

Regulations relating to registration

Regulations came into force in relation to the registration of births and deaths in 1988 which consolidated, with minor amendments, the previous regulations with the statutory forms for completion (Registration of Births and Deaths Regulations SI 1987). The regulations cover the registration of stillbirths (see *Chapter 4*), the disposal of bodies of stillborn children, the registration of deaths, the disposal of bodies of deceased persons, the correction of errors, and birth and death certificates.

The registrar is required to report a death to the coroner on an approved form if the death occurred in specified circumstances. These are set out in *Table 12.1* of *Chapter 12*.

New regulations enable the introduction of an electronic method of communication between registrars, the Superintendent Registrar and the Registrar General and the storage of information electronically (Registration of Births and Deaths (Amendment) Regulations 2006).

Co-operation between hospital and Registrar's Office

The guidance from the Department of Health (2005) suggests that with so many deaths occurring within hospitals, a close link between the hospital bereavement services and the Registrar of Death's office would be beneficial. It puts forward the suggestions shown in *Box 2.2*.

Verification of death

Verification that death has occurred is a different activity than certification and this can be the subject of delegated activity. All the principles of the expanded

Box 2.2 Co-operation between hospital and registrar of deaths

- Provision of jointly organised service to cover evenings and weekends for those whose religious and cultural backgrounds require a quick burial
- Hospital bereavement officers making appointments with the registrar of deaths on behalf of the next of kin when they meet
- The registrar of deaths going to the hospital to register a death in certain cases such as stillbirths or where the next of kin is also a patient
- Location of a registrar of deaths within the hospital for all or part of their working week

role and scope of professional practice apply to this. The Royal College of Nursing (1996) has provided a paper on verification of death by registered nurses. It states that experienced registered nurses will have the authority to verify death, notify the relatives, and arrange for last offices and the removal of the body to the mortuary. Education is necessary to ensure nurses have the confidence, competence, knowledge and skills to equip them for undertaking this role. Their records should document the action they have taken and contain information relating to the date, time and any other information required by hospital policy. Where nurses expand their scope of professional practice to include such activities as the verification of death, they should ensure that their employers are in agreement with this role expansion and approve the training they have received or intend to receive. If the employers have approved the

Box 2.3 Key points to observe when undertaking expanded roles

- Always work within the scope of your professional practice.
- Identify any training or supervised practice needs and take steps to ensure that these are met
- Be aware that the law does not accept a principle of team liability: all individual practitioners are personally and professionally accountable for their own actions
- Do not obey orders, except in an extreme emergency, unless you are satisfied that they constitute reasonable professional practice
- Be prepared to refuse to undertake any activity unless it is within your competence
- Do not accept an undertaking that someone else will accept responsibility for what you do (I'll take responsibility)
- Ensure that any development in your professional practice takes place in the context of multidisciplinary discussions, with full management support and an awareness of the need to educate the patient and others to the new situation

nurse carrying out verification of death, they would be vicariously liable should the nurse be negligent and cause harm. Key points for the expansion of the scope of professional practice are shown in *Box 2.3*.

Nursing and Midwifery Council advice

The Nursing and Midwifery Council (NMC) (2006) in its A–Z advice sheet on confirmation of death states that:

> *A nurse cannot legally certify death. This is one of the few activities required by law to be carried out by a registered medical practitioner; in the case of an expected death, a registered nurse may confirm or verify when death has occurred, providing there is an explicit local policy or protocol in place to allow such an action.*
>
> ***The policy or protocol must only be used in situations where the death is expected.***
>
> *Nurses undertaking this responsibility should only do so providing they have received appropriate education and training and have been assessed as competent. They must also be aware of their accountability when performing this role.*
>
> ***It is advised that local policies should be developed or amended using the information outlined above. Information on updated advice sheets will be published in NMC news.***

Mistakes in identifying death

Inevitably there are failures in correctly identifying that death has occurred as the case in *Box 2.4* illustrates.

Box 2.4. Fatal diagnosis (Wilkinson, 2000)

The son of Mrs Maureen Jones summoned a GP when he found his mother collapsed in her bedroom. The GP said that she had died and advised the relatives to notify the police. The undertakers were summoned. A policeman called to the scene saw the woman's leg move and applied mouth-to-mouth resuscitation until the paramedics arrived. She then made a full recovery in hospital. She had been in a diabetic coma. A county court judge found the doctor negligent in making a diagnosis of death. Damages were agreed with the Medical Defence Union at £38 500. The Health Authority, following an investigation, agreed that the doctor could continue in practice, but was given an official reprimand, told to comply more closely with her terms of service and was required to undergo educational assessment and support.

Another example of a mistake in identifying death occurred in Dublin in 2007. Doctors had spent 30 minutes trying to save a patient in the Mater Hospital before pronouncing him dead. However a member of staff saw his hand move before he was placed in the mortuary refrigerator. An investigation into the identification of death was being carried out by the hospital (Sharrock, 2007).

Viewing the body

The Department of Health (2005) in its guidance on action to be taken when patients die in hospital has suggested that hospital staff should facilitate the viewing of the deceased by relatives and friends. It put forward the advice shown in *Box 2.5*.

Box 2.5. Guidance on viewing the deceased

- Ensure procedures and personnel are in place during evenings and weekends to allow viewings to take place
- Develop a policy on who has the right to view the deceased, including the criteria used and the legal basis for refusing a viewing
- Ensure facilities and procedures take into account the variations in family structures, family disputes, the ages of those who have been bereaved and differing religious and cultural needs
- Ensure that transportation of the deceased from the mortuary to the viewing area is included within porters' job descriptions and contracts with external service suppliers
- Develop a policy on children viewing the deceased and make available specialist bereavement support services for children, and childcare facilities
- Accompany people who have been bereaved to the viewing area and stay with them or nearby for as long as is required in case someone is needed
- Utilise volunteers and/or the chaplain service to support those who have been bereaved while they view the deceased
- Ensure that the room, facilities, environment and presentation of the deceased are in line with professionally accepted codes of practice
- Ensure that the conditions of viewing for special cases, such as those involving the coroner or infectious diseases, are fully understood
- Develop a policy and procedures to identify who can remove the body and when, dealing with circumstances where the hospital has the right to refuse to allow the body to be removed, such as if the transportation and storage arrangements are thought to be insecure under health and safety regulations

Application of the law to situation in *Box 2.1*

It would appear from the facts that Daisy is not trained in the verification of death and therefore would have to wait for a doctor to certify the death before allowing Gwen's body to be removed, according to the community hospital procedures. However if Daisy is able to obtain the training to take on this expanded role, then it would clearly be in the interests of the existing patients and any new admissions for the body to be removed from the ward. Should Daisy secure the necessary training, it is her personal and professional responsibility to ensure that she is competent, and that she works within this field of competency and takes steps to keep up to date. It would also be her responsibility to discuss with senior management the amendment of the policy relating to removal of the body, so that provision is made for verification of the death by a competent registered practitioner.

Future changes

As a consequence of the investigations into the deaths caused by Shipman, major changes are proposed to the coroner's jurisdiction and office. The third Shipman Inquiry also recommended changes to the system of certification of death. It suggested that two persons will be required to certify that death has occurred: the first form could be completed by an appropriately registered heath professional and would record the fact and circumstances of death, the second would be a medical practitioner who would give the background of the facts leading to the death and an opinion as to the cause of death. All deaths would be reported to the coroner. (At present the certification of one doctor only is necessary if burial is intended, and of two doctors if cremation is required and only those deaths caused in specified circumstances are reported to the coroner, see *Chapter 12*.)

In spite of these strong recommendations reforms to the procedure for the certification of death were not included in the draft Coroners' Bill. This omission was criticised by the Department for Constitutional Affairs Select Committee (2006) as follows:

> *Recommendation 6: We strongly recommend that the Government revise its policy not to reform death certification in order to address reform of death certification in tandem with reform of the coronial system. It should return to the proposals on death certification put forward by the Home Office in 2004 ensuring they are supported with sufficient resources*

To this recommendation the UK Government (2006) replied:

> *The Government is not convinced that to have all deaths reported to the coroner service would be effective in terms of targeting resources where the risk is greatest. Such a system could bring unnecessary delay to families wishing to proceed quickly with funeral arrangements. The improved focus of the coroner service under the proposals in the Bill, the changes the Department of Health has made on controlled drugs, and the changes it is consulting on in relation to professional regulation (eg. doctor revalidation every 5 years, an independent tribunal to adjudicate on fitness to practice) will, we believe, reduce the likelihood of a Shipman type figure operating undetected in the future, and will curb or deter other potential abuses. The structural changes we are proposing to the coroner service do not preclude further changes to the processes for validating and using death certificate information in the future and we are exploring the options as set out in our response to recommendation 5.*
>
> *In the interim, as part of the implementation of the Bill, we will look further at how coroners can better interact with registrars. In most areas there are good working relationships between local offices. Plans are for registrars to become local government employees in the future, when legislation allows, and a number of shire counties are looking at local organisation of offices. There may be opportunities to look at more instances of co-location, and the sharing of administration facilities. In the longer term, it may be possible to introduce electronic exchanges of information to further enhance co-operation and to facilitate more efficient working relationships. The Government rejects this recommendation.*

The Government did however accept recommendation 7 of the Select Committee relating to the reporting of deaths to the coroner. See *Chapter 12*.

At present therefore the existing system for death certification will continue, but there will be considerable pressure upon the Government to review the situation in the light of the Shipman Inquiry and the Department for Constitutional Affairs Select Committee recommendations.

Guide on what to do after a death

Practical advice on what to do after a death has been provided by the UK Government (2006) as part of its public services directory. The UK Government website provides information on the rights and responsibilities after someone dies and other useful information including the following:

- What to do in the first five days
- Who else to contact as soon as possible
- Documents and information needed when someone dies

- Registering a death
- When someone dies abroad
- When someone dies in hospital or care home
- Notifying the DVLA of a bereavement
- Arranging a funeral
- What to do if there is no will

Conclusion

Tragically there have been cases where a diagnosis of death has proved incorrect, resulting in considerable distress to relatives and staff. It is vital that verification is only carried out by a competent, trained person. Major changes are proposed in our system of death certification and the role of the coroner as a consequence of the Shipman Inquiry and these are considered in *Chapters 12–14*.

References

Births and Deaths Registration Act 1953 S16, S17(3), S22

Department for Constitutional Affairs Select Committee (2006) *Report on the Reform of the Coroners' System and Death Certification*. London: Department for Constitutional Affairs

Department of Health (2005) *When a Patient Dies: Advice on Developing Bereavement Services in the NHS*. London: Department of Health

Nursing and Midwifery Council (2006) *Confirmation of Death. A-Z Advice Sheet*. London: Nursing and Midwifery Council

Registration of Births and Deaths Regulations SI 1987 2088

Registration of Births and Deaths (Amendment) Regulations 2006. SI 2006 2827; Registration of Births and Deaths (Electronic Communications and Electronic Storage) Order 2006. SI 2006 2809

Royal College of Nursing (1996) *Verification of Death by Registered Nurses*. Document No: 000 594. London: Royal College of Nursing.

UK Government (2006) *Response to the Constitutional Affairs Select Committee's Report: Reform of the Coroners' System and Death Certification*. Cm 6943. London: UK Government

Wilkinson P (2000) £38,500 for woman given up for dead. *The Times*: **27 September**

Sharrock D (2007) Easter 'miracle' as dead man returns to life. *The Times* **9 June**

www.direct.gov.uk/Over50s/EndOfLife/WhatToDoAfterADeath

CHAPTER 3

Disposal of the body

Box 3.1. Eccentric disposal

Ray had always been an eccentric character and when his mother, with whom he had lived all his life, died he wished her to be buried under her favourite tree in their garden. What is the law?

Understandably the way in which a body is disposed of is an extremely important aspect of many different religions and even those who do not believe in an after life may have decided views on the arrangements they would wish for their body after death. Individuals have no control over their dead body – such control is vested in the person in lawful possession of the body. Thus individuals in their will cannot require their executors to make any arrangements with the body that is not according to the law, and cannot bequeath body parts except as is permitted under the Human Tissue Act 2004 (which is considered in later chapters).

This chapter considers the various ways in which different religions treat the dead body and what the law requires. In some hospitals there are nurses who have been trained to fulfil the last offices. Where such practitioners exist it is a great advantage to the nursing team. However some readers, especially students, may not have cared for a dying person or even seen a dead person. It is hoped that this chapter will alert nurse practitioners to the complexity of this area and the varied practices and beliefs that exist, and to make them acquainted with sources for future advice and support. It is considered helpful if nurses are aware of different religious and legal requirements and know what may be requested or required, even if they are not required to carry them out.

Cremation

The Cremation Act 1902 (as amended by the Cremation Act 1952 together with the Regulations drawn up under it in 1930) sets out the provisions controlling the incineration of deceased persons.

Amendments that came into force on 14 February 2006 amend the definition of body parts to extend its application to all parts of bodies from deceased persons. Previously the Regulations only allowed for body parts removed during post mortem to be cremated, and parts severed from a body during the course of death or prior to death were not covered by the Regulations. The change allows the cremation of parts of someone identified after the rest of the body has been buried, eg. where a body has been severely damaged in a bomb blast. The definition now includes parts of a stillborn child.

In addition the new Regulations authorise the incineration of body parts where an incinerator has a specific permit for that purpose. This amendment brings into the ambit of the Regulations the incineration of body parts by hospitals and other such establishments in possession of parts of a deceased body, where the retention of that part of the body is no longer necessary and the families do not wish cremation or burial of that part, eg. tissue for forensic testing. The 2006 Regulations also allow midwives to certify a stillbirth. In addition it is recognised that the forms apply to civil partnerships in the same way as they apply to matrimonial relationships.

Christians

If there is a hospital chaplain, it is advantageous if he or she is informed by nursing staff when a patient is dying or receiving terminal care or when there is a sudden emergency such as an admission to the accident and emergency department where the patient is considered unlikely to survive, or an unforeseen deterioration, a cardiac arrest or a decision to switch off artificial ventilation or feeding. However a ruling by the Commissioner for Information advises that since hospital chaplains are not registered health care professionals they can only access data under the Data Protection Act with the explicit informed consent of a patient (MacAskill, 2006). It is important for nursing staff to ascertain whether a patient would wish to be visited by a chaplain and document the patient's consent, where appropriate.

After death Christians are normally clothed in a shroud and wrapped in a cloth or sheet. The arms and hand are placed at the sides. There is no religions objection to a post mortem or cremation. Roman Catholics and other Christian denominations may seek to have the rite of extreme unction or rite of the anointing of the sick. Since 1972 a new rite has been used within the Roman Catholic church, which is not necessarily associated with the imminence of death. The booklet *Anointing Christ's Healing Touch* (Betram, 2004) recommends that

> *The ideal moment for the sacrament is before an operation, not afterwards. It is routine that patients preparing for anaesthetic must not receive anything by mouth … so they should not receive Holy Communion, but can and should be anointed.*

Clearly the sooner a chaplain is notified about the possible requirements of anointing the sick, the easier it is to make the appropriate arrangements. The booklet also provides useful information about conducting the rite in an emergency when the patient is unconscious. Relatives may or may not wish to be present.

Jews

A Jewish Rabbi may be on call in the hospital and the local synagogue should be contacted in the circumstances listed above. Special rites and prayers are given and special facilities are available for Jews to register a death at the local Registry Office on Saturdays and for burials on Sundays. If relatives cannot be traced, the Jewish Burial Society or synagogue should be contacted immediately to make funeral arrangements. Post mortems are allowed on Jewish persons only if they have been ordered by the coroner and only very liberal Jews would permit cremation. The body should not be touched until the views of the relatives or local synagogue are known.

To Jews death is seen as a natural process and Jewish practices relating to death and mourning have two purposes: to show respect for the dead and to comfort the living. After a person dies, the eyes are closed, the body is laid on the floor and covered, and candles are lit next to the body. The body is never left alone until after burial, as a sign of respect. Volunteers may be available to provide care for the dead. Prior to burial the body is thoroughly cleaned and wrapped in a simple, plain linen shroud. The body is not embalmed, and no organs or fluids may be removed. However in some sects organ donation is permitted, because the subsequent burial of the donee will satisfy the requirement of burying the entire body. The body must not be cremated. It must be buried in earth. Coffins are not required, but if they are used, they must have holes drilled in them so that the body comes in contact with the earth. The body is never displayed at funerals; open caskets are forbidden by Jewish law. Further information about the processes of mourning can be obtained from the jewfaq website and a book by Maurice Lamm (2000).

Muslims

If the death of a Muslim is expected, the Muslim Imam should be called so that special prayers can be given to the dying patient. Following the death, the body should normally be left untouched. When it is removed to the mortuary, it should be washed by another Muslim of the same sex and then left uncovered. The body should, if possible, face Mecca (South East). Prayers which follow the death should preferably be said at the Mosque, and it is therefore important to release the body to the undertakers as soon as possible. If relatives cannot be traced, the local Mosque should be notified immediately. Post mortems are against the belief of the Muslim faith, but cannot be refused if a coroner orders one. The body is not left alone between death and burial. Muslim rules relating to a dying person can be obtained from the al-islam website.

Sikhs

There are no particular arrangements which should be observed on the death of a Sikh. However post mortems are not normally allowed and cremation is the preferred method of disposal, although if it is not possible, any other method such as burial or submergence at sea is acceptable. Death is considered a natural process and God's will and any public displays of grief at the funeral such as wailing or crying out loud are discouraged. The body is usually bathed and clothed by family members and taken to the cremation grounds. Hymns are recited. The ashes are disposed of by immersing them in the nearest river.

Hindus

Hindu priests very often wish to perform the last rites but in their absence anyone may read to the patient from the *Bhagavad Gita* if this is desired by the patient. Although there are no particular rules about post mortems, often relatives will refuse consent. It is usual for cremation to take place rather than burial. Further information is available from the Hinduism Today International website.

A Hindu approaching death works diligently to finish all his business in his lifetime. Since Hindus consider a conscious death to be the ideal, they will avoid excessive drugs or mind numbing medical measures and cultivate detachment as death approaches, knowing that loss is not suffered when something is given up voluntarily, only when it is taken by force. Death at home, rather than in hospital, is the preferred option. Dying people are placed with the head facing east. A lamp is lit near the head and dying people are urged to concentrate on their mantra. Holy ash or sandal paste is applied to the forehead, Verdic verses are chanted and a few drops of milk, Ganga or other holy water are trickled into the mouth. After death, if the Hindu dies at home, the body is laid in the home's entryway, with the head facing south on a cot or near the ground. A lamp is kept lit near the head and incense burned. A cloth is tied under the chin and over the top of the head. The thumbs are tied together, as are the big toes. When death occurs in hospital, the relatives will attempt to get the death certificate signed immediately so that they can transport the body home. The body should not be embalmed or organs removed. Religious pictures are turned to the wall and in some traditions mirrors are covered.

Buddhists

Buddhists believe that the dead are reborn at higher or lower places of existence, depending on merits they have built up in this life and former lives. Entering death in a positive state of mind in the company of monks and family members can contribute to rebirth on a higher level. Buddhism has no dogmatic rules for what kind of care the body of the dead person should be given, apart from the process being handled in a worthy and respectful way. The family may agree to a post mortem. The deceased may be cremated or buried, depending on the wishes of the family. White clothing and white headbands are symbols of mourning during the ceremony. More information is available from the buddism website.

Open air cremations for Hindus and Sikhs

The Anglo-Asian Friendship Society reported in February 2006 that a ban on the use of funeral pyres, dating back to 1930, unfairly penalised both Hindus and Sikhs. The Society has approached Newcastle City Council to seek land for open air cremations and is threatening to take the case to the European Court of Human Rights (Norfolk, 2006). The Society's president maintains that open-air cremations are considered essential to the process of reincarnation.

Other religious sects

Where a patient from another religion is dying, advice should be sought from family members or the local church community to ascertain any specific requirements about the care of the body.

Persons without a specified religion

Many patients when admitted to hospital may state that they are Church of England (C of E) even though it is many years since they have attended a service. If they should die, the family would probably care for them according to Christian traditions. However there are some patients who may on admission declare themselves to be atheist, agnostic or humanist.

The British Humanist Association (BHA) represents the interests of people in the UK who are ethically concerned but non-religious and works for an open and inclusive society with freedom of belief and speech and for an end to the privileged position of religion in law, education, broadcasting and elsewhere. The BHA describes humanism as:

> *the belief that we can live good lives without religious or superstitious beliefs. Humanists make sense of the world using reason, experience and shared human values. We seek to make the best of the one life we have by creating meaning and purpose for ourselves. We take responsibility for our actions and work with others for the common good.*

The British Humanist Association provides advice on funerals on the humanism website. In a humanist funeral there is no suggestion that the person has gone on to another life – it is the life that was lived that is celebrated and the person people knew who is talked about and said goodbye to. The BHA trains officiants or celebrants to conduct funerals (and baby namings and weddings).

The Natural Death Centre

The Natural Death Centre, a charity set up in 1991, aims to support those dying at home and their carers and help people arrange inexpensive, family organised and environmentally-friendly funerals. It also has a more general aim of helping improve the quality of dying. It provides assistance on living wills, and a befriending network. Its details and publications can be accessed via its website and its publications include *The Natural Death Handbook* (Weinrich and Speyer, 2003). The Association of Natural Burial Grounds was set up by the Natural Death Centre in 1994 to support schemes of natural (also known as woodland or green) burial grounds and over 200 sites are now available around the UK. It has a code of practice and rules of membership to ensure that the sites are properly maintained and the graves appropriately located and marked.

Disposal of the body: The law

It is a requirement of law that the executors of the deceased arrange for the proper disposal of the body. Where a person dies in hospital without known relatives, it is the duty of the hospital authority to arrange for the cremation or burial of the deceased. In its updated guidance on patients who die in hospital, the Department of Health (2005) states that:

> *It is clear that the circumstances of people who die in hospital vary enormously and a death may present trusts with complex, time consuming*

and sometimes costly decisions. The situation may arise where trusts have to consider making funeral arrangements for patients who die in hospital because:

- *relatives cannot be traced*
- *relatives cannot afford to pay for the funeral and do not qualify for Social Fund Funeral Payments (*Department for Work and Pensions, 2005*) or*
- *relatives are unwilling to take responsibility for funeral arrangements.*

The Department of Health's guidance recommends that in the above circumstances, it will be particularly important for trusts to consider having a formal policy that takes account of the interests and/or responsibilities of other partners. For example the local authority in whose area the body lies may arrange for burials or cremation under Section 46(1) of the Public Health (Control of Disease) Act 1984. However practice will vary widely depending on local circumstances and trusts may wish to liaise closely and develop protocols with local authorities and others to establish responsibilities and help ensure the most respectful burial or cremation takes place as quickly as possible.

Under the Public Health (Control of Disease) Act 1984 S46(1) where any person who dies or has been found dead in a local authority's area, then the local authority has a duty to cause the body to be cremated or buried. The local authority can recover the costs from the dead person's estate. The Department of Health guidance was updated in 1997 to explain the minimum standards for funerals and burial or cremation arrangements where NHS Trusts take responsibility for them. The guidance has now been replaced (Department of Health, 2005).

Where NHS trusts take responsibility for a funeral

The Department of Health (2005) advises that where trusts do take responsibility for a funeral (including meeting the costs) or assist others in arranging a funeral, the following points should be noted:

- It is important to be sensitive to the wishes of the family and friends of the deceased and to take account of any known cultural or religious beliefs of the deceased. The choice between burial or cremation should be made only after taking into account any known views of the deceased, including religious preferences; the views of relatives close to the deceased; and, in the case of long-stay patients with no relatives, the views of any friends in the hospital, including both patients and staff. Where there is no known preference, and the faith of the deceased does not indicate any preference, cremation should be considered as the preferred choice.

- The funeral arrangements should be made by a funeral director who will be responsible for the service, burial or cremation.
- A minister of religion or appropriate religious representative of the faith of the deceased should be present to conduct the service in accordance with that faith. Depending upon the faith of the deceased, the appropriate hospital chaplain, religious representative or adviser could be consulted at an early stage to advise about any special faith observances.
- Arrangements should respect and meet the needs of families and carers from differing religious and cultural groups. For example the needs of prayer and facilities appropriate to the faith of the deceased should be observed, which might include washing of the body by a designated person, dressing of the body and the length of time the body lies in state. Some faiths require the burial to be within a time limit and arrangements need to be sensitive to such requirements.
- The deceased may have been known to many people. However, even when there are no known relatives, other patients and staff members may regard themselves as family. They may wish to attend the funeral and should be given the opportunity to attend the funeral service. If the funeral is by cremation, the ashes should be scattered or interred in a suitable place.

Transport of deceased patients

No specific advice is given in the new guidance (Department of Health, 2005) on meeting the costs of transport of deceased patients and the above list of points would apply. (In its earlier guidance the Department of Health (1992) advised that while there was no obligation on purchasing health authorities (these would now be the primary care trusts) or provider units to meet the cost of transport of the dead body to a funeral in the home area (which may be some distance from the hospital) but if the relatives were unable to afford the cost of transport, they might ask the provider unit to meet the cost. It suggested that this request might be met where the patient had been referred to a hospital distant from his or her home. A request should not normally be met where the patient was admitted to a distant hospital, because the patient happened to be visiting that area. This did not apply if someone was prepared to assume responsibility for a funeral in the home area and where the cost of disposal would otherwise have fallen upon the hospital and the cost of transport was less than the cost of the NHS arranging the funeral.)

In May 2006 (Sapsted, 2006) it was reported that a daughter expressed outrage after a crematorium told her that it would not cremate her mother because she was too large. At 22 stone she was too big to fit into the incinerator. The body could be taken 100 miles to a crematorium with a larger incinerator.

In May 2006 the Government announced that old graves may be opened to allow more bodies to be buried in the same plot (Petre, 2006). The space problem was particularly acute in London and a report in 2004 Planning for Burial Space in London had recommended that only graves more than 100 years old should be disturbed.

Laws relating to disposal of the body

Any cremation must take place according to the Cremation Acts of 1902 and 1952 and subsequent regulations. Burials in churchyards come under ecclesiastical law and non-Church of England burials come under statutory provisions (Burial Laws Amendment Act 1988). In August 2004 the Leicester Consistory court of the Church of England ruled that a faculty for a burial which was contrary to the policy of the diocese and the parochial church council could only be granted where there were powerful medical reasons, which could not be shown in the present case. The churchyard had been closed since June 1974 and had a garden and remembrance book in accordance with diocesan regulations (*Re St James and Great Birstall*). There have been several cases recently where relatives have asked the church to permit the removal of their dead relative from the existing graveyard to a graveyard nearer to the relative's new home. The consistory courts have ruled that once buried, the deceased must be allowed to rest in peace, unless there are medical reasons (Gledhill, 2006).

Since 1974 burials in public cemeteries have come under local authority control under which burial authorities are required to provide and maintain public cemeteries, whether inside or outside their areas (Local Government Act 1972, S214). Private cemeteries are not covered by statutory provisions, but if consecration of the area is wanted a private act would be required.

Procedure following notification of the death

Any person receiving the certificate for disposal from the registrar must give it to the person who is to arrange for the disposal of the body (Births and Deaths Registration Act S24(3)). The person who disposes of the body has a duty to notify the registrar within 96 hours of the disposal of the date, place and means of the disposal of the body (ibid S3(1)). If the registrar fails to receive this notification, he or she can inquire of the person to whom the certificate of disposal was issued details about the disposal of the body. If it is discovered that the body has not been disposed of (and the Human Tissue Act 2004 does not apply) then the registrar must report the failure to dispose of the body to environmental health department.

Two undertakers were charged at York Crown Court in June 2007 with conspiring to prevent the lawful burial of a baby boy. They had sent a baby's empty coffin to be buried and then covered up their mistake by hiding the body between the legs of an elderly woman who was about to be cremated. They were sentenced to 18 months in prison suspended for two years and were each fined £5000 (*The Times*, 2007).

Identification of the body

It is vital that clear procedures for the identification of the body are followed meticulously to ensure that the labelling of the body in the mortuary and then the correct transfer to the undertakers takes place. Mistakes in following the correct procedure can cause considerable distress to relatives and cannot always be rectified when discovered. Correct documentation must be completed and retained at all times. The Department of Health (NHS Estates, 2001) recommends that NHS trusts have in place:

- Secure systems for the identification of bodies, in order to ensure that the correct body is prepared for viewing and/or released for cremation or burial.
- Adequate facilities for the storage of bodies. Guidance is available on what to take account of when improving or rebuilding mortuary facilities .

Application of the law to the situation in *Box 3.1*

Returning the situation at the start of the chapter, as long as there are no restrictive covenants limiting the use of the land, a place of burial may be established by any person without statutory authority, in private ground, provided that no nuisance is caused thereby. If consecration of the site is required, then a Private Act would have to be passed by Parliament. Neighbours may well object to such use of the land. In a case in 1877 (*Lord Cowley v. Byas*) it had been assumed that actual interment in a private cemetery within a certain distance of a dwelling house was prohibited by the Burial Act 1855 but this was not followed in a later case (*Clegg v. Metcalfe*).

In Ray's case he would have to comply with public health requirements relating to the disposal of a body. Ray would need to obtain the registrar's certificate for disposal of the body and satisfy the registrar that the body would be disposed of appropriately. Ray then has to notify the registrar of the date, place and means of the disposal. While planning permission is not required for non-commercial sites for a limited number of burials for family, friends and those living in the house, there are various legal requirements and recommendations relating to burial on private land. It would therefore be advisable for Ray to contact the local authority about his intentions. He should also take into account possible problems in relation to selling the property at a later date. Ray would be well advised to contact the Natural Death Centre, who would provide advice on burying his mother in woodlands or similar natural burial ground.

Conclusions

Sensitivity is essential in those who care for the dying with an appreciation of the importance of observing the correct rituals to assist relatives and friends in their bereavement. Dignity, understanding of different customs and religious practices and flexibility to assist in their scrupulous observation is essential. Insensitive handling and disposal of dead bodies can be the subject of complaints and investigations (Department of Health, 2001).

References

Bertram J (2004) *Anointing Christ's Healing Touch*. London: Catholic Truth Society

Births and Deaths Registration Act 1926 S3(1), S24(3)

Burial Laws Amendment Act 1880

Clegg v. Metcalfe [1914] 1 Ch 808

Department of Health (1992) *Patients Who Die in Hospital HSG(92)8*; www.dh.gov.uk/PolicyAnd Guidance/Organisation

Department of Health (1997) *Patients who Die in Hospital HSG(97)43*. London: Department of Health

Department of Health (2001) *Report of an Investigation into Mortuary Arrangements at Bedford Hospital NHS Trust*. London: Department of Health

Department of Health (2005) *When a Patient Dies: Advice on Developing Bereavement Services in the NHS*. London: Department of Health

Department for Work and Pensions (2005) *What to Do After a Death in England and Wales Leaflet D49*. London: Department for Work and Pensions

Gledhill R (2006) Homeowners on the move want to take dead relatives. *The Times* **2 December**

Lamm M (2000) *The Jewish Way in Death and Mourning*. New York: Jonathan David

Local Government Act 1972 S214

Lord Cowley v. Byas (1877) 5ChD 944 CA

Macaskill M (2006) Data protection 'stops last rites'. *The Sunday Times* **3 December**

NHS Estates (2001) *Facilities for Mortuary and Post-Mortem Room Services. NHS Estates HBN* 2. www.nhsestates.gov.uk

Norfolk A (2006) Hindus and Sikhs call for the right to open-air cremations. *The Times* **1 February**: 5

Public Health (Control of Disease) Act 1984 S47(1)

Re St James the Great, Birstall The Times 14 August 2006 Consistory Court

Weinrich W, Speyer J (eds) (2003) Natural Death Handbook (4th edn). London: Natural Death Centre

The Times (2007) Baby cremated to cover error. *The Times* **14 June**

Sapsted D (2006) Too big for crematorium. *The Daily Telegraph* **30 May**

Petre J (2006) Old graves may be used for double and vertical burials. *The Daily Telegraph* **31 May**

Regulations as to Cremation 1930 SR and O 1930/ 1016 as amended by the Cremation (Amendment) Regulations 2000 SI 2000/58

Resources

British Humanist Association, 1 Gower Street, London WC1E 6HD. Tel: 020 7079 3580, Fax: 020 7079 3588. Email: info@humanism.org.uk

Natural Death Centre 6 Blackstock Mews Blackstock Road London N4 2BT. Tel: 0871 288 2098. Email: ndc@alberyfoundation.org

Cremation (Amendment) Regulations 2006 SI 2006 No 92

www.al-islam.org/laws/

www.buddhismfarewell.htm

www.dh.gov.uk

www.hinduismtoday.com

www.humanism.org.uk

www.jewfaq.org/death.htm

www.naturaldeath.org.uk

www.sikhismhomepage

CHAPTER 4

Pregnancy, stillbirths and miscarriages and disposal

Box 4.1. A miscarriage

Brenda was 5 months pregnant when she miscarried. She was seriously ill but when she recovered, she asked for the fetal remains to be made available to be buried in her local churchyard. She subsequently discovered that they had been incinerated and she wished to sue the hospital.

Since the amendments to the Abortion Act 1967, the significance of 28 weeks, after which date the ending of a pregnancy is notifiable as a stillbirth, has been changed to 24 weeks. This has considerable procedural consequences for the woman, but it should be remembered by staff, that even where the fetus is less than 24 weeks gestation, the woman may feel as bereaved as she would following a longer pregnancy, even though there are not the same legal formalities for the fetus's disposal.

Legal status of the fetus

The fetus is not regarded in law as having an independent legal personality. As a result of this principle, actions cannot be brought in its name before its birth. Only after the fetus is born, can legal action be brought on his or her behalf. Once discharged from the womb, the legal position depends upon the length of gestation.

Fetus of less than 24 weeks

If a fetus of less than 24 weeks is delivered without any signs of life, then no registration of the event is necessary. The fetus may be disposed of without formality in any way that does not constitute a nuisance or an affront to public decency. If the fetus shows signs of life and then dies, it would have to be treated as both a birth and a death and therefore both the birth and the death would have to be registered (see below). Health professionals should be sensitive to the fact that parents may suffer the same feelings of bereavement whatever the period of gestation and should therefore arrange for counselling and support as they would if the baby were full term.

The use of fetal tissue comes under the provisions of the Human Tissue Act 2004 and the appropriate consent must be obtained to its retention, storage and use. This is discussed further in *Chapter 17* and full guidance is given in Appendix B of the Human Tissue Authority's (2006) *Code of Practice on Removal, Storage and Disposal of Human Organs and Tissue Retention.*

Fetus of more than 24 weeks: A stillbirth

A stillbirth according to the Stillbirth Act 1992 is defined as

> *Where a child issues forth from its mother after the 24th week of pregnancy, and which did not at any time after being completely expelled from its mother breathe or show any signs of life.*

The stillbirth has to be registered as such and the informant has to deliver to the registrar a written certificate that the child was not born alive. This must be signed by the registered medical practitioner or the registered midwife who was in attendance at the birth or who has examined the body. The certificate must state, to the best of the knowledge and belief of the person signing it, the cause of death and the estimated duration of the pregnancy (Registration of Births and Deaths Act 1953 S11(1)(a)). Where the midwife is in sole attendance at the confinement, whether in a home or in a hospital, she must complete the certificate.

Alternatively, a declaration in the prescribed form giving the reasons for the absence of a certificate and that the child was not born alive could be made (ibid S11(1)(b)). Where registrars (of births and deaths) are given information of an alleged stillbirth and they have reason to believe that the child was born alive they must report the matter to the coroner on the approved form Registration of Births and Deaths Regulations 1987 S33(1)(2)). Registrars must not register a stillbirth which to their knowledge has been reported to the coroner until they have received either a coroner's certificate after inquest or a notification from the coroner that he or she does not intend to hold an inquest.

A stillbirth should be disposed of by burial in a burial ground or churchyard or by cremation at an authorised crematorium. The certificate must be taken to the registrar within 42 days of the day of delivery of the stillborn child. The certificate of disposal for burial or cremation will then be issued by the registrar.

Rule 12 of the *Midwives Rules and Standards* (Nursing and Midwifery Council, 2004) requires midwives to have a named supervisor appointed by the local supervising authority covering their main area of practice. The local supervising authority must ensure that all practising midwives within its area have 24 hour access to a supervisor of midwives. It is implied that midwives should inform the supervisor of midwives of any maternal death, stillbirth or neonatal death occurring when they are the midwife responsible for the care of that mother and her baby. Further guidance on the statutory duties of the midwife is given in the *Midwives Rules and Standards* (NMC, 2004). Under the supplementary information and legislation placed by the Nursing and Midwifery Council (NMC) at the end of this publication, the NMC sets out the provisions of the Births and Deaths Registration Act and outlines the duties of the midwife. The guidance contained in the earlier *Midwife's Code of Practice* paragraph 39 (UKCC, 1998) that midwives must inform their supervisor of midwives of any maternal death, stillbirth or neonatal death occurring when they are the midwife responsible for the care of that mother and her baby is not included in the updated standards. However the need for this communication would be implied from the relationship of the midwife and supervisor as set out in the NMC guidance.

Disposal of stillbirth

A Health Authority should not dispose of a stillbirth without the consent of the parents. In October 1993 the manager at the Bishop Auckland General Hospital, Co. Durham, admitted causing distress to Tracey Turner for burying her stillborn baby without her permission. It was stated that there would be an investigation into how the mistake occurred (The Times, 1993). Under the Births and Deaths Registration Act 1953 the informant in the case of a stillborn child found exposed is the person who found the child (Births and Deaths Registration Act 1957 added by Children Act 1975 Schedule 3 Para. 13(2)).

The change of time from 28 weeks to 24 weeks for the definition of stillbirth also affects the right of the mother to maternity allowances. The meaning of confinement for the purposes of benefits under the Social Security and Benefits Act 1992 now covers confinements of 24 or more weeks rather than 28 weeks.

Abortion

The Human Fertilisation and Embryology Act 1990 Section 37 changed the law relating to abortion. It substituted a new section for the Abortion Act 1967 and apart from some exceptional circumstances shown in *Table 4.1*, the rule now is that the pregnancy must not have exceeded its 24th week and that the continuance of the pregnancy would involve a risk greater than if the pregnancy were terminated to the physical or mental health of the pregnant woman or any existing children of her family. In the exceptional circumstances shown in

Table 4.1 it is possible for an abortion to take place after 24 weeks' gestation. The statutory requirements are shown in *Table 4.1*.

Abortion after 24 weeks

What happens in the very exceptional circumstances when an abortion takes place after 24 weeks' gestation? This is possible under the amendments to the Abortion Act 1967 by the Human Fertilisation and Embryology Act 1990 which are shown in *Table 4.1*. If a termination took place after 24 weeks under sections 1 (b), (c) and (d) then the proceeds would be seen in law as a stillbirth and the legal provisions relating to stillbirths would have to be followed. Very few abortions now take place after 24 weeks' gestation. Figures from the Department of Health (2005a) show that 42 women had terminations at 28 weeks or more gestation in 2004 compared with 49 the year before. There were 18 cases that involved pregnancies of 32 weeks or more, compared with 22 in 2003.

How is the length of gestation determined?

The midwife or doctor have to use their professional judgement in determining whether the fetus comes within the provisions of the stillbirth regulations. If

Table 4.1. Abortion Act 1967 Section 1(1) as amended by the Human Fertilisation and Embryology Act 1990

A person shall not be guilty of an offence under the law relating to abortion when a pregnancy is terminated by a registered medical practitioner if two registered medical practitioners are of the opinion, formed in good faith

(a) that the pregnancy has not exceeded its 24th week and that the continuance of the pregnancy would involve risk, greater than if the pregnancy were terminated, of injury to the physical or mental health of the pregnant woman or any existing children of her family; or
(b) that the termination is necessary to prevent grave permanent injury to the physical or mental health of the pregnant woman; or
(c) that the continuance of the pregnancy would involve risk to the life of the pregnant woman, greater than if the pregnancy were terminated; or
(d) that there is a substantial risk that if the child were born it would suffer from such physical or mental abnormalities as to be seriously handicapped

the fetus is considered to be less than 24 weeks the parents could still arrange a ceremony and formal disposal of the body if they so wish.

Should the fetus survive a termination and breathes, then every reasonable care should be taken of the baby. Speeding up the death of the baby would be considered to be manslaughter or murder.

Live birth followed by death

A fetus of 24 weeks or more gestation which is born alive but subsequently dies is not a stillbirth but must be registered as a birth and a death. The registered medical practitioner who attended the baby must issue a medical certificate giving cause of death. The parents will be required to register both the birth and death. The registrar will then issue a disposal certificate to permit burial or cremation.

Maternal death

In the rare event of a maternal death, health professionals should be conversant with the legal requirements for the certification and registration of the death and the requirements when the family request a cremation rather than a burial. They should also ensure that they are familiar with specific ethnic and religious requirements when appropriate.

Department of Health guidance

The Department of Health (2005b) has provided guidance on patients who die in hospital. It suggests that NHS trusts will wish to consider putting in place arrangements for the respectful disposal of fetal tissue resulting from pregnancy losses prior to 24 weeks, including ectopic pregnancies, early or late miscarriages, early intra-uterine fetal deaths and terminations. Arrangements for the respectful burial or cremation of the bodies of babies following stillbirth or neonatal death also need to be considered (involving the hospital chaplaincy service and others as appropriate). Trusts will wish to ensure that women (or couples) are informed about these arrangements and are enabled to express their own wishes about what happens to their baby's body or products of conception and, if they want to, to make their own funeral or cremation arrangements. Further guidance is available from the Department of Health website in the form of a question and answer briefing. The Stillbirth and Neonatal Death Society has published a booklet: *Pregnancy Loss and the Death of a Baby. Guidelines for Professionals* (Henley and Schlott, 2007). See also the Royal College of Nursing (2001) publication *Sensitive Disposal of All Fetal Remains*.

Legal status of the fetus

Until a fetus is born, it does not have a legal personality and actions cannot be brought in its name. Certain protection is provided for the fetus by means of the Abortion Act 1967 (as amended), so unless the conditions of the Abortion Act are complied with, it is a criminal offence to bring about a miscarriage. Protection of the fetus in terms of implantation and research is also provided by the Human Fertilisation and Embryology Act 1990.

A dispute arose over the continuation of the life of frozen embryos in the Evans case. Natalie Evans and her partner had agreed that, following a diagnosis of pre-cancerous ovaries, they would undergo one cycle of in-vitro fertilisation treatment before surgical removal of her ovaries. Six embryos were created and stored. Subsequently, the relationship between the couple broke up and her partner withdrew his consent to the continued storage of the embryos. The continuing consent of both partners to the storage of the embryos is a requirement under the Human Fertilisation and Embryology Act 1990. Natalie Evans brought an action in the High Court seeking an injunction to compel him to restore his consent but her claim was refused (*Evans v. Amicus Healthcare Ltd 2003*). She appealed to the Court of Appeal which upheld the judgement of the High Court (*Evans v. Amicus Healthcare Ltd 2004*). Natalie Evans then took her case to the European Court of Human Rights (ECHR) (*Evans v. United Kingdom*). The ECHR held that there had been no violation of the right to life in Article 2 of the European Convention on Human Rights, since under English law an embryo did not have independent rights or interests and could not claim or have claimed on its behalf a right to life under Article 2. Nor was there any breach of Article 8 and the right to private and family life.

Application of the law to situation in *Box 4.1*

Even though Brenda's pregnancy does not last 24 weeks, and therefore, as long as the proceeds are disposed of with dignity and decency, no specific formalities must be complied with and no registration is required, for Brenda that loss could seem like a bereavement. She is entitled to request that the body is disposed of according to her wishes. She may want a small ceremony. It would be the duty of the hospital to ensure that as far as practicable her wishes were acceded to and she was supported in her grief and bereavement. She should initially take up her concerns with the designated officer of complaints. She may eventually be able to obtain compensation, especially if she can show that she has suffered psychiatric disorder as a result of the actions of the NHS trust.

Conclusions

The Stillbirth and Neonatal Death Society (SANDS) offers support for bereaved parents and families where a baby dies at or soon after birth. It also runs a network of self-help groups that are run by and for bereaved parents and it provides information for the bereaved and health professionals. Staff should have details of these organisations and offer support to any woman who has lost her baby whatever the length of gestation and whether legal formalities are required or not.

References

Births and Deaths Registration Act 1957 added by Children Act 1975 Schedule 3 Para. 13(2)

Department of Health (2005a) Stastics available from www.dh.gov.uk

Department of Health (2005b) *When a Patient Dies: Advice on Developing Bereavement Services in the NHS*. London: Department of Health

Evans v. Amicus Healthcare Ltd The Times 2 October 2003 HC

Evans v. Amicus Healthcare Ltd The Times 30 June 2004 CA, [2005] Fam 1

Evans v. United Kingdom (Application No 6339/05) The Times 17 March 2006; [2006] 1 FCR 585 [2007] ECHR 264 No 6339/05

Henley A, Schlott J (2007) *Improving Bereavement Care* (3rd edn). London: Stillbirth and Neonatal Death Society

Human Tissue Authority (2006) *Code of Practice 5. Removal, Storage and Disposal of Human Organs and Tissue Retention*. London: Human Tissue Authority

Nursing and Midwifery Council (2004) *Midwives Rules and Standards*. London: Nursing and Midwifery Council

Registration of Births and Deaths Act 1953 Section 11(1)(a), 11(1)(b) and Section 41 as amended by Section 1 of the Stillbirth Act 1992.

Registration of Births and Deaths Regulations SI 1987 2088 regulation 33(1) and(2)

Royal College of Nursing (2001) *Sensitive Disposal of All Fetal Remains*. London: RCN

UKCC (1998) *Midwives Rules and Code of Practice*. London: UKCC

The Times (1993) News item. *The Times*, **11 October**

Resources

Stillbirth and Neonatal Death Society Helpline: 020 7436 5881; www.uk-sands.org/

www.dh.gov.uk

CHAPTER 5

Health and safety considerations on death of patient

> **Box 5.1 An explosive time**
>
> Arthur, who had spent all his life in Liverpool, came to live with his niece in Brighton. He was in his 80s and systematically prepared for his death. He told her that he would like to be cremated and the ashes returned to Liverpool. On his death in hospital, the family made arrangements for him to be cremated. Unfortunately no one remembered or checked about the fact that a heart pacemaker had been inserted many years before, and when questioned by funeral directors, no warnings were given by the family. The pacemaker exploded in the crematorium and the local authority who was responsible for its upkeep claimed compensation from the family or NHS trust. Who, if anyone is liable?

There are certain circumstances where public health considerations must be taken into account when a person dies. These may add to relatives' distress, and health professionals have the difficult task of ensuring that the law is followed in relation to the prevention of outbreaks of infection or threats to health and safety and at the same time taking steps to minimise any further the additional distress that relatives could suffer.

Public health considerations

Public health legislation gives powers to a justice of the peace to take precautions to secure the safety of the public in the event of certain deaths. Thus if a justice of the peace (acting if necessary without notice) is satisfied on a certificate of the proper officer of the local authority for the district in which the dead body lies, or on a certificate of any other registered medical practitioner on the staff of the health authority of that district, that the retention of the body in any building would endanger the health of the inmates of that building, or of any adjoining or neighbouring building, he may order that the body be removed by, and at the cost of the local authority, to a mortuary (Public Health (Control of Disease) Act 1984 S48(1)). He may also order that the necessary steps be taken to secure that the body is buried within the time limited by the order, or, if he considers immediate burial necessary, immediately. Friends or relatives could secure compliance with the order on the local authority, by arranging for the body to be cremated within the time set in the order or immediately.

Every person who is responsible for premises where the body of a person who has died while suffering from a notifiable disease is lying, must take such steps as may be reasonably practicable to prevent persons coming unnecessarily into contact with, or proximity to, the body, and if he or she fails to do so is liable to prosecution (ibid S44).

It is a criminal offence to hold a wake over the body of a person who has died while suffering from a notifiable disease, and the occupier of any premises who permits or suffers any such wake to take place, and every person who takes part in the wake, is liable on summary conviction to a fine (ibid S45).

If a person dies in hospital while suffering from a notifiable disease, and the proper officer of the local authority or any registered medical practitioner certifies that in his or her opinion it is desirable, in order to prevent the spread of infection, that the body should not be removed from the hospital except for the purpose of being taken direct to a mortuary or being forthwith buried or cremated, it is unlawful for any person to remove the body from the hospital except for that purpose (ibid S43(1)). When the body is removed for burial or cremation in such a case it must be taken direct to the crematorium or a place of burial and there buried or cremated (ibid S43(2)). Failure to obey these rules is a criminal offence (ibid S43(3)).

The Secretary of State has power to make further regulations relating to the means of disposal of dead bodies other than by burial or cremation, the period of time a body may be retained after death on any premises, and on embalming or preservation, as appear desirable in the interests of public health or public safety (ibid S47(1)).

Guidance on the disposal of bodies with dangerous pathogens

The Department of Health has an advisory committee that provides guidance on dangerous pathogens. Special arrangements should be followed when handling bodies which contain dangerous pathogens. It is imperative to wear full protective clothing, wrap the body in a special cadaver bag and to make all necessary arrangements to avoid the spread of infection. The cadaver bag should be clearly labelled as a high risk infectious body. Nursing staff should have training in cross infection controls and ensure that relatives do not breach cross infection control guidelines.

Implants and removal of cardiac pacemakers

The Department of Health guidance (Department of Health and Social Security, 1983) on the ownership of implants and cardiac pacemakers states:

> *An implant is any device or prosthesis implanted surgically in and intended to remain within the patient's body. An implant becomes the property of the person in whom it has been implanted and it remains his or her property even if it is subsequently removed. Following the patient's death, it forms part of his or her estate unless there is any specific provision to the contrary. It is neither desirable nor necessary for implants to be removed after the patient's death, except in the case of cardiac pacemakers.*

Clearly in the light of the advice following the Alder Hey scandal discussions must take place with relatives over anything that is to be removed from the body and the appropriate information must be given to relatives and any necessary forms must be completed.

Removal of cardiac pacemakers

The Department of Health advice further states:

> *Where a patient fitted with a cardiac pacemaker has died it is desirable for the pacemaker to be removed and returned to the cardiac department which implanted it for checking and evaluation of its performance, so that knowledge gained can be applied for the benefit of future patients. If the patient is to be cremated it is also essential that the pacemaker should first be removed since if heated to high temperature, pacemakers are liable to explode and give off toxic fumes and could be hazardous to cremation staff or premises.*
>
> *If the patient dies in hospital, removal of the pacemaker will normally be carried out by a mortuary technician, unless for clinical reasons a hospital doctor decides to remove it himself. Funeral directors may also remove cardiac pacemakers, who have been given guidance by the Home Office via the National Association of Funeral Directors.*

Radioactive materials

Care must be taken in carrying out post mortems, and burying or cremating a body which contains radioactive substances. Guidance is provided by the

Institute of Physics and Engineering in Medicine (2001). This sets out the good practice to be followed to ensure that there is no breach of Ionising Radiation Regulations 1999 or the Radio Substances Act 1993. It recommends that the Radiation Protection Adviser (RPA) should be contacted for advice on whether or not there is any requirement for whole body or extremity dose monitoring. The guidance covers the dosages over which special precautions should be taken and the different procedures that are to be followed when a patient dies within 48 hours of diagnostic quantities of radioactive substances or within 48 hours of therapeutic quantities of radioactive substances.

Recording cause of death

It used to be the situation where a doctor, instead of recording on the death certificate that a patient had died from an AIDS-related disease, would write the immediate cause of death (eg. bronchopneumonia) and also tick Box B to indicate that they could provide further information. Now however the General Medical Council (quoted in Terrence Higgins Trust, 2003) has made it clear that doctors are required to disclose information about serious communicable diseases:

> *You must disclose information about serious communicable diseases in accordance with the law. For example, the appropriate authority must be informed where a notifiable disease is diagnosed. Where a communicable disease contributed to the cause of death, this must be recorded on the death certificate. You must also pass information about serious communicable diseases to the relevant authorities for the purpose of communicable disease control and surveillance.*

Since the registration of a death is a public document, it is impossible for relatives at present to conceal the cause of death even where they would wish to preserve confidentiality such as the death of a person from AIDS/HIV.

Applying the law to the situation in *Box 5.1*

A clear procedure should have been followed by the undertakers so that a body with a cardiac pacemaker could not be cremated until the dangerous object had been removed. Clearly it is insufficient to rely on the family's knowledge or memory. Since the patient died in hospital, it is highly likely that it was recorded in his documentation that he had a cardiac pacemaker fitted, even if cardiac problems were not the reason for his admission or death. The hospital staff would have had a duty to ensure that the existence of the pacemaker was made known to the family and to the undertakers, so that steps could be taken for its removal. Compensation may be sought from the NHS trust by the local authority for the damage that has been caused as a result of the breach of its duty of care.

Conclusion

Public health and safety considerations cannot be ignored when death occurs, but such issues place considerable strain on staff, who, as well as supporting relatives in their bereavement, must ensure that the legal requirements are followed and that no danger to the health and safety of the public arises from the disposal of the body. Any risks of contamination in the movement of the body must be controlled.

References

Department of Health and Social Security (1983) *Ownership of Implants and Removal of Cardiac Pacemakers After Death HN(83)6*. London: DHSS

Institute of Physics and Engineering in Medicine (2001) *Medical and Dental Guidance Notes: A good practice guide to implement ionising radiation protection legislation in the clinical environment*. London: Institute of Physics and Engineering in Medicine

Ionising Radiation Regulations 1999 SI 1999 No 3232

Public Health (Control of Disease) Act 1984

Terrence Higgins Trust (2003) *Disclosure of HIV on Death*. London Terrence Higgins Trust

Resources

www.gmc-uk.org/standards

CHAPTER 6

Preparation for death

> **Box 6.1. information overheard**
> Maggie O'Farrell, the writer, recounts that when she was a child she was severely ill in hospital. She heard a nurse say to another child outside the room, 'Be quiet. There's a little girl dying in there.'
> At first she had not understood, but as she stared and stared at the nurse who now would not look her in the eye, slowly she realised that this person had been talking about her (Wark, 2004). What are the legal implications?

Similar stories to the above situation could probably be told by many patients who have overheard about the seriousness of their situation by such indirect, and possibly very hurtful (albeit unintentional) means. Another comparable situation which some patients experience is 'the other ward round', where patients find that they cease to be visited by doctors who attend other patients, since they have reached a time when they are beyond medical help and are left to the palliative care of the nursing staff. Doctors no longer have a role to play. Overheard conversations are also reported by those who have been 'flatliners', ie. people with no respiration, heartbeat or brain function who may not survive following resuscitation. They subsequently report how they have memories of the time after life has apparently left their bodies (Rogers, 2002).

This chapter explores the duty of care in relation to informing patients and relatives about a patient's prognosis and possible early demise.

Right of patient to be told

At present there is not an absolute right for a patient to be told everything about his condition. Statutory provisions such as the regulations drawn up under the Data Protection Act 1998 enable people to access their own health records but there are exceptions to this right and therefore the right of access is not absolute. Under the Data Protection (Subject Access Modifications) (Health) Order the right of access to health records is modified so that access is not permitted where the access *would be likely to cause serious harm to the physical or mental health or condition of the data subject or any other person (which may include a health professional).*

Nor under common law (ie. judge-made law or case law) is there an absolute right of access to all information available about a person and the proposed treatment. Thus in the Sidaway case (*Sidaway v. Bethlem Royal Hospital Governors and others*), the House of Lords held that there was a duty to inform a patient of significant risks of substantial harm which could arise following recommended treatment. However the duty to inform had to comply with reasonable professional practice (ie. the Bolam test was applied (*Bolam v. Friern Barnet HMC*). Lord Scarman recognised the right of therapeutic privilege where, in exceptional circumstances, information could be withheld if providing the patient with this would have an adverse effect out of all proportion to its significance. Lord Scarman said that even if there was a material risk of harm arising from proposed treatment:

Even if the risk be material, the doctor will not be liable if on a reasonable assessment of his patient's condition he takes the view that a warning would be detrimental to his patient's health.

However withholding important information from a patient is a dangerous step and may be seen as an infringement of his human rights as set out in the European Convention on Human Rights Article 8. This states that:

- Everyone has the right to respect for his or her private and family life, home and correspondence.
- There shall be no interference by a public authority with the exercise of this right except such as is in accordance with the law and is necessary in a democratic society in the interests of national security, public safety or the economic wellbeing of the country, for the prevention of disorder or crime, for the protection of health or morals, or for the protection of the rights and freedoms of others.

Therefore where any health professional decides that it would be in the interests of a patient who was terminally ill, not to be told of his or her condition, the health professional has to be satisfied that withholding this information is justified under paragraph 2 of article 8 and also under the Data Protection (Subject Access Modifications) (Health) Order.

Research from the Marie Curie Palliative Care Institute in Liverpool is reported as showing that only 45% of patients know that they are in 'the dying phase' compared with 80% of their carers (*The Times*, 2007). The

Box 6.2. Am I dying nurse?

Harry Downs had been admitted for surgery and the surgeon had diagnosed inoperable cancer. The surgeon notified Harry's wife and daughter of the result, and they immediately said that Harry should not be told, since he could not cope with that information. Harry was informed that the operation had been successful and he would be discharged within a week. He suspected that he was seriously ill, and told the nurses that he hoped to go to America the following year and asked them if it was worth booking. The nurses, who had been told not to tell Harry about the diagnosis, did not know how to reply. What is the law?

research also showed that the spiritual needs of dying patients were assessed in only one third of cases and the appropriate hospital procedures after death were documented as having been followed in just as half of cases.

Confidentiality of patient information

Patients are entitled to have information relating to their medical condition kept confidential and so in the situation in *Box 6.2*, it should have been the patient who was notified first about the findings during the operation of the diagnosis and the prognosis. However if the patient is mentally incapable of receiving such information, it would be lawful to notify the relatives if that were in the best interests of the patient. Unfortunately relatives may be given confidential information when the patient is capable of receiving it and where the patient may wish to exercise the right to keep it to him or herself.

The duty to maintain the confidentiality of patient information arises from many sources: the trust relationship between patient and health professionals, the ethical duty laid down in many codes of professional practice of registered health professionals, an implied duty in the contract of employment between employer and employee, and many statutory provisions also require respect for confidentiality especially the Data Protection Act 1998 which applies to both computerised and manually held records. Clearly however in the situation in *Box 6.2* it is extremely unlikely that the patient would seek to enforce his rights to confidentiality and once the relatives have been told, there is little point in taking action against the staff or the NHS trust, except possibly to ensure that in the future other patients may have their confidentiality better respected.

Communications with a dying patient

It may be that staff find it easier to communicate with relatives than the patient about the terminal condition of the patient or about the patient being close to death. Thus whatever the legal right of the patient to be notified, relatives may be informed first. It is probable that more training (and possibly more staffing resources) is essential so that staff can communicate directly with patients, so that they can answer any questions from the patient and so that they can ensure the patient is given the support to have the dignified, peaceful death following the customs he or she would wish to be in place.

Dying at home

It has become increasingly common for people to die in hospital rather than at home, although some religious groups such as Hindus prefer to die in their own home. A report by Marie Curie Cancer Care (Hawkes, 2004) stated that most terminally ill people would prefer to die at home, yet only a minority are given the chance. The charity is campaigning to increase the availability of palliative care at home and increase the number of people dying at home rather than in hospital from 25% to 50%. It was estimated that this could save £100 million. The campaign has been backed by the Department of Health, which stated that it had already provided £6 million over three years for additional training and committed a further £12 million. A letter to *The Times* (Knight, 2004) described how in a small community in the South Midlands a charity was set up six years ago to allow anybody in the area to die at home. During the last two months of life, they supplied free nurses trained in palliative care for up to 24 hours a day, when needed, thereby saving hospital and hospice beds and reducing the pressure on district nurses and local doctors. The letter encouraged other local communities to do the same. A research report on an evaluation of hospital at home for palliative care was published by the Department of Health (2003) which concluded that Hospital at Home appeared to offer better quality home care than standard care and reduced the number of GP out of hours visits required. It was evaluated very positively by local health professionals, although it was not found to have increased the number of patients dying at home.

Department of Health guidance

In 1992 the Department of Health provided guidance on patients who die in hospital. This was superseded by a new publication in 2005. Part 1 of the new guidance provides advice on developing bereavement services in the NHS and Part 2 gives practical solutions. The principles shown in *Box 6.3* are put forward for underpinning the development of services and professional practice around the time of a patient's death and afterwards.

In addition to the principles set out in *Box 6.3*, the Department of Health

Box 6.3. Principles underpinning the development of services and professional practice at the time of death

- Respect for the individual
- Equality of provision
- Communication
- Information
- Partnership
- Recognising and acknowledging loss
- Environment and facilities
- Staff training and development
- Staff support
- Health and safety
- Review and audit

Box 6.4. Core elements in a bereavement service

- The recognition that grief is normal after bereavement but many bereaved people lack an understanding of grief and should therefore be offered information on how to access sources of support if needed.
- Some bereaved people may require a more formal opportunity to look at their experience. This need not involve professionals. Volunteer groups, self-help groups, faith groups and others can provide much support at this level.
- The recognition that a minority of people may require specialist interventions and proper referral in these cases is essential.

also identifies critical elements considered necessary in providing a good quality bereavement service. These core elements are shown in *Box 6.4*.

Part 2 of the Department of Health guidance

Part 2 of the Department of Health guidance describes some of the experiences of users of hospital bereavement services in order to highlight some questions and issues that could be considered when reviewing and developing these services. These issues include:

- An open, equal and respectful culture
- The purpose of a hospital bereavement service
- Being there when someone dies in hospital
- Informing the next of kin
- Arriving at the hospital

- Creating an appropriate environment
- Who will I see? Role of specialist bereavement staff
- Documentation
- The deceased's property
- What else should happen?

Death bed marriages

Where a patient is dying but indicates that he or she wishes to be married, the hospital should assist in providing the appropriate support and advice. The Registrar of Births, Marriages and Deaths should be informed and the appropriate chaplain if a religious service is required.

Financial provision for terminally ill patients

Terminally ill patients may be entitled to additional funds from social security and nurses should be aware of sources of information on financial provision for patients and relatives. This topic is considered in *Chapter 21.*

Legal issues arising from situation in *Box 6.1*

Several legal issues arise in the situation in *Box 6.1*. One is whether children should be told that they are close to death or terminally ill and what are their legal rights in this respect. It cannot be assumed that those under 16 years are incapable of being told of their condition. Those children suffering from a chronic condition may be able to handle very grave information, but much depends upon the extent to which the child has been kept informed and also his or her level of maturity. For example it was reported in October 2006 (Lister, 2006) that a boy of 14 with leukaemia planned his own funeral. A British Medical Association (2001) publication supports the active development of the autonomy of the child by ensuring that as much information as appropriate is given to the child, according to his or her mental capacity. Another issue which arises is the duty of confidentiality and the fact that information about one child should not be given to another child on the ward. There are exceptions to the duty of confidentiality but disclosure to the other child in the ward would not be justified in these circumstances, irrespective of the insensitivity of the feelings of the seriously ill child.

Applying the law to the situation in *Box 6.2*

There is a presumption in favour of Harry being informed about his health and prognosis. It could be argued that the surgeon should not have informed his wife and daughter before him. By telling the relatives first, she has deprived Harry of the chance of keeping this information to himself before notifying his relatives when he felt the time was right. It is Harry's right of confidentiality to decide when information should be disclosed to others. When the nurse is asked directly by Harry about his prognosis, if she is under instructions from the consultant that Harry should not yet be informed, she should not go against those instructions, but suggest to Harry that he should talk to the consultant. The nurse should then ensure that the consultant visits Harry to answer his questions and give him information about his condition. It is highly likely that when Harry and the consultant meet face to face the latter is more likely to give him a full explanation of his condition.

Conclusions

Many legal and ethical issues arise when patients are facing death, and the competence and skill of the staff in handling questions from the patient and the relatives may have a significant impact upon the nature and manner of the death and also of the ability of relatives and friends to cope with the bereavement. Nor do the duties of the nursing and medical staff in relation to the relatives necessarily end with the death of the patient. An investigation by Help the Aged which reported in April 2006 found that many people are prevented from having a 'good death' because health staff are not always equipped to deal with their needs. Failure to follow procedures and a lack of good staff training add up to inadequate care for old people. Of those responding 57% said that they would benefit from more support or training in working with older patients. It is hoped that the new guidance from the Department of Health on developing bereavement services in the NHS will meet some of these criticisms and shortfalls. In 2006 a Palliative Care Bill was introduced to make provision for those who were terminally ill and had its first reading in the House of Lords on 16 November 2006.

It may be that the UK will follow the example of Germany where a Death TV channel has been set up to give people more information about funeral packages and preparation for death in an attempt to remove the taboos about discussion on death (Boyes, 2007).

References

Bolam v. Friern Barnet Hospital Management Committee [1957] 2 All ER 118

Boyes R (2007) Good mourning, you're watching Death TV. *The Times* **2 November**

British Medical Association (2001) *Consent, Rights and Choices in Health Care for Children and Young People*. London: BMJ Books

Data Protection (Subject Access Modifications) (Health) Order Statutory Instrument 2000 No 413

Department of Health (1992) *Patients who Die in Hospital HSG(92)8*. London: Department of Health

Department of Health (2003) *Hospital at Home for Palliative Care: An Evaluation*. PSI 10-19. London: Department of Health

Department of Health (2005) *When a Patient Dies: Advice on Developing Bereavement Services in the NHS*. London: Department of Health

Hawkes N (2004) NHS could save £100m by letting people die at home. *The Times* **2 March**

Help the Aged (2006) *End of Life Care for Older Persons*. London: Help the Aged

Knight A (2004) Letter. *The Times* **4 February**

Rogers L (2002) Flatline patients bring back evidence of life after death. *The Sunday Times* **8 September**

Sidaway v. Bethlem Royal Hospital Governors and others 1985 1 All ER 643

The Times (2007) Patients not told they are dying. *The Times* **5th December**

Wark P (2004) A Sense of Difference. Quoting from Maggie O'Farrell The Distance Between Us. *The Times* **3 March**

Lister D (2006) Boy with leukaemia planned own funeral. *The Times* **5 October**

Resources

www.dh.gov.uk/PolicyAnd Guidance/Organisation; supplemented by HSG(97)43 Patients who die in hospital

www.helptheaged.org.uk/

CHAPTER 7

Death, stress and health service professionals

Box 7.1. No let up

Margaret worked in an adolescent unit for sufferers from cystic fibrosis. The unit was under considerable pressure since it served the whole region, and often teenagers were brought in at a very serious stage of their illness and died in the unit.

One Christmas they had had a particularly stressful time, with several youngsters suffering long and painful deaths and Margaret, who had grown close to many of them over the years they had been attending the unit, found the work becoming more stressful. Sometimes she was given the time to attend the funerals, but at other times, the unit was too busy for staff to be released and they had to carry on with their work. Margaret found it difficult to cope with the pressure. She told her colleagues that she was not sleeping well and was advised to get some medication from the doctor. She did not like to miss work, since her loyalty to her colleagues meant that she was aware of the additional pressure that they would be under if she failed to get to work. One day she broke down in uncontrollable tears at work, and found it difficult to continue. She was advised to go home early, but found that her condition deteriorated, until she found herself shaking and too unsure of herself to do the simplest task. Her doctor advised her that she was suffering a form of mental breakdown and would refer her to a specialist. She was advised that she would be unlikely to be able to return to work in the near future. She is concerned about her loss of income and inability to work. What is the law?

The fact that health professionals, particularly nurses, may have considerable difficulties in coping with the death of their patients has not been given a high priority by employers in the health service. Sometimes staff counselling sessions may be arranged, but these are resource sensitive and it may not always be possible to provide counselling facilities, or, if they are provided, give staff the time off to be able to attend. This is an unsatisfactory situation. The law however recognises that the employer has a duty to take reasonable action.

Employer's duty

The employer has a duty to take reasonable care of the health and safety of the employee. The duty derives from statutory provisions as well as common law (judge made or case law) sources. The duty is statutory since it is a requirement under section 2 of the Health and Safety at Work Act 1974 that:

> *It shall be the duty of every employer to ensure, so far as is reasonably practicable, the health, safety and welfare at work of all his employees.*

This statutory duty is enforced by inspections by the Health and Safety Inspectorate and by prosecutions in the criminal courts.

In addition, under the contract of employment, an employer has a duty to take reasonable care of the health and safety of the employee. This duty is recognised as an implied term in a contract of employment at common law by decided cases (*Wilsons and Clyde Coal Co Ltd v. English*). It is enforceable by the employee in the civil courts by claiming compensation if the employee has been harmed as a result of a breach of this duty by the employer, or through employment tribunals if the employee claims that the employer has constructively dismissed the employee by failing to take reasonable precautions for the employee's health and safety.

Court for employer's liability for stress

One of the first cases where the High Court recognised that the employer's duty of care covered mental health as well as physical health is shown in *Box 7.2*.

The Walker case has been followed by further reports of payments for compensation for stress across a wide range of employment.

Box 7.2. Stress at work: *Walker v. Northumberland County Council*

A social worker obtained compensation when his employer failed to provide the necessary support in a stressful work situation when he returned to work following an earlier absence due to stress. The employer was not liable for the initial absence, but that put the employer on notice that the employee was vulnerable and its failure to provide the assistance he needed was a breach of its duty to provide reasonable care for his health and safety as required under the contract of employment.

Court of Appeal rulings

The Court of Appeal has recently clarified the law relating to compensation for stress at work (*Hatton v. Sutherland; Barber v. Somerset County Council; Jones v. Sandwell Metropolitan Borough Council; Baker v. Baker Refractories Ltd*). Four appeals were heard together by the Court of Appeal. In each one the employer appealed against a finding of liability for an employee's psychiatric illness caused by stress at work. Two of the claimants were teachers in public sector comprehensive schools, the third an administrative assistant at a local authority training centre and the fourth a raw material operative in a factory.

In determining whether the employer was liable or not, the Court of Appeal held that the ordinary principles of employer's liability applied to an allegation of psychiatric illness caused by stress at work. The threshold question was whether the particular kind of harm – an injury to health (as distinct to occupational health) which was attributable to stress at work (as distinct from other factors) – to the employee was reasonably foreseeable. Foreseeability depended upon what the employer knew or ought reasonably to have known about the individual employee. Because of the nature of mental disorder, it was harder to foresee than physical injury, but might be easier to foresee in a known individual than in the population at large. An employer was usually entitled to assume that the employee could withstand the normal pressures of his job unless he knew of some particular problem or vulnerability. The test was the same whatever the employment: there were no occupations which should be regarded as intrinsically dangerous to mental health.

The relevant factors identified by the Court of Appeal in determining the reasonable foreseeability of stress were:

- The nature and extent of the work done by the employee.
- The signs from the employee of impending harm to his health.

The employer was entitled to take at face value what he was told by an employee; he did not have to make searching inquiries of the employee or seek to make further inquiries of the employee's medical advisors.

If there were indications of impending harm to health arising from stress at work and these indications were plain enough for any reasonable employer to realise that he should do something about it, then the duty of the employer to take steps would be triggered. The employer could only be in breach of duty if he failed to take the steps which were reasonable in the circumstances, bearing in mind the magnitude of the risk of harm occurring, the gravity of the harm which might occur, the costs and practicability of preventing it and the justifications for running the risk. The factors to be taken into account in determining what was reasonable action by the employer included:

- The size and scope of the employer's operation, its resources, and the demands it faced.
- The interests of other employees.
- The need to treat other employees fairly (for example, in any redistribution of duties).

An employer could be reasonably expected to take steps which were likely to do some good, and the court was likely to need expert evidence of that.

An employer who offered a confidential advice service, with referral to appropriate counselling or treatment services, was unlikely to be found in breach of duty. If the only reasonable and effective step would have been to dismiss or demote the employee, the employer would not be in breach of duty in allowing a willing employee to continue in the job.

In all cases, therefore, it was necessary to identify the steps which the employer both could and should have taken before finding him in breach of his duty of care. The claimant had to show that the breach of duty had caused or materially contributed to the harm suffered. It was not enough to show that the occupational stress had caused the harm. Where the harm suffered had more than one cause, the employer should only pay for that proportion of the harm suffered which was attributable to his wrongdoing, unless the harm was truly indivisible. It was for the defendant to raise the question of apportionment. The assessment of damages would take account of any pre-existing disorder or vulnerability and of the chance that the claimant would have succumbed to a stress-related disorder in any event.

On the actual facts of the appeals before it, the Court of Appeal allowed the appeals by the employers in three cases and dismissed the appeal in the case of *Jones v. Sandwell Metropolitan Borough Council.*

House of Lords decision

One of the claimants succeeded in an appeal before the House of Lords which overruled the Court of Appeal decision.

Mr Barber, the head of the Maths Department at East Bridgwater Community School, was involved in a restructuring of staffing at the school following which he became 'mathematical area of experience co-ordinator' and in order to maintain his salary level he had also taken on the post of project manager for public and media relations. In order to discharge all his responsibilities he was working between 61 and 70 hours a week. Stress took its toll and in the summer term of 1996 he was off sick for three weeks with sick notes showing 'overstressed/depression' and 'stress'. On his return to work he had filled in the council's form of sickness declaration stating his troubles as 'overstressed/depression'. He initiated a meeting with the headmistress, but found that she treated him unsympathetically by telling him that all the staff were under stress. Similarly meetings with the two deputy heads, although more sympathetic, resulted in no steps being taken to improve or consider the situation beyond urging him to prioritise his work. In the autumn he found himself with the same or even possibly slightly heavier workload. In November he lost control of himself and found himself shaking a pupil. He left school that day and never returned. Since then he had been unable to work as a teacher or do any work other than undemanding part-time work. He took early retirement in March 1997 aged 52 years.

The House of Lords held that the guidance issued by the Court of Appeal that unless the employer knows of some particular problem or vulnerability, he is usually entitled to assume that his employee is up to the normal pressures of the job, was only guidance and not a rule of law. Every case had to be decided on its own facts. The House of Lords quoted the principle established in an earlier case (*Stokes v. Guest*):

> *The overall test is still the conduct of the reasonable and prudent employer taking positive thought for the safety of his workers in the light of what he knows or ought to know.*

The House of Lords held (in a majority decision) that on the facts there it had not been a flagrant breach of duty by the employer, but nor was it an obviously hopeless claim. It decided that there was insufficient reason for the Court of Appeal to set aside the decision of the High Court. At the very least the school's senior management team should have taken the initiative in making sympathetic inquiries about him when he returned to work in June 1996 and in making some reduction to his workload to ease his return. Even a small reduction in workload, coupled with the feeling that the team was on his side might have made a difference. In any event his condition should have been monitored and if it did not improve some more drastic action should have been taken.

The Barber ruling was followed in a case where a teacher claimed compensation for a severe clinical depression on two occasions as a result of pressures at work (*Vahidi v. Fairstead House School Trust Ltd*). The court held that her two bouts of depression were not caused by any breach of duty on the part of the defendants.

Need for employee to establish significant mental harm

The Court of Appeal allowed the appeal of employers against a finding of liability for stress and an award of £30 856 (*Bonser v. UK Coal Mining Ltd*). The court held that for an employee to recover damages for psychiatric injury caused by stress at work, it had to be demonstrated that the employee had exhibited sufficient signs for it to be reasonably foreseeable by the employer that injury to health would result from the stress caused. The fact that in this case the employee was on an occasion tearful and upset did not make it reasonably foreseeable to the employer that stress would cause her to crack, as the trial judge had considered.

Stress suffered by a nursing auxiliary

The principles laid down in the Barber case were followed by the Court of Appeal in a case involving a nursing auxiliary. The facts are shown in *Box 7.3*.

When looking at the facts in Hartman's case, the Court of Appeal held that there was no basis for concluding that caring for children with learning disabilities imposed on her employer a higher standard of alertness to the risk that its employees would sustain psychiatric injury. The fact that Ms Hartman might be vulnerable had been confidential information and her employer could not be fixed with knowledge of it. Despite general complaints of staff shortages, in the absence of signs that she was particularly vulnerable, there had been nothing to indicate that Ms Hartman could not cope with her work.

Box 7.3. ***Hartman v South Essex Mental Health and Community Care NHS Trust [2005]***

Ms Hartman worked as a nursing auxiliary in a centre for children with learning difficulties and her employment was terminated as a result of her ill health from depression and anxiety. The judge accepted evidence that, but for pressures at work, her condition would not have become chronic or lasted so long. He found that H was in a high risk occupation that Imposed on employers a higher than the normal standard of alertness in respect of the risk of psychiatric injury and that the employer had failed to protect her from foreseeable harm as it was aware of her pre-existing vulnerability and there had been complaints about staff shortages. The employers appealed.

The Court of Appeal held that the general principles had to be applied in claims for psychiatric injury arising out of stress at work. It was foreseeable injury flowing from the employer's breach of duty that gave rise to liability for injury caused by stress at work.

It was not reasonably foreseeable to her employer that she would suffer psychiatric injury, so it was not in breach of duty to her.

Providing counselling is not a complete defence

In a case in 2007 it was held that the mere fact that the employers had provided counselling services did not relieve them of the duty to take reasonable care of an employee who was being subjected to considerable stress because of overwork, lack of clear management controls, The Court of Appeal dismissed the employer's appeal against the finding of a breach of the duty of care and the award of £134 000 (*Daw v. Intel Corp (UK) Ltd*)

Grounds for obtaining compensation for stress

In order to establish grounds for compensation for stress induced by work, an employee would have to show on a balance of probabilities that:

- He or she was under an unacceptable level of stress at work.
- The employer was aware of this situation.
- There was reasonable action which the employer could have taken to relieve this pressure.
- The employer failed to take that action.
- As a reasonably foreseeable result the employee has suffered a serious mental condition.

In other words, like any other situation of health and safety in the workplace, the employee must establish on a balance of probabilities the four elements necessary in any negligence action, ie. duty owed by the employer to safeguard the health and safety of the employee, breach of the duty, causation and harm.

Following the inquest on a hospital consultant who was exhausted from working up to 100 hours a week and who died after injecting himself with anaesthetic while on duty at hospital, the British Medical Association announced that it was stepping up its campaign to restrict doctors' hours (Wright, 2003a).

Health and safety prosecutions and stress

In August 2003 the Health and Safety Executive issued its first enforcement notice against an NHS hospital for failing to protect doctors and nurses from stress at work (de Bruzelles et al, 2003).

Dorset Hospitals NHS Trust was given until 15 December 2003 to assess stress levels among its 1100 staff and introduce a programme to reduce it. If it failed to act it would face court action and fines under the Health and Safety at Work Act 1974. In June 2003 the Health and Safety Executive (HSE) published draft management standards (risk assessment tool) which suggest methods by which employers could reduce stress in the workplace. The standards were piloted in 2003. The management standards for work-related stress are available from the HSE website together with free leaflets on how to apply the standards. The HSE has also launched *Real Solutions, Real People. A Manager's Guide to Tackling Work-Related Stress*, which is based around a series of case studies and which can be downloaded from the HSE website.

Surveys are to be carried out by the Commission for Health Improvement (after April 2004 the Commission for Audit and Inspection, known as the Healthcare Commission) as part of its inspections to monitor stress levels. The HSE estimated that British industry loses £370 million a year because of stress, while the cost to society as a whole could be £3.75 billion (Wright, 2003b).

The Department of Health, in its guidance on when a patient dies, suggests that one of the principles that should underpin the development of services and professional practice around the time of a patient's death and afterwards include that of health and safety. (See *Chapter 5* for all the principles.) It states that

> *Consideration should be given to the health and safety of both the bereaved and of staff working with the bereaved to ensure that the health and safety of an individual is not compromised by issues relating to the cause of death (eg. infectious disease or similar) or by the reaction of the bereaved to the death.*

Claim by widow following suicide caused by husband's stress at work

In a significant decision the House of Lords held that the widow of a man who had committed suicide as a direct result of a depressive illness brought on by an accident at work (for which the employers were responsible) could claim compensation from his employers under the Fatal Accidents Act 1976 (*Corr v. IBC Vehicles Ltd*).

Application of the law to the situation in *Box 7.1*

Margaret will have to show that it was a reasonably foreseeable consequence of the situation at work that she could suffer from a psychiatric injury, that the employer was aware of this and that there were steps which her employer both could and should have taken and as a consequence of the employer's failure she has suffered harm. She can refer to the Department of Health

(2005) guidance *When a Patient Dies* to establish what her NHS employer should have put in practice for the support of staff involved in caring for dying patients. In addition she could refer to the Health and Safety Executive guidance on stress at work. She would have to identify what steps her employer should have taken. In this way she could establish that there was a breach of its duty of care. Margaret would then have to show that this breach of duty had caused or materially contributed to the nervous breakdown which she had suffered. The fact that there was no counselling support or time off given for such assistance would be of some evidential value that the NHS trust as employer was not fulfilling its legal duty to take reasonable care of her mental as well as her physical health. It is also important for Margaret to show that the effects of the employer's failure to provide support and counselling have caused a serious mental illness.

Conclusion

Assisting nursing staff (especially in certain specialties) and other health professionals to deal with death is an essential part of the role of any employer in fulfilling its health and safety duties. It cannot be assumed that coping with death is an automatic ability of all registered health professionals and there is a danger that in any macho work environment, to seek or wish to have support in the form of counselling is seen as weak or lacking, ie. a failure on the employee's part. Just as employers should ensure that health professionals have the training and skills to support relatives before and following a death, they should also take steps to assist staff who, if they had the appropriate help, would thereby become even more effective in supporting the bereaved.

References

Barber v. Somerset County Council 2004 The Times Law Report 5 April 2004 HL; [2002] EWCA Cuv 76; [2002] 2 All ER 1

Bonser v. UK Coal Mining Ltd (Formerly RJB Mining (UK) Ltd) The Times Law Report 30 June 2003 CA

Corr v. IBC Vehicles Ltd The Times Law Report 28 February 2008

Daw v. Intel Corp (UK) Ltd [2007] EWCA Civ 70; (2007) 104(8) L.S.G 36

de Bruzelles S, Wright O, Rumbelow H (2003) Bosses will be fined for workers' stress. *The Times* **5 August**

Department of Health (2005) *When a Patient Dies: Advice on Developing Bereavement Services in the NHS.* London: Department of Health

Hartman v. South Essex Mental Health and Community Care NHS Trust [2005] EWCA Civ 6 [2005] I.C.R. 782

Hatton v. Sutherland; Barber v. Somerset County Council, Jones v. Sandwell Metropolitan

Borough Council, Baker v. Baker Refractories Ltd (2002) The Times Law Report 12

Health and Safety Executive (2003) *Real Solutions, Real People – A Manager's Guide to Tackling Work-Related Stress*. London: Health and Safety Executive

Stokes v. Guest, Keen and Nettlefold (Bolts and Nuts) Ltd [1968] 1 WLR 1776

Vahidi v. Fairstead House School Trust Ltd [2004] EWHC 2102; [2005] P.I.Q.R. P9

Walker v. Northumberland County Council (1994) The Times Law Report 24 November, Queen's Bench Division; [1995] 1 All ER 737

Wilsons and Clyde Coal Co Ltd v. English [1937] 3 All ER 628

Wright O (2003a) Doctor worn out by 'crazy hours' took fatal overdose. *The Times* **17 May**

Wright O (2003b) CBI backs employers over new stress law. *The Times* **6 August**

Resources

www.hse.govuk/pubns/stresspk.htm

www.hse.gov.uk/stress/issues.htm

www.hse.gov.uk/stress/standards

CHAPTER 8

Murder, manslaughter and other criminal offences

> **Box 8.1. Death due a mistake**
>
> Martha Brown by mistake administered twice the dosage of painkiller which was prescribed for Ted Snow. He convulsed and she realised immediately that something was amiss and called the doctor and pharmacist. However he died before they were able to take remedial action. Since it was only a small mistake (admittedly with horrendous consequences), she is wondering what the consequences in law might be.

It cannot be assumed in law that if death results without any intention to kill on the part of the health professional, then there is no liability for a criminal offence. If a person dies, there could be prosecutions for murder, manslaughter, grievous bodily harm or even no prosecution if the death was completely accidental. The purpose of this chapter is to identify these various offences and examine the implications for health professionals.

The elements of a crime

In order to establish guilt, the prosecution must be able to show that each element of the crime charged is proved beyond all reasonable doubt. Each crime thus has its ingredients which make up that particular offence. There is a further breakdown of the elements that have to be established to prove that a crime has taken place, ie. between the *actus reus* and the *mens rea*. The *mens rea*, or mental element, includes all those elements that relate to the mind of the accused. The *actus reus* are all the other elements. There are some crimes where there is no requirement to show a mental element and these are known as offences of absolute liability. In order to secure a conviction, all the elements, mental and physical, must be shown to have existed at the time it was alleged that the crime was committed.

For example, if a person discovered when they unpacked their shopping goods at home that two packets of ham had been stuck together and they had only paid for one, that would not be theft, since there was no intention to steal. However if they were aware at the time of purchase that two packs were stuck together and failed to point this out to the cashier, there would have been an intention to permanently deprive the owner of those goods, ie. the *mens rea* of theft.

Murder

The definition of murder derives from a 17th century case (Dine and Gobert, 2000):

> *Murder is when a man of sound memory, and of the age of discretion, unlawfully killeth within any country of the realm any reasonable creature in* rerum natura *under the King's peace, with malice aforethought, either expressed by the party or implied by law, so as the party wounded, or hurt, etc. die of the wound or hurt, etc…*

The original definition set a time limit of a year and a day in which the person must die of the wound or hurt. This limitation of time was removed in 1996. Where there has been a plea or conviction of guilty of murder, at the present time the judge has no discretion: there is a mandatory life sentence for murder. The judge has power however to identify what he or she would consider to be the maximum time the accused should serve in prison and gives reasons for this. There is currently discussion on whether the mandatory life sentence for murder should be abolished. The Law Commission published a report in 2006 entitled *Murder, Manslaughter and Infanticide* which can be downloaded from its website. It made significant recommendations for the reform of the law. It was followed by a consultation exercise by the Ministry of Justice launched on 12 December 2007 to obtain feedback on the Law Commission recommendations. Legislation may follow in the summer of 2008.

Manslaughter

In certain circumstances what could have been a crime of murder may be reduced to manslaughter. Manslaughter is divided into two categories: voluntary and involuntary. Voluntary covers the situation where there is the mental intention to kill or complete disregard as to the possibility that death could arise from one's actions, ie. there is the mental requirement (*mens rea*) but there are extenuating factors. For example:

- provocation,
- death in pursuance of a suicide pact, or
- diminished responsibility.

The effect of these extenuating facts is that a murder verdict could not be obtained but the defendant could be guilty of voluntary manslaughter.

Involuntary manslaughter exists when the *mens rea* (ie. the mental element) for murder is absent. Such circumstances would include:

- gross negligence
- killing recklessly may or may not be insufficient to be murder
- an intention to escape from lawful arrest.

Defences to a charge of murder or manslaughter include:

- killing in carrying out the sentence of the court
- killing in the course of preventing crime or arresting offenders
- killing in the defence of one's own person or that of another
- killing in defence of property.

Use of excessive force will negate the defence of protecting one's own person or that of another or defending property.

The House of Lords has held that it was never appropriate to find someone guilty of manslaughter where that person had been involved in the supply of a class A controlled drug (in this case heroin), which was then freely and voluntarily self-administered by a fully informed and responsive adult to whom it had been supplied and the administration of the drug then caused his death (*R v. Kennedy*).

Where the accused is convicted of manslaughter the judge has complete discretion over sentencing in contrast to where there is a murder conviction, where at present there is a mandatory life sentence.

Box 8.2. *R v. Adomako. Manslaughter by an anaesthetist*

At approximately 11.05 a.m. a disconnection occurred at the endotracheal tube connection. The supply of oxygen to the patient ceased and led to a cardiac arrest at 11.14 a.m. During this period, the defendant failed to notice or remedy the disconnection. He first became aware that something was amiss when an alarm sounded on the Dinamap machine, which monitors the patient's blood pressure. From the evidence it appeared that some four and a half minutes had elapsed between the disconnection and the sounding of the alarm. When the alarm sounded, the defendant responded in various ways by checking the equipment and began administering atropine to raise the patient's pulse. But at no stage before the cardiac arrest did he check the integrity of the endotracheal tube connection. The disconnection was not discovered until after resuscitation measures had been commenced.

An example of manslaughter on the grounds of gross negligence

Gross professional negligence can constitute both a criminal offence of manslaughter and also grounds for an action for compensation in the tort of negligence as the case of Dr Adomako shows. Dr Adomako was an anaesthetist who failed to realise during an operation that a tube had become disconnected as a result of which the patient died. He was prosecuted in the criminal courts and convicted of manslaughter (*R v. Adomako)*. The facts are set out in *Box 8.2*.

Box 8.3. House of Lords ruling in Adomako case

1. The ordinary principles of the law of negligence should be applied to ascertain whether or not the defendant had been in breach of a duty of care towards the victim who had died.
2. If such a breach of duty was established, the next question was whether that breach caused the death of the victim.
3. If so, the jury had to go on to consider whether that breach of duty should be characterised as gross negligence and therefore as a crime. That would depend on the seriousness of the breach of duty committed by the defendant in all the circumstances in which the defendant was placed when it occurred.
4. The jury would have to consider whether the extent to which the defendant's conduct departed from the proper standard of care incumbent upon him, involving as it must have done a risk of death to the patient, was such that it should be judged criminal.

The judge was required to give the jury a direction on the meaning of gross negligence as had been given in the present case by the Court of Appeal.

The jury might properly find gross negligence on proof of:

(a) indifference to an obvious risk of injury to health or

(b) actual foresight of the risk coupled either

(i) with a determination nevertheless to run it or

(ii) with an intention to avoid it but involving such a high degree of negligence in the attempted avoidance as the jury considered justified conviction or

(c) of inattention or failure to advert to a serious risk going beyond mere inadvertence in respect of an obvious and important matter which the defendant's duty demanded he should address.

[Lettering and numbering are the author's]

Dr Adomako accepted at his criminal trial that he had been negligent. The issue was whether his conduct was criminal. He was convicted of involuntary manslaughter, but appealed against conviction. He lost his appeal in the Court of Appeal and then appealed to the House of Lords.

The House of Lords clarified the legal situation (*R v. Adomako)*. The stages that the House of Lords suggested should be followed are set out in *Box 8.3*. The House of Lords held that the Court of Appeal had applied the correct test and the appeal was dismissed.

There would also be vicarious liability on Dr Adomako's employers in the civil courts for his negligence in causing the death of the patient. The Law Commission (1996) has recommended that the law should be changed to enable it to be made easier for corporations and statutory bodies to be prosecuted for manslaughter and this may lead to more charges being brought in connection with deaths that arise from gross negligence. The Government accepted the recommendations and proposed that there should be a new corporate killing offence with the Health and Safety Executive responsible for its enforcement. A Corporate Manslaughter and Corporate Homicide Act was passed in 2007 and came into force on 6 April 2008. It creates an offence of corporate manslaughter (corporate homicide in Scotland) by an organisation (as defined in the Act) (see below) if the way in which any of its activities are managed or organised by its senior managers:

- causes a person's death, and
- amounts to a gross breach of a relevant duty of care owed by the organisation to the deceased.

A senior manager is defined as a person who plays a significant role in:

- the making of decisions about the whole or a substantial part of its activities to be managed or organised, or
- the actual managing or organising of the whole of a substantial part of those activities.

The definition of duty of care covers both the duty owed to employees and others working for the organisation or performing services for it, the duty owed as occupier of the premises and a duty owed in connection with the supply of goods or services, carrying out of construction or maintenance operations, carrying out of commercial activities and the use or keeping of any plant, vehicle or other thing.

Organisations covered by the Act include a corporation, a department or other body listed in Schedule 1, and a police force. Schedule 1 lists many Government departments including the Attorney General's Office and the Department of Health, Department for Education and Skills and the Department of Trade and Industry (now the Department for Business, Enterprise and Regulatory Reform). Under Section 22 the Secretary of State has the power to amend Schedule 1 by statutory instrument. There is no crown immunity. Proceedings for an offence of corporate manslaughter may not be commenced without the consent of the Director of Public Prosecutions.

Individuals cannot be guilty of aiding, abetting, counselling or procuring the commission of an offence of corporate manslaughter.

The common law offence of manslaughter by gross negligence is abolished in its application to corporations (but is still retained in relation to individuals).

Failure by an organisation to ensure that health and safety regulations are implemented and monitored and that staff are trained in health and safety procedures which leads to the death of an employee, member of the public or other individual could result in a prosecution under the new Act.

Determination by jury

Once it is established that an organisation owes a relevant duty of care to a person, then the jury has to determine whether there was a gross breach of that duty. The Act specifies that the jury must consider whether the evidence shows that the organisation failed to comply with any health and safety legislation that relates to the alleged breach, and if so:

- how serious that failure was, and
- how much of a risk of death it posed.

The jury may also consider the extent to which the evidence shows that there were attitudes, policies, systems or accepted practices within the organisation that were likely to have encouraged any such failure as its mentioned in Subsection (2), or to have produced tolerance of it. The jury may also have regard to any health and safety guidance that relates to the alleged breach and other matters they consider relevant.

The court has the power, following conviction of an organisation for corporate manslaughter, to order it to take specified steps to remedy the breach of the duty of care and any matter that appears to the court to have resulted from that breach and to have been a cause of the death. The order must specify a period within which the steps must be taken.

The Act came into force on 6 April 2008 and is not retrospective and the common law of manslaughter applied to acts committed before the Act came into force.

Liability for suicide bill

Under the 10 minute rule Ian Duncan Smith introduced, as a private member's bill, a Liability for Suicide Bill into the House of Commons. The Bill would have created an offence where an abusive husband drove his wife to suicide. It would also cover bullies who torment children to death and rapists who drive their victims to kill themselves. Research suggests that over one-third of women who kill themselves have been assaulted by their partners (Browne, 2006). At the time of writing it has not been published and it seems unlikely that it will proceed.

Attempted murder

In the case of *R v. Arthur* the accused was a consultant paediatrician who had prescribed dihydrocodeine for a baby suffering from Down's syndrome whose parents did not wish the baby to survive. The baby died on 1 July 1980 about 69 hours old. The prosecution alleged that the drug had caused lung stasis and the baby died from this. During the trial the judge, after legal argument, withdrew the charge of murder and the trial proceeded on the charge of attempted murder. This followed medical evidence given by a pathologist called for the defendant which was considered to show that the evidence given by the pathologist for the Crown was incomplete. Dr Arthur was acquitted by the jury.

The case of Dr Nigel Cox who was convicted of attempted murder of a patient to whom he had administered potassium chloride is considered in *Chapter 9 (R v. Cox).*

Grievous bodily harm

Grievous bodily harm is a statutory offence under Section 20 of the Offences Against the Person Act 1861 under which a person can be convicted if it has been shown beyond reasonable doubt that the defendant was unlawfully and maliciously guilty of wounding or inflicting any grievous bodily harm upon any other person, either with or without any weapon or instrument.

Breach of health and safety laws

A death resulting from negligence and breach of health and safety laws can also result in criminal proceedings as in the case of a confused 93-year-old widow who suffered from dementia who died after a minibus ambulance taking her home from hospital dropped her off at the wrong house. The driver let her in with a key found under the doormat. She broke a leg while trying to leave the house and died five weeks later in hospital. The ambulance service and the NHS trust were prosecuted in the magistrates court by the Health and Safety Executive and they admitted failure to discharge their duty of care by exposing patients to serious risk of injury and were sentenced in the crown court.

Coroner's case

A coroner criticised hospital staff whose catalogue of mistakes led to the death of a mother who was given penicillin despite telling doctors she was allergic to it (Cazzulino, 2006). Teresa Innes lapsed into a coma in September 2001 after a surgeon at Bradford Royal Infirmary prescribed Magnapen which contains penicillin as she was about to undergo a routine procedure to drain fluid from an abscess on her thigh. She was wearing a red allergy band on her wrist and her medical notes had been marked to reflect her acute aversion to the antibiotic. She suffered anaphylactic shock, which stopped her heart for 35 minutes, resulting in permanent brain damage. She was left in a persistent vegetative state from which she never recovered. She died two years later. In a narrative verdict, the coroner stated that a simple labelling tool on drugs and more comprehensive checks by surgeons were needed to ensure that patients' allergies were taken into account when doctors were prescribing antibiotics.

In another inquest into the death of a patient following surgery, the coroner ruled that a swab was left in the patient accidentally and the patient died as a result of malnutrition due to the retained surgical pack. He also suffered from ischaemic heart disease and jejunal diverticulitis (Devlin, 2006). The coroner in another case was told that a grandmother had starved to death after a lack of mindfulness by welfare services. Ivy Allen, aged 79 years, was found in her home emaciated with no food in the house and had probably been dead for two days. The coroner ruled that she died of natural causes to which neglect – including self-neglect – contributed. It is a summation of a lack of mindfulness of those undertaking their duties as they saw fit. The biggest single failing was one of communication (Times Newspaper, 2006).

As will be seen in *Chapter 12* the coroner is not able to determine whether a criminal offence has taken place. It is however possible that criminal and civil proceedings could follow the inquest as well as disciplinary actions by the employer, and fitness to practice proceedings by the General Medical Council can take place against the staff at fault.

The case of Dr Shipman

On 31 January 2000, Dr Shipman, a general practitioner, was found guilty of the murder of 15 patients and was suspected of having killed at least

215 persons. The atrocious offences raised serious concerns about the inadequacy of professional regulation and control. An inquiry set up by the Secretary of State has published six reports. The first considered how many patients Shipman killed, the means employed and the period over which the killings took place. The second report examined the conduct of the police investigation. The third report considered the present system for death and cremation certification and for the investigation of deaths by coroners. This is discussed in *Chapter 14*. The fourth report which was published in July 2004 considered the regulation of controlled drugs in the community. The fifth report concerned complaints against general practitioners and future professional regulation. The sixth report considered how many patients Shipman killed during his career as a junior doctor at Pontefract General Infirmary and during his time at Hyde.

Administration of drug by epidural instead of intravenous injection

In 2003 a junior doctor in Nottingham pleaded guilty to the manslaughter of a patient suffering from leukaemia. Instead of administering the drug intravenously, he administered it epidurally and the patient died. The doctor was given a prison sentence. The National Patient Safety Agency has aimed at preventing the recurrence of such mistakes.

Application of law to the situation in *Box 8.1*

Martha Brown may not have intended that Ted should die and may see her mistake as only a small error. However the repercussions would be considerable. She could be prosecuted for the manslaughter of Ted. The prosecution would have to establish beyond reasonable doubt that her actions were so grossly negligent that they amounted to a criminal offence. The prosecution would also have to establish that her grossly negligent actions caused the death of the patient. The jury would have to be satisfied beyond reasonable doubt of both the gross negligence and also of the causation. If they brought forward a verdict of guilty of manslaughter, the judge in determining his sentence could take account of her previous conduct and any character witnesses and could exercise his discretion over sentencing in her favour if he considered that justified. He would also take note of the fact that she would have to face fitness to practice proceedings before the Nursing and Midwifery Council and may well be struck off the register. She would also face disciplinary proceedings before her employer and would probably lose her job. She could apply to an employment tribunal for unfair dismissal, but provided that the employer has followed the correct procedure and acted reasonably, she would probably be unsuccessful in being reinstated. In addition the employers would probably have to pay compensation to Ted's relatives because of its vicarious liability for the actions of a negligent employee in the course of her employment.

If there are failures by the senior management within the organisation which caused the death, then a prosecution under the Corporate Manslaughter and Corporate Homicide Act 2007 could be sought.

Conclusion

It may seem unjust to some health professionals that they could face criminal proceedings should patients die in their care, even though the health professional did not intend that death. However, accountability to the public through the criminal courts for gross negligence and error leading to death, would appear to be justified from the perspective of the victims' families. Health professionals now have to be alert to the possibility that a colleague is guilty of criminal acts against patients. While the possibility of another Dr Shipman is extremely unlikely, staff have to remain vigilant in the protection of the patient. It is also essential to remember that, at the time of writing, it is a criminal offence to assist someone who wishes to die and it is to this topic that we turn in the next chapter.

References

Dine J, Gobert J (2000) *Cases and Materials on Criminal Law*. 3rd edn. Blackstone Press, London

Browne A (2006) Abusive husbands face jail for wives' suicides. *The Times* **18 October:** 35

Cazzulino M (2006) Doctors blamed in penicillin death. *The Times* **25 March:** 13

Devlin H (2006) Patient starved to death after operation blunder *The Times* **1 September**

Law Commission (1996) *Report No 237 Legislating the Ciminal Code: Involuntary manslaughter*. London: Stationery Office

Law Commission (2006) *Murder, Manslaughter and Infanticide*. London: Law Commission. Available from www.lawcom.gov.uk/murder.htm

R. v. Adomako [1995] 1 AC 171; [1994] 3 All ER 79

R. v Arthur Med Sci Law (1982) Vol 22 No 2 page 148

R v. Cox (1992) 12 BMLR 38. Winchester Crown Court (1992) The Times 22 September

R v. Kennedy (No 2) The Times Law Report 19 October 2007

Shipman Inquiry First Report (2002) *Death Disguised* published 19 July 2002. Available from: www.the-shipman-inquiry.org.uk/reports.asp

Shipman Inquiry Second Report (2003) *The Police Investigation of March 1998* published 14 July 2003. Available from: www.the-shipman-inquiry.org.uk/reports.asp

Shipman Inquiry Third Report (2003) *Death and Cremation Certification* published 14 July 2003. Available from: www.the-shipman-inquiry.org.uk/reports.asp

Shipman Inquiry Fourth Report (2004) *The Regulation of Controlled Drugs in the Community* published 15 July 2004 Cm 6249 Stationery Office. Available from: www.the-shipman-inquiry.org.uk/reports.asp

The Shipman Inquiry Fifth Report (2004) *Safeguarding Patients: Lessons from the Past – Proposals for the Future*. Command Paper CM 6394 December 2004. Stationery Office. Available from: www.the-shipman-inquiry.org.uk/reports.asp

The Shipman Inquiry Sixth Report (2005) *The Final Report* published January 2005 Stationery Office. Available from: www.the-shipman-inquiry.org.uk/reports.asp

The Times (2006) Woman starved to death, age 79. *The Times* **8 September**

CHAPTER 9

Euthanasia and assisted suicide

Box 9.1. Assisted suicide

Trevor suffered from motor neurone disease and was concerned about the late stages of the illness. He had heard reports of people being unable to swallow or move and being in considerable pain and he wanted to ensure that he would die a dignified, pain free and peaceful death. He therefore asked his son, a diabetic, to set aside insulin for him so that when he wished to end his life his son would help him die. His son was prepared to do that for him, but was concerned at the possibility of his being prosecuted. What is the law?

In contrast to The Netherlands, the laws of this country make it a criminal offence to assist another person to die. According to the Suicide Act 1961 and Offences Against the Persons Act 1861, any person involved in the death of another could face the laws of murder or manslaughter. These apply even when the victim has made the request for help with full mental capacity. The consent of that individual does not constitute a defence to any of these offences. These offences are considered in the previous chapter. They will be considered in the light of Trevor's situation in *Box 9.1*.

The case presented in *Box 9.2* is one where a doctor was found guilty of attempted murder. It is noticeable that in this case Dr Cox was not charged with murder. Had he been so and found guilty of that, then the judge would have had no choice other than to impose a sentence of life imprisonment. (The current mandatory sentence for life imprisonment following a conviction for murder is at present under discussion). The case came to light because a nurse, in fulfilment of her professional duty, reported to senior management the fact that potassium chloride had been administered. Management then brought in the police. As the case of Dr Cox shows, voluntary euthanasia, by which is meant the killing of a person with that person's consent, is unlawful. The fact that the patient had pleaded with the doctor for her life to be ended was not a defence against attempted murder.

The Cox case contrasts with that of Dr Bodkin Adams who was charged with the murder of an elderly patient in Eastbourne (*H Palmer Adam's Trial for Murder*). The judge directed the jury that a doctor was not guilty of murder if he or she prescribed medication for pain relief appropriate to the patient's needs, even if incidentally the medication shortened the patient's life (see below).

The outcome in the case of Dr Cox can also be contrasted with a case where a husband killed his wife who was suffering from motor neurone disease (see below).

Assistance in a suicide bid

If the act of a person in causing a person's death amounts to assistance in a suicide bid, then it is illegal under section 2(1) of the Suicide Act 1961:

> *A person who aids, abets, counsels or procures the suicide of another or an attempt by another to commit suicide, shall be liable on conviction on indictment to imprisonment (up to 14 years).*

Before the Suicide Act 1961 people who attempted to commit suicide and failed could be prosecuted for the attempt to take their own life (of course, if they succeeded, they were beyond the reach of the laws of this country). The Suicide Act 1961 made it no longer a criminal offence to attempt to commit suicide, but retained the criminal offences of aiding and abetting another person's suicide. If two persons enter into a suicide pact and one survives, the survivor would be able to plead the defence of voluntary manslaughter if charged with murder (see *Chapter 8*). It was reported in November 2004 in *The Times* that a woman died in a suicide pact with her husband, a cancer patient, after they took pills and tried to gas themselves with car exhaust

Box 8.2. The case of Dr Cox (*R v. Cox 1992*)

Lillian Boyes was 70 years old and terminally ill with rheumatoid arthritis, gastric ulcer and gangrene and in considerable pain. She asked her consultant Dr Cox a rheumatologist in Winchester, and others to kill her. Her relatives were concerned at her condition. Dr Nigel Cox administered a lethal dose of potassium chloride, after repeated doses of heroin failed to control her pain. He was convicted of attempted murder and was given a prison sentence of one year suspended for 12 months. Dr Cox was also brought before his employers, the Wessex Regional Health Authority, to face disciplinary proceedings, but retained his post. He was also brought before professional conduct proceedings of the General Medical Council, who admonished him but noted that he acted in good faith and allowed him to stay on the register.

fumes. The husband survived, recovered and raised the alarm. A verdict of suicide was recorded upon the wife.

There have been other cases that have not as yet led to criminal proceedings where patients have travelled to Switzerland to attend a clinic where they have been given a lethal injection. For example Dave Richards gave an interview with a journalist before travelling to the Dignitas clinic in Zurich Switzerland to die (Templeton, 2006). He had been diagnosed with Huntingdon's disease four years before.

Presumably if such one way trips are advertised, prosecutions of those assisting would follow. The retired GP who helped him travel to Zurich wrote to *The Sunday Times* advocating doctor-assisted suicide which is widely accepted with adequate safeguards in Belgium, The Netherlands, Oregon, USA, and Switzerland (Irwin, 2006). In a recent case the judge held that a woman, who had a degenerative brain condition, could not be prevented from travelling to Switzerland for her life to be ended, since she had the mental capacity to make that decision (*Re Z*). An inquest was told in July 2007 that a paralysed huntsman indicated that he wanted his life-support machine turned off through a series of eyelid blinks. He had broken his neck in a hunting accident. The coroner recorded a verdict of accidental death (*The Times*, 2007). (See also the case of *Re B* considered below)

Letting die and killing

While assisting a person to die is illegal in this country, it may in certain circumstances be lawful to allow a person to die, ie. to let nature take its course. This could arise where either a mentally capacitated person had refused treatment or it was considered to be in the best interests of the person to be allowed to die.

The Tony Bland case (*Airedale NHS Trust v. Bland*) is an example where the House of Lords held that it was in the best interests of this person who was in a persistent vegetative state to be allowed to die and for artificial feeding to cease.

Patients with mental capacity

Where patients have the necessary mental capacity, then they are entitled to refuse life-saving treatment. Thus in the case of Ms B who was paralysed, because she was held to have the necessary mental capacity, she was able to refuse to be ventilated, and the judge declared it lawful for the ventilator to be switched off. It was a trespass to her person to place her on a ventilator contrary to her wishes. Even young persons below 18 years may have the capacity to refuse life-sustaining treatment. Thus Josie Grove, a 16-year-old girl with cancer, chose to die at home rather than continue to undergo further treatment in hospital. She had had two bone marrow transplants and a course of aggressive anti-cancer drugs which all proved unsuccessful. Her parents respected her refusal (Bannerman, 2006).

Treatment that reduces life expectancy

This issue arose in the trial of Dr Bodkin Adams who was charged with the murder of an elderly woman who was receiving 24-hour nursing care in Eastbourne by giving her excessive amounts of morphine (*R v. Adams (Bodkin)*). The trial judge made it clear to the jury that a doctor has a duty to care for a dying patient and is able to ensure that the patient is given appropriate pain relief, even if the effect of the medication is to reduce the life expectancy of the patient. If, however, the doctor administered medication with the intention of reducing the life of the patient that would be unlawful. What would be reasonable levels of medication would be determined according to the Bolam Test (*Bolam v. Friern Barnet*) as to what is reasonable practice.

The Netherlands

Several countries have brought in legislation to decriminalise voluntary euthanasia, so that mentally competent people who are dying can have assistance in ending their life, which is recognised as lawful. In The Netherlands, for example, a doctor will not be prosecuted if he or she has assisted a dying person to die, provided that the doctor has followed specific requirements, including obtaining the written consent of a mentally capacitated patient (Battin, 1992).

The House of Lords

The House of Lords in a Select Committee report (1993–1994) has strongly advocated against any relaxation of the laws which would permit voluntary euthanasia in the UK. This has also been the stance of the Government in its White Paper on decision making on behalf of mentally incapacitated adults (Lord Chancellor, 1999).

The case of Diane Pretty

In a well-publicised case (*R (On the application of Pretty) v. DPP*), Diane Pretty, a sufferer of motor neurone disease, appealed to the House of Lords that her husband should be allowed to end her life, and not be prosecuted under the Suicide Act 1961. The House of Lords did not allow her appeal. It held that if there were to be any changes to the Suicide Act to legalise the killing of another person, then these changes should be made by Parliament. As the law stood, the Suicide Act made it a criminal offence to aid and abet the suicide of another person and the husband could not be granted immunity from prosecution were he to assist his wife to die. The House of Lords held that there was no conflict between the human rights of Mrs Pretty as set out in the European Convention on Human Rights. Mrs Pretty then applied to the European Court of Human Rights in Strasbourg, but lost. The Court held that there was no conflict between the Suicide Act 1961 and the European Convention of Human Rights. The Council of Europe issued a press release entitled Chamber judgement in the case of *Pretty v. the United Kingdom* published on 29 April 2002. It stated that,

> *The European Court of Human Rights has refused an application by Diane Pretty, a British national dying of motor neurone disease, for a ruling that would allow her husband to assist her to commit suicide without facing prosecution under the Suicide Act 1961 section 2(1). The applicant is paralysed from the neck downwards and has a poor life expectancy, while her intellect and decision making capacity remain unimpaired. She wanted to be given the right to decide when and how she died without undergoing further suffering and indignity. The court unanimously found the application inadmissible with no violations under the European Convention of Human Rights under Art. 2 the right to life; Art 3 prohibition of human or degrading treatment or punishment; Art 8 the right to respect for private life; Art 9 freedom of conscience and Art 14 prohibition of discrimination.*

It was subsequently reported that Diane Pretty had died.

Mercy killing

Even though the law treats voluntary euthanasia as a criminal offence the actual punishment given to offenders depends upon the attitude taken by the judge in sentencing. A conviction for murder is followed by life imprisonment; the judge has no discretion. However there have been cases where a person found guilty of manslaughter in a mercy killing situation has been given a non-custodial sentence. For example in a recent case (Peek, 2002), Lionel Bailey, the husband of a woman suffering from motor neurone disease, smothered his wife with a pillow to release her from pain. He pleaded guilty to manslaughter on the grounds of diminished responsibility. A plea of not guilty to murder was accepted by the prosecution. The judge sentenced him to a three year community rehabilitation order. The judge said,

In my view, the interests of justice do not require me to impose a custodial sentence in this case. I accept that the strain you were under watching a much-loved wife deteriorate due to the cruelty of illness must have been well-nigh unbearable. You were in your 70s, in poor health, and yet continued to do your loving best to care for her as a loyal husband should. That anguish must have been intense. You couldn't bear to see her suffering any longer. I'm sure you did what you did to end her suffering without a thought for yourself and I make that quite plain.

Mental Capacity Act 2005

This Act which came fully into effect in October 2007 makes provision for decision making on behalf of those adults who are incapable of making their own decisions. Decisions have to be made in the best interests of such people.

Where a decision relates to life-sustaining treatment the person acting on behalf of the mentally incapacitated adult must not, in considering whether the treatment is in the best interests of the person concerned, be motivated by a desire to bring about his death (S.4(7)). Where a person wishes to make an advance decision to refuse treatment at a later time when he or she may not have the requisite mental capacity, there are specific conditions which must be satisfied if the refusal relates to life-sustaining treatment. These include the requirements that the request must be in writing and signed and witnessed and specifically cover the refusal of treatments that could lead to death (S.25(5) and (6)). A person acting under a lasting power of attorney could only refuse life-sustaining treatment on behalf of that individual if there is specific provision for such a refusal in the instrument setting up the attorney and other statutory conditions. A deputy appointed by the Court of Protection and acting in the best interests of the mentally incapacitated person could not refuse life-sustaining treatment.

There is a new Court of Protection with the jurisdiction to hear cases relating to the personal welfare decisions as well as property and finance of those lacking mental capacity. Serious treatment decisions and treatments which are disputed will go before that court and if a relative or friend is not available an independent mental capacity advocate must be appointed. A Code of Practice on the Mental Capacity Act is available from the Ministry of Justice website, which also provides additional guidance on the Act.

Application of the law to the situation in *Box 9.1*

If Trevor were able to end his own life without the assistance of any other person it would not be a criminal offence. Trevor, if he was deemed to have the necessary mental capacity could also refuse any life-saving treatment. The situation is, therefore, that if Trevor succeeds in taking his own life without the involvement of any other person, then no crime has been committed. Yet, if his son helps him in any way at all (and it will be noted that the words 'aids', 'abets', 'counsels', 'procures' or 'attempts' any such action in the Suicide Act are extremely wide), then such help would constitute an offence under the Suicide Act 1961. The words used in the Act would cover Trevor's son obtaining a publication giving advice on suicide, or leaving insulin by Trevor's bed if he knew that Trevor wanted to take his own life, and any other form of encouragement or assistance by the son. Trevor, if mentally capacitated, could refuse any further treatment in the hope that he would die quicker. If Trevor were in extreme pain it may become necessary to increase his level of morphine to such a point that the medication would actually reduce his life expectancy. However, if the intention is to control the pain and not to bring about the death and the level of medication is in accordance with reasonable medical practice, then giving the medication would not constitute a criminal offence of murder or manslaughter.

Conclusion

At present the law is clear: health professionals cannot deliberately shorten the lives of their patients or assist them in a suicide attempt. They must, however, respect the wishes of their mentally capacitated patients to refuse treatment. The Mental Capacity Act 2005 now applies to those who are mentally incapable of making their own decisions. Legislation has been debated in Parliament several times to legalise euthanasia but has been rejected, despite a considerable pressure for limited euthanasia to be introduced into the law. Lord Joffe in particular has introduced several bills to legalise assisted suicide and failed. At the time of writing the chances of a new Bill to legalise assisted suicide being passed seem slight.

References

Airedale NHS Trust v. Bland [1993] 1 All ER 821

Bannerman L (2006) Take me home to die, says cancer girl. *The Times* **7 December**

Battin M (1992) Voluntary euthanasia and the risk of abuse: Can we learn anything from the Netherlands. *Law Med Health Care* **20**(1–2): 133–43

Bolam v. Friern Barnet Hospital Management Committee [1957] 2 All ER 118

House of Lords Select Committee on Medical Ethics (1993–1994) HL Paper 21, House of Lords Select Committee on Medical Ethics, London

H Palmer Adam's Trial for Murder [1957] Crim LR 365

Irwin M (2006) Letter: Accepting suicide. *The Sunday Times* **3 December**

Lord Chancellor (1999) *Making Decisions: The Government's Proposals for Making Decisions on Behalf of Mentally Incapacitated Adults*. London: The Stationery Office

Peek L (2002) Mercy for husband who killed wife in pain. *The Times* **7 September**

Pretty v. the United Kingdom [2002] ECHR 427 2346/02

Templeton SK (2006) Last meal with the man who chose death. *The Sunday Times* **19 November**

The Times (2004) Suicide verdict. *The Times* **5 November**

The Times (2007) Deathbed request. *The Times* **14 July**

R (On the application of Pretty) v. DPP [2001] UKHL 61, [2001] 3 WLR 1598

R v. Adams (Bodkin) [1957] Crim LR 365

Re B (consent to treatment: capacity) Times Law Report 26 March 2002; [2002] 2 ALL ER 449

R v. Cox (1992) 12 BMLR 38. Winchester Crown Court (1992) The Times 22 September

Re Z [2004] EWHC 2817

Ministry of Justice website: www.justice.gov.uk

CHAPTER 10

Not for resuscitation instructions: Adults and children

Box 10.1. Tired of life

Marion, aged 55 years, had suffered from multiple sclerosis for 10 years and had reached the stage where she was wheelchair bound and had become extremely depressed. She was admitted to hospital for review of her medication and treatment plan. She discussed with a nurse what should happen in the event of her suffering a cardiac arrest and stated that she would not wish to be resuscitated. She had not discussed this with her relatives, nor had she put the instructions in writing. Two days later, when her daughter was visiting her, she had a cardiac arrest. Her daughter was anxious that every effort should be made to resuscitate her and asked the nurse to call the arrest team. However the nurse said that Marion had told her that she did not want to be resuscitated and that was therefore binding upon her. The daughter disagreed. What is the law?

Life and death decisions over whether or not a person is to be resuscitated, if not considered before an emergency arises, can lead to a difficult situation for nursing staff and others. Clarity of instructions based firmly on the legal principles is essential both to protect the rights of the patient and to protect the position of staff.

Patient's rights

A patient has a right to be resuscitated, if the procedure is reasonably likely to be successful and if he or she has a reasonably good prognosis following resuscitation.

European Convention on Human Rights

Under article 2 of the European Convention on Human Rights, every person has a right to life. It could be argued that failure to resuscitate in circumstances favourable to the patient is a denial of this right. Article 2 states:

> *Everyone's right to life shall be protected by law. No one shall be deprived of his life intentionally save in the execution of a sentence of a court following his conviction of a crime for which this penalty is provided by law.*

Recent decisions of the courts show how this right is interpreted. For example, in a recent case (*A National Health Service Trust v. D*), parents lost their attempt to ensure that a severely handicapped baby born prematurely was resuscitated if necessary. The judge ruled that the hospital should provide him with palliative care to ease his suffering, but should not try to revive him as that would cause unnecessary pain.

In another case (*NHS Trust A v. Mrs M and NHS Trust B v. Mrs H*), the President of the Family Division, Dame Elizabeth Butler-Sloss, held that the withdrawal of life-sustaining medical treatment was not contrary to article 2 of the Human Rights Convention and the right to life where the patient was in a persistent vegetative state (PVS). The ruling was made on 25 October 2000 in cases involving Mrs M, a 49-year-old woman, who suffered brain damage during an operation abroad in 1997 and was diagnosed as being in a PVS in October 1998, and in the case of Mrs H, aged 36, who fell ill in America as a result of pancreatitis during Christmas 1999. In the light of these decisions, it would appear that failure to resuscitate a patient when circumstances justify the decision would not amount to a breach of article 2. However where those circumstances are not present, and it would be in the best interests for the patient to be resuscitated, then that could be seen as a breach of article 2.

Article 3 of the European Convention of Human Rights states:

> *No one shall be subjected to torture or to inhuman or degrading treatment or punishment.*

Failure to resuscitate when all the circumstances (likely success and good prognosis) are favourable may be defined as inhuman treatment.

Duty of care in the law of negligence

A duty of care is owed by medical and nursing staff for their patients. The standard of care of this duty, as defined by the Bolam Test (*Bolam v. Friern Barnet Management Committee*), would require staff to follow a reasonable standard of care conforming to the acceptable approved practice of a competent body of professional opinion.

If in a case such as Marion's reasonable practice would have indicated resuscitation, then it could be argued that failure to resuscitate was a breach of the duty of care (unless of course Marion was mentally competent and had refused resuscitation, see below). If, as a result of this failure, Marion suffered harm (ie. death), then her relatives could sue in her name for breach of the duty of care owed to her.

The mentally capacitated patient

If the patient is able to express his or her views over whether resuscitation should be attempted, then those wishes are binding upon health professionals. Clearly it is important to ascertain that the patient has the requisite mental capacity. Professionals have a duty when a person refuses what could be life-saving treatment to ensure that the person is mentally competent (*Re T*). If, however, it is clear that Marion in *Box 10.1* has the necessary mental capacity and clearly indicates that she does not wish to be resuscitated then it is her legal right to refuse treatment (*Re MB*). In the case of *Re B 2002* the President of the Family Division emphasised the right of the mentally competent person to refuse even life-saving treatment (see *Chapter 9*).

The mentally incapacitated patient

If the patient is mentally incapacitated, then the Mental Capacity Act 2005 applies and staff would have to decide what was in the patient's best interests in determining whether or not not for resuscitation (NFR) instructions were appropriate. The Mental Capacity Act 2005, which came fully into force in October 2007, establishes a statutory framework for decision making on behalf of mentally incapacitated adults. It replaces the common law (ie. judge-made law) with statutory provisions. The House of Lords had laid down the principle that health professionals have a duty in law to act out of necessity in the best interests of a mentally incapacitated adult person (*Re F*).

What rights do the relatives have?

The Mental Capacity Act 2005 applies to relatives who are bound to act in the best interests of a mentally incapacitated adult (in the absence of an advance decision refusing treatment, or a lasting power of attorney under which a donee is appointed). However in disputed situations where there is a conflict over whether the best interests of the patient require that life-sustaining treatment should be given, there is likely to be a referral to the Court of Protection. The Act states specifically:

> *S. 4(5) Where the determination relates to life-sustaining treatment he (ie. the person making the decision about treatment) must not, in considering whether the treatment is in the best interests of the person concerned, be motivated by a desire to bring about his death.*

It is, of course, important to discuss potential treatment plans with relatives because they may be able to shed light on the patient's views, and the beliefs, values and views of the patient must be considered in determining what is in the patient's best interests. Form 4 of the Department of Health's implementation guidance on consent to examination and treatment is useful where the patient lacks the mental capacity to make decisions (Department of Health, 2001). It should be revised in the light of the Mental Capacity Act 2005. The rights of parents in relation to children and the recent case of Ms Glass are considered below.

Dispute between experts

In a case (*A National Health Service Trust v. X*) which preceded the bringing into force of the Mental Capacity Act 2005, there was a dispute between doctors. R the expert consulted by the Official Solicitor on behalf of the patient X and the patient's son Y considered that life-sustaining treatment should not be withheld from the patient, an elderly man who suffered from acute chronic renal failure, peripheral oedema and a total lack of urine production. The clinicians caring for X, supported by the independent expert evidence of B, considered that it was in his best interests for treatment to be discontinued and palliative care provided. Y argued that the Bolam Test of reasonable practice as described by R their expert should be followed and therefore the treatment should be continued. In addition X and Y were practising Muslims and discontinuing the treatment would be contrary to Islam and X's religious beliefs.

The Court of Appeal dismissed the appeal holding that it was for the court to determine what was in the best interests of the patient. The trial judge had concluded, on the basis of the evidence, that discontinuing the treatment was in the best interests of X and had concluded to a high standard of probability that the evidence of those treating X supported by the independent evidence of their expert B was preferable to R's evidence. The judge had decided that the key issue was whether there was any chance of X recovering any quality of life so as to justify his continued discomfort. Once he had formed that view, it was difficult for religious views and the views of Y and the family to overcome the fact that continued treatment was not in X's best interests. It is suggested that similar principles will apply when the Court of Protection hears cases following the implementation of the Mental Capacity Act 2005.

Withholding treatment: A legal challenge

Leslie Burke, a patient suffering from a degenerative brain condition, brought an action against the General Medical Council (GMC) arguing that their guidance for doctors, *Withholding and Withdrawing Life-prolonging Treatment: Good Practice in Decision Making* (General Medical Council, 2004) was illegal. Counsel for the GMC argued that there is no obligation to provide treatment that would enable a patient to survive a life-threatening condition regardless of the suffering involved in the treatment and regardless of the quality of life the patient would experience thereafter. Counsel also stated that no evidence existed that Mr Burke would ever be denied life-prolonging treatment. Withdrawing artificial feeding and hydration in his case would be entirely inappropriate (Horsnell, 2004).

Mr Burke won his case before the High Court. The judge granted judicial review holding that once a patient had been admitted to an NHS hospital there was a duty of care to provide and go on providing treatment, whether the patient was competent or incompetent or unconscious. This duty of care, which could not be transferred to anyone else, was to provide that treatment was in the best interests of the patient. It was for the patient, if competent, to determine what was in his or her best interests. If the patient was incompetent and had left no binding and effective advance directive, then it was for the court to decide what was in his or her best interests. To withdraw artificial nutrition and hydration at any stage before the claimant finally lapsed into a coma would involve clear breach of both Article 8 and Article 3 because he or she would thereby be exposed to acute mental and physical suffering. The GMC guidelines were therefore in error in emphasising the right of the claimant to refuse treatment, but not his or her right to require treatment.

The GMC appealed against this ruling and the Court of Appeal's reserved judgment was given on 29 July 2005 (*R (on the application of Burke) v. General Medical Council etc*) . The Court of Appeal held that doctors are not obliged to provide patients with treatment that they consider to be futile or harmful, even if the patient demands it. Autonomy and the right of self-determination do not entitle the patient to insist on receiving a particular medical treatment regardless of the nature of the treatment. However where a competent patient says that he or she wants to be kept alive by the provision of food and water, doctors must agree to that. Not to do so would result in the doctor not merely being in breach of duty in the law of negligence but also guilty of the criminal offence of murder.

Professional guidance

Before the implementation of the Human Rights Act 1998, the Department of Health drew attention to guidance that had been drawn up by the

Resuscitation Council, the Royal College of Nursing and the British Medical Association (1999) (this guidance has since been updated in 2001 and again in 2007). The guidance was commended to NHS trusts in September 2000 by the NHS Executive in an NHS circular (NHS Executive, 2000).

By this circular, chief executives of NHS trusts are required to ensure that appropriate resuscitation policies which respect patients' rights are in place, understood by all relevant staff, and accessible to those who need them, and that such policies are subject to appropriate audit and monitoring arrangements. The action required to be taken by NHS trusts is shown in *Table 10.1*.

The Commission for Health Improvement (CHI) (Since April 2004 the Commission for Health Audit and Inspection known as the Healthcare Commission) has been asked by the Secretary of State to pay particular attention to resuscitation decision-making processes as part of its rolling programme of reviews of clinical governance arrangements put in place by NHS organisations. Guidance emphasises that there must be no blanket policies, each individual patient must be assessed personally and policy cannot depend solely on the age of the patient. The most recent guidance on resuscitation decision making adds a suitably experienced nurse to the

Table 10.1. Resuscitation policies

Action to be taken by NHS trusts must ensure:

- Patients' rights are central to decision making on resuscitation
- The trust has an agreed resuscitation policy in place that respects patients' rights
- The policy is published and readily available to those who may wish to consult it, including patients, families and carers
- Appropriate arrangements are in place for ensuring that all staff who may be involved in resuscitation decisions understand and implement the policy
- Appropriate supervision arrangements are in place to review the resuscitation decisions
- Induction and staff development programmes cover the resuscitation policy
- Clinical practice in this area is regularly audited
- Clinical audit outcomes are reported in the trust's annual clinical governance report
- A non-executive director of the trust is given designated responsibility on behalf of the trust board to ensure that a resuscitation policy is agreed, implemented, and regularly reviewed within the clinical governance framework

consultant and GP in identifying those responsible for making decisions on cardiopulmonary resuscitation (CPR). It will be the responsibility of individual nurses to ensure they have the requisite competence to make such a decision.

Withholding of resuscitation

According to the guidelines, CPR should only be withheld in the following four situations:

- The mentally competent patient has refused treatment.
- A valid living will covering such circumstances has been made by the patient.
- Effective CPR is unlikely to be successful.
- Where successful CPR is likely to be followed by a length and quality of life which would not be in the best interests of the patient to sustain.

A request for resuscitation

A situation may arise where the patient is asking for resuscitation and the medical view is that it would not succeed or the prognosis of the patient is so appalling that it would not be a justification for resources to be used. For example, imagine the situation of Marion in *Box 10.1*. She is suffering from the final stages of cancer of the pancreas and asks to be resuscitated, but medical staff know that she has very few days left and in her very poor state of health CPR may not succeed. In such circumstances, while Marion may want the treatment, medical staff may consider that it is unjustified. It is clear that following the Burke judgment, a patient cannot insist upon treatment which would not be in accordance with the professional judgement of health staff. This also applies to parents seeking treatment for their child (see below). In the case discussed above (*A National Health Service Trust v. D*), the court held that the decision by doctors that a child should not be placed upon a ventilator was not an infringement of the child's right to life and parents could not compel the doctors to act contrary to their professional discretion.

Application of the law to the situation in *Box 10.1*

In the situation in *Box 10.1* the nurse's failure to call out the team would be criticised by the daughter and by the medical staff who would say that in the absence of clear written instructions by Marion the presumption must be in favour of resuscitation. It would be dangerous to take the nurse's word for Marion's wishes. There have been clear failures on the part of the medical and nursing team. On admission, the possibility of DNR instructions should have been discussed with Marion so she could have expressed her wishes and these could then have been recorded in writing. From the daughter's perspective since Marion had not told her that she would not want to be resuscitated, it is natural that her daughter would want all efforts to be made to keep her alive. However the daughter does not have a choice. If Marion's wishes have not been clearly expressed, whether or not resuscitation is to proceed will depend upon the best interests of Marion. Had these wishes been made known before two witnesses or put in writing, then Marion's wish not to be resuscitated should have prevailed. Alternatively had the nurse recorded Marion's wishes in writing and brought them to the attention of the multi-disciplinary team, there would have been sufficient evidence to ensure that Marion's wishes should be carried out, whatever the views of the daughter. The statutory provisions relating to the drawing up of advance decisions are considered in the next chapter.

Not for resuscitation (NFR) instructions: Children

Parents are able to make decisions on behalf of their children up to the age of 18 years. In addition, a child or young person of 16 or 17 has a statutory right to give consent to treatment including medical, surgical and dental treatment, anaesthetics and diagnostic procedures (Family Reform Act 1969 S.8). However the refusal of a young person of 16 or 17 to life-saving treatment can be overruled, in exceptional circumstances, if it is in the best interests of that person (*Re W*). A child or young person of any age also has a right to give consent which is recognised at common law if it is established that they have the mental capacity to make the decision (*Gillick v. West Norfolk and Wisbech AHA and the DHSS*). Where the prognosis of the child is such that the recommended medical treatment is that the child should not be resuscitated it is essential that, if there is a dispute with the parent over this decision, there should be reference to court as the case in *Box 10.2* shows.

The Court of Appeal held that it would be inappropriate to grant a declaration in anticipation and indicate to doctors at a hospital what treatment they should or should not give in circumstances that had not yet arisen. The best course was for the parents of a child and the medical staff to agree on the approach to be taken for the treatment of that child, but if that was not possible and a grave conflict arose, then the actual circumstances must be brought before the court so that the court could resolve what was in the best interests of the child in the light of the facts existing at that time. The principles recognised by the Court of Appeal were as follows.

- The sanctity of life.
- The non-interference by the courts in areas of clinical judgement in the treatment of patients where that could be avoided.

Box 10.2. Dispute over treatment. *R v. Portsmouth Hospitals NHS Trust ex p. Glass*

David Glass a boy of 13 was severely disabled with only a limited life span. The mother wished him to receive whatever medical treatment was necessary to prolong his life. Following an incident in which the hospital gave the child morphine against the mother's wishes, family members resuscitated the child and prevented him from dying. There was a complete breakdown of trust between the family and the hospital. His mother, Ms Glass sought a declaration as to the course doctors in the hospital should take if the boy were admitted for emergency treatment and disagreements arose as to the treatment to be given to or withheld from the child. The judge refused the mother's application for judicial review and she appealed to the Court of Appeal.

- The refusal of the courts to dictate appropriate treatment to a medical practitioner, subject to the court's power to take decisions in the child's best interests.
- Treatment without consent save in an emergency was a trespass to the person.
- The court would interfere to protect the interests of a minor or a person under a disability.

The Court of Appeal dismissed the appeal.

Members of the family were prosecuted for their violence in the hospital and sentenced to imprisonment.

Glass and the European Court of Human Rights

Subsequently however Ms Glass won her appeal to the European Court of Human Rights. Ms Glass argued that both the decision to administer diamorphine to the boy against his mother's wishes and to place a DNR notice in his notes without her knowledge interfered with both their rights under Article 8. She also alleged that leaving the decision to involve the courts to the discretion of doctors was a wholly inadequate basis on which to ensure effective respect for the rights of vulnerable patients.

The Court held unanimously that the right to respect of private life, as guaranteed by article 8 of the European Convention on Human Rights (ECHR), was breached where hospital authorities decided to over-ride an applicant's objection to the treatment proposed for her severely disabled son in the absence of authorisation by a court. The ECHR looked at the justifications for an interference with article 8 rights under paragraph 8.2 and held that the interference was in accordance with the law and that there was a regulatory framework in the UK which was firmly based on the duty to preserve the life of a patient, save in exceptional circumstances. The same framework prioritised the requirement of parental consent and, save in an emergency situation, required doctors to seek the intervention of the courts in the event of parental objection. The ECHR considered that the action taken by the hospital staff pursued a legitimate aim and was intended as a matter of clinical judgement to serve David's interests. It rejected any suggestion that it was the doctor's intention unilaterally to hasten David's death whether by administering diamorphine to him or placing a DNR notice in his case notes. The ECHR held that it had not been explained to its satisfaction why the NHS trust did not at the time of the dispute over the diamorphine seek the intervention of the court and held that the onus was on the trust to take the initiative and to defuse the situation in anticipation of a further emergency. The ECHR noted that the trust was able to secure the presence of a police officer to oversee the negotiations with Ms Glass but, surprisingly, did not consider making a High Court application even though it would have been possible at short notice.

It therefore came to the unanimous conclusion that the decision of the authorities to over-ride Ms Glass's objection to the proposed treatment in the absence of authorisation by a court resulted in a breach of article 8. The ECHR did not go on to examine her complaint of the inclusion of the DNR notice in David's case notes, without her consent and knowledge, although it noted that the DNR notice was only directed against the application of vigorous respiratory support and did not exclude the use of other techniques, such as the provision of oxygen to keep David alive. The ECHR awarded Ms Glass 10 000 Euros for non-pecuniary damage and 15 000 Euros for costs and expenses.

Withholding and withdrawing life saving treatment in children

Parents of children under 18 years of age do have decision-making rights on behalf of their child, as long as such decisions are in the best interests of the child. Guidance has been issued by the Royal College of Paediatric and Child Health (2004). The Royal College identified five situations in which withholding or withdrawing treatment may be considered:

- the brain dead child
- the permanent vegetative state
- the 'no chance' situation
- the 'no purpose' situation
- the 'unbearable' situation.

At the present time there are no clear guidelines as to when the approval of the court should be sought for the withholding or withdrawing of treatment in a child and in practice it is probably only where there is a dispute between parents and physicians or surgeons, or a third party wishes to seek a court review of what is being proposed in relation to the treatment or non-treatment of a child that an application is made to court. In the case of *Re J*, the baby suffered from a severe form of cerebral palsy with cortical blindness and severe epilepsy. The Court of Appeal held that the court would not exercise its inherent jurisdiction over minors by ordering a medical practitioner to treat the minor in a manner contrary to the practitioner's clinical judgement. In the practitioner's view, intensive therapeutic measures such as artificial ventilation were inappropriate. The Court of Appeal declared that it would be lawful for doctors in their professional judgement to allow a severely disabled child to die. For further information on this subject see Dimond (2008). The decision of the ECHR in the Glass case illustrates the importance of involving the courts if there is any dispute over whether proposed treatment is in the best interests of the child.

Clash between parents and clinicians

The conflict between parents and clinicians over what is in the best interests of the child, can lead to bitter court battles as the case of Glass above shows. Several other recent cases reveal the judicial thinking in these conflicts and the cases of Charlotte Wyatt and of MB will be briefly discussed.

Charlotte Wyatt

The case of Charlotte Wyatt illustrates the complexity of ensuring that the best interests of a severely disabled child are protected and the case resulted in several court hearings as the parents and the clinicians disputed as to what was in the child's best interests.

The Portsmouth NHS Trust sought permission to decline to give invasive medical treatment to prolong the life of a profoundly disabled baby. Charlotte had been born at 26 weeks' gestation, weighing about one pound. She had chronic respiratory and kidney problems and brain damage that had left her blind, deaf and incapable of voluntary movement or response. She was capable of experiencing pain. The dispute was over what should be done should she deteriorate and required artificial ventilation. The unanimous medical advice was that to give such treatment would not be in her best interests. However her parents' view was that such treatment should at least be instituted and that the treatment could best be prepared for by carrying out an elective tracheotomy. They believed that it was their duty to maintain life as they did not believe that Charlotte was yet ready to die. The high court judge set out in October 2004 a number of declarations as to what was and what was not in the best interests of Charlotte. In particular the declaration authorised the responsible paediatric medical consultants not to ventilate Charlotte in the event that she suffered an infection which had led or might lead to a collapsed lung and which proved resistant to antibiotics. At that time her prognosis was extremely gloomy and she was not expected to survive the forthcoming winter. The court decided that any further aggressive treatment, even if necessary to prolong life, was not in Charlotte's best interests. The doctors still had a duty of care to Charlotte. The order only authorised the doctors not to send Charlotte for artificial ventilation or similar aggressive treatment. The court asked the doctors to give further consideration to an elective tracheotomy on the basis of its possible contribution to her palliative care. The High Court judge made the declarations shown in *Box 10.3*.

The Court of Appeal heard the parents' appeal in respect of Charlotte's medical treatment and decided that the permission to appeal on the declarations on best interests and on the timing would be dismissed, but the review of the continuation of the declarations directed by the judge should, if possible be accelerated. It gave the reasons for its decision in October 2005.

The Court of Appeal emphasised that the case was not about the withdrawal of treatment from Charlotte in order to allow her to die. Nor was it about whether or not Charlotte should be subject to a 'do not resuscitate' policy. Nor was it about the level of care provided for her.

What it was about was what should happen to Charlotte if she contracted an infection or suffered some other crisis which was likely to lead to her death, but which could not be treated by drugs and thus required her to be ventilated if she was to stand any chance of remaining alive. The Court of Appeal decided that the judge's declarations should continue pending their review.

Subsequently Charlotte appeared to progress and expert evidence was given that there were certain circumstances in which it would be appropriate to ventilate Charlotte in the event of respiratory distress. In those circumstances the judge declared that it was not possible to frame a conventional declaration to deal with the medical problems that had arisen (*Wyatt Re 2005*). The court held that no declaration was required for the doctors to act in accordance with their professional judgement in determining what was in the best interests for her. Where a parent was requesting treatment that would be an affront to a clinician's conscience, the clinician was entitled to refuse to act. This was sufficient protection for the clinicians in the instant case.

After that decision Charlotte's condition significantly deteriorated in that she developed an intermittent rasping cough and it was likely that she was suffering from a viral infection. The medical experts were of the opinion

Box 10.3. Declarations made by Judge Hedley 1 October 2004 in Charlotte Wyatt's case

1. Charlotte, as a child, lacks capacity to make decisions about medical treatment to be delivered to herself for her physical health care.
2. Having regard to Charlotte's best interests, and in the event that the paediatric medical consultants responsible for Charlotte's case, at (the Trust) the Southampton University Hospitals NHS Trust or any NHS Trust treating Charlotte, consider that she is suffering an infection which has or may lead to a collapsed lung, it shall be lawful for the doctors treating Charlotte to provide all suitable medical care including antibiotics.
3. That in the events anticipated in paragraph 2 above, and having regard to Charlotte's best interests:
   - In the event that the responsible paediatric medical consultants reach a decision that Charlotte's medical condition shall have deteriorated to such an extent that she is unable to maintain oxygen and carbon dioxide exchange, it shall be lawful for responsible paediatric medical consultants to reach a decision that she should not be intubated and/or ventilated.
   - While the responsible paediatric medical consultants may reach a decision that it is appropriate to administer continuous positive airways pressure (CPAP) or help keep Charlotte's airways open and to ease Charlotte's breathing, if she is visibly distressed by CPAP, it shall be lawful for the responsible paediatric medical consultants to reach a decision that CPAP shall be withdrawn.
   - The responsible paediatric medical consultants shall be entitled to reach a decision to use symptomatic relief which may be in the form of opiates in the knowledge that this may depress Charlotte's efforts to breathe while making her more comfortable

that the only intervention, if Charlotte continued to deteriorate, would be intubation and ventilation but that it would not be in her best interests as essentially it would be futile.

The parents appealed maintaining that it was in Charlotte's best interests for her to be ventilated since that could lead to a recovery. The judge held that the circumstances had arisen where the court should make it clear that, in the best interests of Charlotte, the medical profession should be free to refrain from intervention by way of intubation and ventilation. That was a permissive and not mandatory declaration; therefore at the moment the decision arose the medical authorities were required to use their best judgement, in Charlotte's best interests, as to whether to desist. Accordingly a decision to desist would be lawful (*Wyatt Re 2006*).

In October 2006 it was reported that social services were searching for foster parents for Charlotte whose parents had split up and Charlotte, although still very ill, would be able to leave hospital if arrangements could be made.

Re MB (2006)

In contrast to the case of Charlotte Wyatt, the judge in the case of *Re MB* decided that the terminally ill child could be kept on a life-support machine against the wishes of his doctors (Smith, 2006). The boy suffered from spinal muscular atrophy (SMA), a degenerative muscle-wasting disease. He could not smile, make a sound, swallow or move his arms or legs. He was expected to die within a year. The doctors claimed that the boy's quality of life was so poor that it was intolerable and that it was in his best interests to be allowed to die peacefully. His parents challenged this pointing out that MB enjoyed watching television, listening to music and being read stories. They said that he was able to communicate his likes and dislikes by moving an eyebrow, looking away or twitching the corners of his mouth. The judge decided that despite being in almost constant discomfort and frequent pain, MB derived pleasure from seeing, hearing and being stroked by family members. He made the following declarations:

- The paramount consideration was the welfare of the child. Considerable weight had to be attached to the prolongation of life, but it was not absolute or necessarily decisive
- It was probable and had to be assumed that M continued to see and to hear and to feel touch; to have an awareness of his surroundings and in particular his family and to have the normal thoughts and thought processes of a small child of 18 months, albeit limited by the fact that he had never left hospital.
- It was not in M's best interests to discontinue ventilation with the inevitable result that he would die.
- However, it would not be in M's best interests to undergo procedures that went beyond maintaining ventilation, required the positive infliction of pain and would mean, if they became necessary, that M had moved naturally towards death, despite the ventilation. These procedures were cardiopulmonary resuscitation, electrocardiogram monitoring, administration of intravenous antibiotics and blood sampling. It was in M's best interests and lawful to withhold or not to administer any of those forms of treatment. The declaration reflecting that decision would be permissive in effect and therefore would not prevent a doctor giving such treatment.

The significant difference between MB and Charlotte was that the former was on a life-support machine and to remove him would be to end his life and the judge ruled that he could stay on it. In contrast Charlotte was not on life support at the time of the hearing.

Statement by Royal College of Obstetricians and Gynaecologists

In March 2006 the Royal College of Obstetricians and Gynaecologists in its evidence to the inquiry into premature babies by the Nuffield Council on Bioethics stated that the huge efforts to save babies born under 25 weeks are hampering the treatment of other infants with a better chance of survival and a healthy life (Templeton, 2006a, b). Not surprisingly this has led to considerable controversy with a response in the letters to the editor page the following week where several correspondents wrote of amazing achievements of very premature babies. Clearly length of gestation cannot be the main factor in determining whether intensive care in neonatal units is justified for an individual premature baby.

Conclusion

The circular from the NHS Executive should be of considerable assistance to health professional staff, who are entitled to request that any NFR instructions are in writing and that each patient is individually assessed. Such blanket policies as 'patients over 80 are not for resuscitation' are illegal. The Healthcare Commission has a duty to ensure that NFR policies are in place and are being implemented and this should ensure the protection of patients' rights and also benefit staff.

As far as children are concerned, it is important that children or young people are involved in treatment decisions according to their mental capacity and this can only be developed if they are given the necessary information about their condition, prognosis and recommended treatments. The rights of the child under the European Convention on Human Rights can only be respected if the child is not kept ignorant of significant facts about his or her condition, but clearly this information must be imparted with sensitivity and be appropriate to the child's mental capacity. A British Medical Association publication (2001) provides useful guidance on the rights of the child in giving consent and emphasises the importance of ensuring that the child or young person is kept informed so that they can partake fully in the decision making in so far as their level of maturity and mental capacity permit. For younger children and neonates it is likely that there will be continuing legal controversy as parents and clinicians dispute what is in the best interests of a particular child. A young person under 18 years cannot draw up a binding advance decision and it is to this topic we turn in the next chapter.

References

A National Health Service Trust v. D [2000] The Times Law Report 19 July

A National Health Service Trust v. X [2005] EWCA Civ 1145; [2006] Lloyd's Rep Med. 29

Bolam v. Friern Barnet Management Committee [1957] 1 WLR 582

British Medical Association (2001) *Consent, Rights and Choices in Health Care for Children and Young People*. London: BMJ Books

BMA/RCN/Resuscitation Council (UK) (2007) *Decisions Relating to Cardiopulmonary Resuscitation. A Joint Statement from the British Medical Association, the Resuscitation Council (UK) and the Royal College of Nursing*. London: BMA/RCN/ Resuscitation Council (UK)

Department of Health (2001) Good Practice in Consent Implementation Guide. London: Department of Health. www. doh.gov.uk/consent

Dimond BC (2008) *Legal Aspects of Nursing* (Ch 14, 5th Edn) Harlow: Pearson Education

Family law Reform Act 1969 Section 8

General Medical Council (2002) Withholding and Withdrawing Life Prolonging Treatment: Good Practice in Decision Making. London: General Medical Council

Gillick v. West Norfolk and Wisbech AHA and the DHSS 1985 3 All ER 402

Glass v. United Kingdom The Times Law Report 11 March 2004 ECHR

Horsnell M (2004) Feeding a terminal patient 'is treatment'. *The Times* **28 February**

NHS Executive (2000) *Resuscitation Policy HSC 2000/028*. London: NHS Executive

NHS Trust A v. Mrs M and NHS Trust B v. Mrs H Family Division The Times 25 October 2000; [2001] 1 All ER 801; [2001] 2 F.L.R. 367

R (On the application of Burke) v. General Medical Council and Disability Rights Commission and Official Solicitor to the Supreme Court [2004] EWHC 1879; [2004] Lloyd's Rep. Med 451; [2005] EWCA Civ 1003, 28 July 2005

Re B (consent to treatment: capacity) Times Law Report 26 March 2002; [2002] 2 ALL ER 449

Re F (mental patient: sterilisation) [1990] 2 AC 1

Re J (a minor) (wardship, medical treatment) [1992] 4 All ER 614

Re MB 2006 EWHC 507 15 March 2006; [2006] 2 FLR 319

Re T (adult: refusal of medical treatment) [1992] 4 All ER 649, (1992) 9 BMLR 46 CA

Re W (a minor) (medical treatment) [1992] 4 ALL ER 627

R v. Portsmouth Hospitals NHS Trust ex p. Glass [ ] 2 FLR 905; [1999] Lloyds Law Report Medical 367

Royal College of Paediatric and Child Health (2004) *Withholding or Withdrawing Life Saving Treatment in Children; a Framework for Practice*. London: Royal College of Paediatric and Child Health

Smith L (2006) Victory for dying boy's family. *The Times* **16 March**

Templeton SK (2006a) Doctors call premature babies bed blockers *The Sunday Times* **26 March**

Templeton SK (2006b) Doctors: Let us kill disabled babies *The Sunday Times* **5 November**

Wyatt Re [2005] EWHC 2293; [2005] 4 All ER 1325

Wyatt Re [2006] EWHC 319

CHAPTER 11

Living wills

Box 11.1. Case scenario

David Browne was suffering from motor neurone disease and was anxious to ensure that, as his disease progressed and he ceased to be mentally capacitated, he would not be given artificial feeding and ventilation. He therefore arranged to draw up a living will in which he gave an advanced refusal of such treatments. The document was duly signed and witnessed. Only three months after signing the living will he was severely injured in a road accident and brought into hospital unconscious. He was carrying his living will in his pocket and doctors were concerned that if they operated and he required ventilation in intensive care would the living will prevent their providing such treatment and care. What is the law?

It is a basic principle of the law on consent that an adult mentally competent person can refuse treatment for a good reason, a bad reason or for no reason at all (*Re MB*). In the case of Ms B, a patient who had, as a result of a haemorrhage in her neck, become paralysed, she won her action for trespass to the person because she was placed on a ventilator against her will and she also succeeded in obtaining a declaration that her ventilator could be switched off, even though it meant her certain death. The only issue before the court was her competence to make that decision (*Re B (consent to treatment: capacity)*).

It was also an accepted principle at common law (ie. judge-made or case law) that where people have, when mentally competent, declared their wishes for a time when they may lack the mental capacity, then those previously declared views are binding upon health professionals caring for them during that time of incapacity. These earlier expressed views are variously known as a living will, an advanced directive, an advance decision or an advance refusal of treatment. The Mental Capacity Act 2005 has enacted statutory provisions to cover advance decisions. Provisions relating to advance decisions came into force in October 2007 and until that time the law derived from decided cases (ie. judge-made law also known as the common law) was applied.

The common law on advance statements

In 1993, the House of Lords discussed the situation relating to the discontinuation of artificial feeding for Tony Bland, the victim of the Hillsborough stadium disaster who was in a persistent vegetative state (*Airedale NHS Trust v. Bland*). It decided that the artificial feeding could be discontinued in his best interests. It also stated that had he made an advanced directive setting out his wishes if he were to become mentally incapacitated then that directive would have been binding upon the health professionals caring for him.

A typical example of an advanced directive is the card carried by Jehovah's Witnesses. This makes it clear what treatments or care the person is refusing and it is signed by both the person refusing the treatment in anticipation, and by another person as a witness.

In the Canadian case of *Malette v. Shulman*, an unconscious woman who was given a life-saving blood transfusion, in spite of the fact that she was carrying a card, won Canadian $20000 against the doctor. The reason was that the doctor was guilty of trespass to the person (ie. battery) in treating her against her express instructions even though she was mentally incompetent at the time of the treatment.

The House of Lords in the Tony Bland case gave approval to the decision in this Canadian case, saying that if the same facts were to occur in this country, such treatment contrary to the advanced directive of the patient would be actionable in law. In the Tony Bland case, Lord Goff stated that:

> *[Respect must be given to the patient's wishes] where the patient's refusal to give his consent has been expressed at an earlier date, before he became unconscious or otherwise incapable of communicating it; although in such circumstances special care may be necessary to ensure that the prior refusal of consent is still properly to be regarded as applicable in the circumstances which have subsequently occurred.*

In the absence of a valid living will, the health professional had a duty to act in the best interests of a mentally incapacitated person (*Re F*).

Mental Capacity Act 2005

These common law principles are now given statutory effect by the Mental Capacity Act 2005. Sections 24–26 in the Act cover the legal provisions for advance decisions to refuse treatment. The specified definition in section 24(1) is that an advance decision means:

A decision made by a person ('P') after he has reached 18 and when he has capacity to do so, that if:

a. at a later time and in such circumstances as he may specify, a specified treatment is proposed to be carried out or continued by a person providing health care for him, and
b. at that time he lacks capacity to consent to the carrying out or continuation of the treatment,
the specified treatment is not to be carried out or continued.

There are no statutory forms for the making of an advance decision. Section 24(2) states that for the purposes of section 24(1)(a) a decision may be regarded as specifying a treatment or circumstances even though expressed in layman's terms.

P may withdraw or alter an advance decision at any time when he has capacity to do so (S.24(3)). A withdrawal (including a partial withdrawal) need not be in writing (S.24(4)). An alteration of an advance decision need not be in writing unless section 25(5) applies (ie. it relates to life-sustaining treatment).

Validity and applicability of advance decisions

An advance decision does not affect the liability which a person may incur for carrying out or continuing a treatment in relation to P unless the decision is at the material time:

- valid, and
- applicable to the treatment (S.25(1))

An advance decision is not valid if P:

- has withdrawn the decision at a time when he had capacity to do so
- has, under a lasting power of attorney created after the advance decision was made, conferred authority on the donee(s) to give or refuse consent to the treatment to which the advance decision relates, or
- has done anything else clearly inconsistent with the advance decision remaining his fixed decision (S.25(2)).

An advance decision is not applicable to the treatment in question if at the material time P has capacity to give or refuse consent to it (S.25(3)).

An advance decision is not applicable to the treatment in question if:

- that treatment is not the treatment specified in the advance decision,
- any circumstances specified in the advance decision are absent, or
- there are reasonable grounds for believing that circumstances exist which P did not anticipate at the time of the advance decision and which would have affected his decision had he anticipated them S.25(4)).

Life-sustaining treatment

An advance decision is not applicable to life-sustaining treatment unless:

- the decision is verified by a statement by P to the effect that it is to apply to that treatment even if life is at risk, and
- the decision and statement comply with subsection (6) (S.25(5)).

The conditions laid down in subsection 6 are that:

- it is in writing,
- it is signed by P or by another person in P's presence and by P's direction,
- the signature is made or acknowledged by P in the presence of a witness, and
- the witness signs it, or acknowledges his signature, in P's presence (S.25(6)).

The existence of any lasting power of attorney other than one of a description mentioned in the second point in subsection (2) does not prevent the advance decision from being regarded as valid and applicable.

Formalities of an advance decision

Apart from those provisions relating to an advance decision refusing life-sustaining treatment and the need to ensure that the advance decision is made by a person over 18 years and is relevant to the situation which exists, there are no specific statutory requirements as to the drawing up of an advance decision. However it is important that there should be clear evidence as to:

- the fact that the person is mentally capable at the time he/she expresses advance refusal,
- what the refusal consists of,
- that this is intended to be binding at a later time when the person lacks the capacity,

- that there is a witness to this directive,
- and (for the refusal of life-sustaining treatment), that it should be in writing, signed and witnessed and state that it is intended to cover the refusal of life-sustaining treatments.

Guidance contained in the British Medical Association's (BMA, 1995) code of practice on advance statements has been specifically commended by the Law Commission (1995) and by the Government (Lord Chancellor's Office, 1999). The BMA's code of practice suggests the minimum information that should be contained in a living will and the value of the name of a person who could speak on behalf of the person who made the living will. It suggests that, as a minimum, the following information is included:

- full name,
- address,
- name and address of GP,
- whether advice was sought from health professionals,
- signature,
- date drafted and reviewed,
- witness signature,
- a clear statement of the person's wishes, either general or specific, and
- the name, address and telephone number of the nominated person, if there is one.

The Voluntary Euthanasia Society has launched a pro-choice living will that was put together after consultation with doctors, nurses and barristers. It includes provisions such as nominating a 'healthcare proxy' whom you would like to take part in medical decisions on your behalf should you become unable to do so. It can be found on their website.

Reliance on the views of relatives

In the case of *Re T* (which is considered in *Box 11.2*), Lord Donaldson warned against reliance upon the wishes of relatives when a patient lacks the requisite mental capacity:

> *There seems to be a view in the medical profession that in ... emergency circumstances the next of kin should be asked to consent on behalf of the patient and that, if possible, treatment should be postponed until that consent has been obtained. This is a misconception because the next of kin has no legal right either to consent or to refuse consent.*

Box 11.2. ***Case of Re T (adult: refusal of medical treatment)***

T, 34 weeks pregnant, was injured in a road accident. She had been brought up by her mother who was a Jehovah's Witness, although she was not herself a member of that religion. After being alone with her mother, she told the staff nurse that she would not want to have a blood transfusion. At that time, it was unlikely that it would become necessary. Shortly afterwards she went into labour and it was agreed that she would have a Caesarean section. Again, after being alone with her mother, she told the medical staff that she did not want a blood transfusion. She signed a form of refusal of consent to a blood transfusion. It was not explained to her that it might be necessary to give her a blood transfusion to save her life. Following the Caesarean section, the doctors, in compliance with her wishes, did not give her blood and she was placed on a ventilator and paralysing drugs were administered. Her father (who was not a Jehovah's Witness) and her boyfriend applied to the court for a declaration that it was lawful to give her a blood transfusion. The High Court judge held at the first hearing that it was lawful for a blood transfusion to be given and at the second hearing that T had neither consented to, nor refused, a blood transfusion in the emergency which had arisen and it was therefore lawful for the doctors to treat her in whatever way they considered, in the exercise of their professional judgement, to be in her best interests.

As a consequence of the Mental Capacity Act 2005 if an advance decision is valid and relevant to the treatment in question the relatives do not have the right to overrule it. Only if there is a dispute as to its validity or applicability to the situation which exists would there be an application to court to determine its validity and applicability (see below).

The effect of advance decisions

The effect of advance decisions is that if an advance decision is valid and applicable to a treatment, then the decision has effect as if P had made it, and had had the capacity to make it, at the time when the question arises whether the treatment should be carried out or continued (S.26(1)).

A person does not incur liability for carrying out or continuing treatment unless, at the time, that person is satisfied that an advance decision exists which is valid and applicable to the treatment (S.26(2)).

A person does not incur liability for the consequences of withholding or withdrawing a treatment from P if, at the time, that person reasonably believes that an advance decision exists which is valid and applicable to the treatment (S.26(3)).

Application to the Court of Protection

Where there are concerns as to the validity or relevance of an advance decision, then an application to the Court of Protection can be made. The court may make a declaration as to whether an advance decision (a) exists, (b) is valid, and (c) is applicable to a treatment (S.26(4)).

Nothing in an apparent advance decision stops a person: (a) providing life-sustaining treatment, or (b) doing any act he reasonably believes to be necessary to prevent a serious deterioration in P's condition while a decision as respects any relevant issue is sought from the court.

Code of Practice

A draft *Code of Practice on the Mental Capacity Act 2005* was published in July 2006 and finalised in February 2007. It can be found on the Ministry of Justice website. Chapter 9 of the Code of Practice provides guidance on advance decisions. It is binding on health and social services professionals, attorneys under a lasting power of attorney, deputies appointed by the Court of Protection and it is anticipated that informal carers will also find its guidance of value and follow it.

Application of the law to the situation in *Box 11.1*

There would appear to be no doubt that David Browne has made a valid living will, but the uncertainty which arises is, does it apply to the circumstances which have arisen here? David was clearly anticipating a situation where his mental and physical condition had deteriorated as a result of the motor neurone disease, not a situation where he has suffered a head injury in a road accident. Because of the doubts which prevail over the application of the living will to the situation which has arisen, it would probably be wise to seek a declaration of the court in the circumstances. David could be kept alive in the meantime since health professionals have a duty under the Mental Capacity Act 2005 to act in the best interests of a mentally incompetent adult. If the Court were to declare that the advance decision is not applicable to the present circumstances, then action must be taken in his best interests. In order to establish what his best interests were relatives could be asked about his views and beliefs and what he would have wanted, had he had the capacity under section 4 of the 2005 Act. If at any time David recovers consciousness and has the requisite mental capacity to make his views known, then he has the right in law to decide whether or not he wishes to continue to be ventilated should that be necessary.

What can P refuse?

The Law Commission had recommended in its 1995 report that a person drawing up an advance decision should not be able to opt out of basic care. Basic care was defined as 'care to maintain bodily cleanliness and to alleviate severe pain, and the provision of direct oral nutrition and hydration'. There is no such provision in the Mental Capacity Act and therefore in theory a patient could refuse all kinds of care and treatment including pain relief. However the effect of section 25(5) is that life-sustaining treatment cannot be withheld or withdrawn unless the person specified in writing that the advance decision was to apply even if life was at risk and all the procedural requirements of section 25(6) are satisfied.

Had the earlier draft of the Mental Incapacity Bill in 1995 been enacted, there would have been no difficulties in deciding what action to take in the situation in *Box 11.3* since Peter could not through an advance direction/decision/refusal refuse pain relief. However in the absence of such provision in the Mental Capacity Act, the court would have to determine whether Peter's advance decision could include alleviation of pain. One view is that the advance decision only covers treatment and cannot cover care. It would therefore be necessary to decide whether pain relief came under the definition of treatment or care. Account would have to be taken of the Buddhist views on pain management.

Absence of a valid advance directive

If it is considered that there are significant doubts as to whether or not the patient has made a clear advance refusal of treatment, then the patient would

Box 11.3. Refusing pain relief by means of an advance decision

Peter is a Buddhist and believes in mind over matter. He had drawn up an advance decision which stated that if he were to be in a situation where he no longer had mental capacity to make his own decisions he would not wish to be given any treatment including life-sustaining treatments, including ventilation or resuscitation. He is in the late stages of pancreatic cancer and had refused all pain relief. He gradually lost his mental capacity to make decisions and was clearly in severe pain. Health professionals caring for him were aware of his advance decision, but felt that it would not cover the administration of pain relief. A dispute arose between the clinical team and his relatives over whether pain relief could be administered.

have to be treated as a mentally incapacitated adult. In such a case care must be provided in the best interests of the patient according to the Mental Capacity Act 2005. Where a document has been drawn up, but there are reasonable doubts as to its validity as an advanced refusal, then a declaration from the court could be sought and treatment given in the meantime, to keep the patient alive until the court's decision was made known.

There are considerable advantages in staff discussing with patients who are at an early stage of a deteriorating illness, but while they still enjoy their mental capacity, their views on active intervention. Clearly, this topic would have to be broached sensitively and the correct time chosen for such communication. It would certainly be preferable to relying entirely upon the relatives telling staff what the patient would not have wished, when this can no longer be confirmed with the patient.

The problem over what constituted a valid refusal arose in the case of *Re T* (see *Box 11.2*). T appealed to the Court of Appeal which held that T's refusal was the result of her mother's undue influence upon her and therefore was invalid. In addition, when she signed the form of refusal (the design of which was criticised by Lord Donaldson) she did so in ignorance of the particular circumstances which later arose (ie. that blood may be needed in a life-saving situation for herself).

Advice from the Lord Chancellor's Office

The Lord Chancellor's Office has published several leaflets that are to be issued to different groups who are involved in decision making by people who have difficulty deciding for themselves. Leaflet 6 is a guide for people wishing to plan for future incapacity and contains the following headings:

- Who is this leaflet aimed at?
- The right to make your own decisions.
- What is capacity?
- What can I do to plan for future incapacity?
- What decisions can't be delegated?
- How should decisions be made on my behalf?
- Safeguards against abuse.
- Further information.

The Ministry of Justice has taken over responsibilities from the Department for Constitutional Affairs and provides guidance on human rights and the Mental Capacity Act 2005.

Conclusion

An advance refusal must be clearly intended to be operative in the circumstances which arise when the patient becomes mentally incapacitated. The existence of statutory provisions in the Mental Capacity Act 2005 is to be welcomed but it is likely that there will be several cases where the interpretation and implementation of the relevant sections are disputed. (In Scotland the Adults with Incapacity (Scotland) Act 2000 is in force and covers the situation of decision making on behalf of incapacitated adults.)

References

Airedale NHS Trust v. Bland [1993] 1 All ER 821

British Medical Association (1995) *Advance Statements About Medical Treatment*. London: BMA

Department for Constitutional Affairs (2007) *Code of Practice on the Mental Capacity Act 2005*. London: Department for Constitutional Affairs

Law Commission (1995) *Mental Incapacity Report No 231*. London: The Stationery Office

Lord Chancellor's Office (1999) *Making Decisions: The Government's Proposals for Making Decisions on Behalf of Mentally Incapacitated Adults*. London: The Stationery Office

Lord Chancellor's Office (2002) *Consultation Paper Making Decisions: Helping People who have Difficulty Deciding for Themselves*. From: www.lcd.gov.uk/consult/family/decision.htm

Malette v. Shulman (1990) 67 DLR (4th) 321

Re B (consent to treatment: capacity), Times Law Report 26 March 2002 [2002] 2 ALL ER 449

Re F (a mental patient: sterilisation) [1990] 2 AC 1

Re MB (adult medical treatment) [1997] 2 FLR 426

Re T (adult: refusal of medical treatment), [1992] 4 All ER 649 (1992) 9 BMLR 46 CA

Resources

www.dca.gov.uk

www.livingwill.org.uk.

www.justice.gov.uk/

Voluntary Euthansia Society: www.ves.org.uk

CHAPTER 12

The coroner's jurisdiction 1: Investigation into deaths

Box 12.1. Reportable death

Ray Dobson fell downstairs during the night and was rushed to hospital by ambulance. He died shortly after his admission and his widow Mary has been advised that the death was being reported to the coroner. She was concerned at the implications for herself and whether that would delay a funeral and cremation. What is the law?

The office of the coroner probably dates back to before the 13th century and was an appointment to deal with actions relating to the Crown (*Halsbury's Laws*, 2001). They are of three kinds: coroners *ex officio*, which applies to all High Court judges who can exercise the functions of a coroner; district coroners, who are appointed for each of the metropolitan counties and local government areas; and franchise coroners such as the Queen's Coroner and Attorney and the Coroner of the Queen's household. (On 18 December 2003 the Coroner for the Royal Household announced that there would be an inquest into the death of Diana Princess of Wales and since the Coroner also happened to be Coroner of Surrey he announced that there would also be an inquest into the death of Dodi Fayed.)

Coroners' powers, jurisdiction and procedures at the time of writing come under the Coroners Act 1988 and statutory regulations. To become a coroner a person must have had the appropriate legal qualification or have been a registered medical practitioner for at least five years. The appointments are made by the Secretary of State upon notification of the vacancy by the relevant local authority which is responsible for paying the salary. The coroner can be removed from office by the Lord Chancellor for any inability or misbehaviour in the discharge of his or her duty. If the coroner is guilty of a criminal offence the court can remove that coroner from office. There are restrictions upon the activities of full-time coroners, so that they cannot provide advocacy or litigation services, provide any conveyancing or probate services, practise as barristers, solicitors, notaries or licensed conveyancers or be indirectly involved in any such practice. An inquest into a death must be held only by the coroner within whose district the body lies. Where a death has occurred abroad and the body has been brought back to England, then the coroner for the district in which the body lies has jurisdiction.

Duties of a coroner

The duties of a coroner are:

- To inquire into the death, including the cause of death and the circumstances surrounding the death of certain persons, either by holding an inquest or by having a post mortem examination.
- To act on occasion in the place of the sheriff.
- To hold inquests into treasure.
- To monitor requests for the removal of bodies out of England and Wales.
- To authorise the exhumation of bodies for the purposes of criminal proceedings

Deaths reportable to the coroner

The coroner must hold an inquest into the following deaths where there is reasonable cause to suspect that the deceased

- has died a violent or an unnatural death,
- has died a sudden death of which the cause is unknown, or
- has died in prison, or in such place or in such circumstances as to require an inquest under any other Act.

These deaths must therefore be reported to the coroner who has no discretion whether to hold an inquest or not and must hold an inquest as soon as is practicable (Coroners Act 1988 S8(1)).

Where coroners are informed that there is a reasonable cause to suspect that a person has died a sudden death (provided that it is not a violent or unnatural death or death of a person in prison) they can order a post mortem to take place and if, as a consequence of the results of the post mortem, they consider that an inquest is unnecessary, they can dispense with the inquest (ibid S19(3)).

Deaths would therefore usually be reported to the coroner in the following circumstances:

- abortion,
- accidents or injuries,

- alcoholism,
- anaesthetics and operations,
- crime or suspected crime,
- drugs,
- ill-treatment,
- industrial diseases,
- infant deaths if in any way obscure,
- pensioners where death might be connected with a pensionable disability,
- persons in legal custody,
- poisoning,
- septicaemias if originating from an injury,
- stillbirths where there may have been a possibility or suspicion that the child may have been born alive.

It is a criminal offence at common law for a person to bury the body of anyone who has died a violent death before the coroner has had the opportunity of holding an inquest on it (*R v. Bond*). It is also a criminal offence for a person to prevent the burial of a dead body or to dispose of a dead body in order to prevent the holding of any inquest over it where the coroner has reasonable grounds for holding an inquest (*R v. Clerk*).

Duty of registrar to inform coroner

The registrar of births and deaths has a duty to inform the coroner of the death, if the death was in one of the circumstances set out in *Table 12.1* (Births and Deaths Regulations 1987).

Registrars cannot register deaths shown in *Table 12.1* until they have received from the coroner a certificate after the inquest or a notification that the coroner does not intend to hold an inquest.

Doctor's duty to report cause of death

The registered medical practitioner who attended the person during his or her last illness is required by law to sign a death certificate in the prescribed form (Births and Deaths Registration Act 1953). The Home Office (1923) has advised that the fact that the doctor is aware that the death will be reported to the coroner or that an inquest will be held is no grounds for refusing to give the certificate. The doctor is also advised to notify the coroner of any deaths coming in the list shown in Table 12.1.

Table 12.1. Deaths the registrar must report to the coroner

- The deceased was not attended during his or her last illness by a registered medical practitioner
- The registrar has been unable to obtain a duly completed certificate of the cause of death from the doctor or where it appears the doctor certifying the death had not seen the deceased within 14 days before death
- The cause of death appears unknown
- The cause appears to have been unnatural or caused by violence or neglect or by abortion or to have been attended by suspicious circumstances
- The death appears to have occurred during an operation or before the recovery from the effect of an anaesthetic
- The death appears to have been due to industrial disease or industrial poisoning
- The death appears to have been an alleged stillbirth, but there is reason to believe the child was born alive

Multiple deaths

Where two or more deaths have occurred as a result of the same incident, the different coroners involved may agree that the inquests will be held by one coroner as concurrent inquests.

Unnatural death

Whether a death is unnatural or not is a question of fact. For example, when a person died of an asthmatic attack that was considered a natural cause of death even though the ambulance did not attend for 33 minutes after the emergency call. The delay of the ambulance did not turn the natural death into an unnatural death (*R v. Poplar Coroner*). However it does depend upon the circumstances and examples are given in *Chapter 13* where there had been an unnatural death. A death would come within the purposes of the Coroners Act 1988 S.8(1)(a) as being 'unnatural' where even, if it had come about by natural causes, there was reasonable cause to suspect that there had been a gross failure to provide basic medical attention and that the need for such attention had been obvious at the time (*R (on the application of Canning) v. HM Coroner for Northampton*).

Definition of body

To constitute a body, there must have been independent life. A non-viable fetus expelled at a stage of pregnancy at which separate existence is impossible does not fall within the coroner's jurisdiction, unless there is doubt over whether separate existence has been achieved. There are special rules for stillbirths (ie. where gestation has exceeded 24 weeks' duration, see *Chapter 4*), where the registrar has reason to believe that the child was born alive (see above).

Post mortem or inquest or both?

If a registered medical practitioner has signed a death certificate and there are no circumstances which appear to demand a public inquiry or post mortem examination, the coroner should notify the registrar that he or she does not consider it necessary to hold an inquest.

Even where doctors have signed death certificates coroners still have the power to order inquests. If coroners consider that a post mortem examination may make an inquest unnecessary they can direct a registered medical practitioner who could be called as a witness in the event of an inquest, or request any other registered medical practitioner to conduct a post mortem examination and to report the results in writing. In the light of the results coronors can decide whether or not to conduct an inquest, and if they consider that no inquest is necessary, they can notify the registrar accordingly. Coroners have a duty (Coroner's Rules 1984 7(1)) to notify specified persons of the fact that a post mortem is to take place. These include any relatives who have notified the coroner of their wish to attend or be represented, the deceased's regular medical practitioner, and the hospital (if the deceased died in hospital). Relatives cannot refuse to permit the post mortem where the coroner orders one. The post mortem must take place in premises that are adequately equipped for the purpose of the examination and, where the deceased has died in hospital, this would usually take place on the hospital premises. Under the present Coroners Rules (1984 9) a person making a post mortem examination must make provision, so far as possible, for the preservation of material which, in his or her opinion, bears upon the cause of death for such period as the coroner thinks fit.

Coroner and certificate

If the coroner has held or decided to hold an inquest into the death, he or she may issue an order for the burial of the body.

Department of Health guidance

The Department of Health (2003) has issued guidance on sudden death and the coroner that recommends the booklet produced by Victims' Voice (2003). This adds to the information provided by the Home Office (2002) by advising people confronted by sudden death about post mortems and questions about coroners' inquiries.

Application of the law to the situation in Box *12.1*

Mary Dobson should be reassured that the coroner will deal sensitively and speedily with any inquiry into Ray's death. The coroner may request a post mortem examination to be undertaken and Mary would have no right to refuse it. In the light of this the coroner may decide that an inquest without a jury should be held. This topic is considered in *Chapter 13*.

Reforms to the office of coroner

Following the Shipman Inquiry significant recommendations were made to reform the office of coroner. The Department for Constitutional Affairs Select Committee on the Reform of the Office of Coroner (2006) made the following recommendation in relation to the reporting of deaths to the coroner as follows:

> *Recommendation 7: As a basic minimum, we recommend that the Government introduce a positive statutory duty for doctors to refer certain categories of death to the coroner and work with the General Medical Council (GMC) and the General Register Office (GRO) to establish suitable guidance and training to improve doctors' knowledge of death certification requirements and procedures (paragraph 72).*

The Government response was as follows:

> *The Government accepts this recommendation. We propose to add a provision to the Bill requiring doctors to refer deaths to coroners providing certain conditions are met. We will work with all interested parties, including the GMC and the GRO to set out in secondary legislation what these conditions will be. At present, the certifying doctor indicates on the MCCD [Medical Certificate of Cause of Death] where he has reported a death and the registrar does not register in these cases until authorised to do so by the coroner. Advice and guidance to doctors*

on reporting deaths is included with the instructions for completing the MCCD. Revised guidance was placed on the GRO website last year. Provision for registrars to report a death is contained in regulations. The DCA [District Coroner's Office] work with the GRO on death certification guidance and will continue to see how this can be improved. Likewise the department is, and will continue to be, in close contact with the DH [Department of Health] and other medical stakeholders on doctor training in death certification.

The provisions of the draft Coroners' Bill are considered in *Chapter 14*.

References

Births and Deaths Registration Act 1953 Section 22(1)

Births and Deaths Regulations 1987 SI 1987/2088 reg. 41(1) and 33(1)

Coroners Act 1988 Section 8(1); Section 19(3)

Coroners Rules 1984 SI 1984/552 rules 7(1), 9

Department for Constitutional Affairs Select Committee (2006) Report on the Reform of the Coroners' System and Death Certification. London: Department for Constitutional Affairs

Department of Health (2003) *Sudden Death and the Coroner*. London: Department of Health 22

Halsbury's Laws (2001) *Volume 9(2)* paragraphs 801 onwards. 4th edn. London: Butterworths

Home Office (1923) *Circular 21* London: Home Office

Home Office (2002) *When Sudden Death Occurs*. London: Home Office

R v. Bond (1717) 1 Stra 22

R v. Clerk (1702) 1 Salk 377

R v. Poplar Coroner, ex p Thomas [1993] QB 610; [1993] 2 All ER 381

R (On the application of Canning) v. HM Coroner for Northampton [2005]

Victims' Voice (2003) *Sudden Death and the Coroner*. Chippenham: Victims' Voice

Resources

Victims' Voice PO Box 110 Chippenham SN14 7BQ; email: vv@coroner-info.org.uk

CHAPTER 13

The coroner's jurisdiction 2: Inquests

Box 13.1. An inquest

Ivy Smith was admitted to accident and emergency following an overdose. The accident and emergency staff attempted to pump her out, but she died despite their efforts. The coroner was informed. Ivy's mother said that she did not feel that she could give evidence at an inquest and wondered if she could be excused. What is the law?

Following a coronor's decision that an inquest is to be held, the coroner must notify the date, hour and place of an inquest to the following people (*Halsbury's Laws*, 2001):

- The spouse, partner, near relative or personal representative of the deceased whose name and address are known to the coroner.
- Any other person, who in the opinion of the coroner, is entitled to examine witnesses, has asked the coroner to notify him or her of such particulars of the inquest and has supplied the coroner with a telephone number or address.
- Any person whose conduct is likely to be called into question at an inquest. This person must be given reasonable notice of the inquest.
- Any persons to be summoned as witnesses

Inquests: Jury or no jury?

There is a statutory requirement upon the coroner to summon a jury where death occurred in the following situations:

- In prison.
- In police custody.
- As a result of an accident, poisoning or disease.
- In circumstances that are prejudicial to the health or safety of the public.

Where coroners commence an inquest without a jury but decide that one is necessary, they may then summon a jury.

Purpose of the inquest

The role of the coroner in holding an inquest, whether or not a jury is summoned, is to establish factual answers to the following questions:

- The identity of the deceased,
- The place of death.
- The time of death.
- How the deceased came by his or her death.

It is not the function of the coroner to determine whether there has been any criminal offence or civil liability, or to blame anyone for the death, nor is it the role of the inquest to gather evidence for subsequent criminal or civil proceedings. Neither the coroner nor the jury may express any opinion on any matter outside the scope of the inquest.

Inquisitorial proceedings

An inquest is inquisitorial as opposed to accusatorial or adversarial in its style. There are no parties arguing against each other as in the criminal courts (prosecution and defence) or the civil courts (claimant and defendant). The coroner assumes control, has the power of summoning witnesses, determining what questions can be asked and rules on the procedure to be followed. In relation to the reporting by the press, inquests are seen as court proceedings subject to the same principles and limitations as govern other courts (*Re LM*). Appeals against a coroner's decisions can be made to the High Court. The inquest must be held in public, but the coroner has the power to exclude members of the public if it is in the interest of national security. The coroner can adjourn proceedings if there are justifiable reasons. Thus the coroner could open an inquest, take evidence of identification, issue the order for disposal of the body and then adjourn the inquest until further information is available. (For example, if the deceased died from an overdose of drugs, the results of pathology tests may be awaited.) In the case of the killing of Jean Charles de Menezes, the High Court stated that the coroner had a discretionary power to adjourn an inquest and in that case the coroner had rational reasons for adjourning the inquest and had given proper respect of the State's article 2 obligations (*R (Pereira) Inner South London Coroner and others*).

If, following the opening of the inquest, the coroner is informed by the court that a person is charged with an offence in relation to the death (murder/manslaughter, etc.) then the coroner must, in the absence of reasons to the contrary, adjourn the inquest until after the conclusion of the relevant criminal proceedings. The Chief Officer of Police or Director of Public Prosecutions can also request an adjournment of the inquest. The coroner can also adjourn the inquest to enable a person who is being criticised in the proceedings to attend.

Witnesses

Legal aid is generally not available for representation in proceedings before a coroner, although advice under the Legal Help Scheme administered by the Legal Services Commission may be possible. The coroner has the power to summon witnesses who are within the district of the coroner to attend. (Witnesses outside the coroner's district can be compelled to attend by a Crown Office subpoena.) Failure to comply with the summons could lead to a fine of up to £1000 by the coroner and the coroner has the power to issue a warrant to a constable to bring the witness to court. Witnesses are not obliged to answer any question that could incriminate them and the coroner should notify witnesses of that fact if asked such a question. Witnesses are examined on oath. The procedure is for the coroner to examine the witness first, and then if there are several others wishing to cross examine the witness, the coroner decides upon the order, and finally, the witness, if represented, may be examined by his or her representative.

The Coroners Rules (1984 rule 20(1)) enable certain persons to examine any witness at an inquest either in person or by counsel or solicitor. These include:

- A parent, child, spouse or personal representative of the deceased.
- Any beneficiary under a policy of insurance issued on the life of the deceased.
- The insurer who issued the policy.
- Any person whose act or omission (or his servant or agent) may have caused or contributed to the death.
- Any person appointed by a trade union to which the deceased belonged, if the death may have been caused by an injury received in the course of his or her employment or by an industrial disease.
- Chief Officer of Police.
- Any other person who in the opinion of the coroner is a properly interested person.

The coroner can ensure that any questioning is directed at the purposes of the inquest and does not widen the inquiry into criminal or civil matters.

Documentary evidence

Coroners may admit documentary evidence instead of calling a person as a witness if they consider that the evidence is unlikely to be disputed. Any person who would wish to challenge that evidence could object to the use of documentary evidence. The Court of Appeal has held that a coroner cannot read disputed hearsay evidence to the jury where the maker of the statement was unable to attend (*R (Paul and Others) v. Assistant Deputy Coroner of Inner West London*). The Coroners Rules (1984 rule 37) set out the procedure which must be followed when documentary evidence is to be used.

Summing up

There are no speeches where a person addresses the coroner or jury on the facts (Coroners Rules 1984 rule 40). Where there is a jury the coroner is required to sum up the evidence to members of the jury and explain the law to them. They should be informed that if it appears that a criminal offence has occurred, they should be satisfied beyond reasonable doubt if they wish to bring a verdict that death occurred by murder or other criminal offence. A finding of a verdict of suicide also requires proof beyond reasonable doubt. For other verdicts, they must be satisfied on a balance of probabilities. An open verdict does not have to satisfy any standard of proof.

Verdict

Where no jury has been summoned, coroners give their verdict and sign an inquisition setting out the particulars required by the Births and Deaths Registration Act 1953. Where there is a jury, the jury gives its verdict and signs an inquisition setting out the relevant particulars. Where the jury fails to agree after being given a reasonable time, a majority verdict can be taken if the minority is two or less. Otherwise the jury is discharged and another jury summoned.

The verdicts usually fall into one of the following categories:

- Deaths from natural causes, industrial diseases, dependency on drugs or non-dependent abuse of drugs, want of attention at birth, lack of care or self-neglect.
- Suicide, deaths from an attempted or self-induced abortion, accident or misadventure, execution of sentence of death, lawful killing and an open verdict.
- Deaths as a result of murder, manslaughter or infanticide.
- Stillbirths.

Where a person has been murdered or died as the result of manslaughter, the verdict does not include a finding that any specific person was guilty of the offence.

An open verdict can be given where the evidence does not disclose the means by which death arose.

An inquest into the death of a woman in labour who was given an epidural anaesthetic into her arm instead of a saline drip brought forward a verdict holding the Swindon and Marlborough NHS Trust responsible for unlawful killing (de Bruxelles, 2008). The inquest was told that there had been a mix-up with bags of intravenous saline solution and bupivacaine. The coroner stated that he would be writing to the Health Minister, the Nursing and Midwifery Council and the General Medical Council recommending staff training and an overhaul of the storage and administration of drugs. He also suggested that the connectors for epidural drugs should be changed so that the mix-up would be unlikely to recur.

Death by neglect

In one case the coroner held in an inquest on a person who committed suicide in prison that the question of neglect should not be left to the jury (*Sacker v. Her Majesty's Coroner for W Yorkshire*). However he wrote to the Director General of the Prison Service expressing his grave concern that the medical officer working within the prison service should not have fully understood the workings and procedures where self-harm was feared and required assurance that in future there would be adequate and appropriate training. The mother of the deceased sought judicial review of the coroner's decision. Her appeal to the Court of Appeal against this decision was allowed on the basis that the coroner's letter was evidence that there was systemic neglect. The inquest decision was quashed and a fresh inquest ordered.

A different result occurred in a case where a youth of 16 was sentenced to a two year detention and training order. It was known that he was at risk of self-harm and he hanged himself. The inquest jury returned a verdict of accidental death, but the Coroner wrote to the Secretary of State recommending a public inquiry. This request was refused and the parent appealed against the refusal alleging that it was a breach of his human rights under article 2 of the European Convention on Human Rights not to investigate the circumstances of the death. The Court of Appeal dismissed the appeal holding that the judge had acted lawfully, there had been a thorough evaluation into the circumstances of his death, and there was no breach of article 2 since the holding of the inquest and the Government's acknowledgement that issues remained to be addressed were sufficient to discharge the State's duty to investigate a death and there had therefore been compliance with article 2 (*R (On the application of Scholes) v. Secretary of State for the Home Department*).

A breach of article 2 rights was also claimed in another case when a coroner refused to resume an adjourned hearing (adjourned pending criminal proceedings) into an inquest into the death of a man who was stabbed and killed in May 2000 even though the death had occurred before the Human Rights Act 1998 came into force in October 2000. The victim's mother claimed that there were failures by the police and local housing authority in failing to avert the death. The Court of Appeal held that the inquest should be resumed and the Commissioner of Police appealed against this decision. The House of Lords found that the coroner's decision was lawful and allowed the appeal (*R (on the application of Hurst) v. London Northern District Coroner*).

In a subsequent case a young man attempted suicide in Feltham Young offenders Institution and was left brain damaged. The Court of Appeal held that in such a situation article 2 rights required that there was a clear obligation on the Secretary of State to ensure that there was an effective inquiry into the near death (*R (on the application of JL) v. Secretary of State for the Home Department*).

In another case (*R (On the application of Touche) v. HM Coroner for Inner North London District*) a coroner appealed against a decision that he had erred in deciding not to hold an inquest into the death of a mother who had died soon after birth from a cerebral haemorrhage. The circumstances suggested that her blood pressure had not been properly monitored immediately after the birth. The coroner accepted that the post-operative monitoring appeared wholly inadequate, he concluded that the defects complained of did not put the case into the category of an unnatural death. He therefore refused to hold an inquest. The husband applied for judicial review and the Divisional Court allowed his application, holding that a death was unnatural whenever it occurred in a hospital and a failure to provide 'routine' treatment was a cause (even a secondary cause) of death. The court also ordered the coroner to pay the husband's costs. The coroner appealed against this ruling. The Court of Appeal held that a death was an 'unnatural death' where it was wholly unexpected and would not have occurred but for some culpable human failing. The coroner should have held an inquest upon the receipt of information suggesting the possibility of neglect in her treatment. The Court of Appeal also held that the coroner should pay the costs as ordered.

A death was held to be a natural death where a child had died of an infarction of the small bowel. The parent had applied for an order that an inquest should be held but the coroner refused on the grounds that she was satisfied that it was a natural death. The High Court judge held that there was no evidence of a gross failure to provide basic medical attention to answer a need that had been obvious at the time and the application for an inquest was rejected (*R (On the application of Canning) v. HM Coroner for Northampton*).

Example of the application of Coroners Rules

It has been held that the coroner, in conducting an inquest, had a discretion to provide disclosure of relevant documents in advance of the inquest to properly interested persons, which had to be exercised fairly in the circumstances of the case. The deceased was a vulnerable drug abuser who was staying under bail conditions at a probation hostel which held itself out as having expertise in drug abuse treatment. She died of acute morphine toxicity thought to have been caused by a heroin overdose. Her brother informed the coroner that he wished him to consider how the deceased had obtained access to drugs at the hostel and the degree of care and supervision of residents there. He sought advance disclosure of the post mortem list of witnesses and witness statements, but his request was refused. At the inquest the coroner invited the police officer to read out statements of witnesses he had interviewed. The brother asked for copies of these and attendance at the inquest of the hostel manager but was refused these requests. The coroner entered a verdict of accidental death due to drug overdose. The High Court considered Coroners Rules 57(1), 37 and 20 and held that the applicant's requests were reasonable and quashed the verdict of the inquest, ordering a new inquest with a different coroner (*R v. Avon Coroner*).

A fresh inquest was ordered by the Court of Appeal where the coroner had failed to address the jury on crucial issues relating to neglect of the deceased who had died in prison four days after admission. He was prescribed detoxification treatment but was only given one dose and was seen by a prison nurse but not examined by a doctor. Following the coroner's summing up, the jury reached a verdict of accidental death. The deceased's mother sought judicial review of alleged failings by the coroner and while the High Court judge decided that the coroner's summing up was inadequate he did not consider it necessary or desirable to quash the verdict and order a fresh inquest. The Court of Appeal held, while recognising that the present coronial system was inadequate and major reforms were being discussed, in relation to procedural obligations under article 2 of the European Convention on Human Rights a fresh inquest should be held (Medical Law Monitor 2003/4).

Application of the law to the situation in *Box 13.1*

It should be clear from the above that coroners have complete discretion (subject of course to any appeal against their decisions to the High Court) over the witnesses to be summoned to the inquest and the questions which can be put to them. Coroners would usually require any persons, who may have information relating to the four questions the inquest is designed to answer, to provide statements of their knowledge of the events. In the light of these statements coroners would then decide what witnesses need to give evidence at the inquest. The relevance of information held by Ivy's mother about the circumstances of Ivy's death would therefore determine whether she was summoned as a witness. For example if she had not lived with Ivy for some time, had no personal knowledge of the circumstances which led to her death, then she may not be called as a witness. She would however be notified of the inquest and could attend. She could arrange for her own lawyer to attend to represent her, but she would not obtain legal aid for this. The coroner would decide what questions, if any, the lawyer could ask.

Conclusions

Health service staff are likely to be called to give evidence at an inquest where unexpected deaths occur during their work. They may be required to give statements to the coroner and should ensure that they receive advice and support from senior management or lawyers to the NHS trust in completing these statements, since it is essential to ensure that these statements are clear, comprehensive, accurate and cover any issues on which they may be questioned at an inquest or subsequent criminal, civil, disciplinary or professional hearing.

Significant changes to the office and role of the coroner have been recommended in one of the inquiries following the Shipman murders and also by a Home Office investigation into the work of the coroner and it is to this we turn in *Chapter 14*.

References

Coroners Rules 1984 SI 1984/552 rules 20(1), 37, 40, 57(1)

de Bruxelles S (2008) Inquest jury blames NHS trust for unlawful killing of mother. *The Times* **6 February**

Halsbury's Laws (2001) *Volume 9(2)* paragraphs 801 onwards 4th edn. London: Butterworths

Medical Law Monitor 2003/January 2004 page 18 EWHC 3125 (2006) 91 B.M.L.R. 32

R (On the application of Canning) v. HM Coroner for Northampton [2005]

R (On the application of Hurst) v. London Northern District Coroner [2007] UKHL 13, [2007] 2 All ER 1025

R (On the application of JL) v. Secretary of State for the Home Department [2007] EWCA Civ 767

R (On the application of Scholes) v. Secretary of State for the Home Department [2006]

EWCA Civ 1343, The Times 10 November 2006; [2001] 2 All ER 752

R (On the application of Touche) v. HM Coroner for Inner North London District [2001] EWCA Civ 383 [2001] QB 1206

R (Paul and Others) v. Assistant Deputy Coroner of Inner West London The Times Law Report 11 December 2008

R (Pereira) Inner South London Coroner and others The Times Law Report 22 June 2007

Re LM (Reporting restrictions: Coroner's inquest) The Times Law Report 20 November 2007

R v. Avon Coroner ex parte Bentley The Times Law Report 23 March 2001

Sacker v. Her Majesty's Coroner for W. Yorkshire Lloyd's Rep. Med [2003] 326

CHAPTER 14

The coroner's jurisdiction 3: Reforms to the coroner's office

Following the conviction of Dr Shipman for 15 murders an Inquiry was set up under the chairmanship of Dame Janet Smith DBE. The first report considered how many patients Shipman killed, the means employed and the period over which the killings took place. The second report examined the conduct of the police investigation into Shipman that took place in March 1998 and failed to uncover his crimes.

The third report considered the present system for death and cremation certification and for the investigation of deaths by coroners, together with the conduct of those who had operated those systems in the aftermath of the deaths of Shipman's victims. The report noted that the present system of death and cremation certification failed to detect that Shipman had killed any of his 215 victims. Even though many of the deaths occurred suddenly and unexpectedly and should, under the present procedures, have been reported to the coroner, Shipman managed to avoid any coronial investigation in all but two of the cases in which he had killed. He did this by claiming to be in a position to certify the cause of death and by persuading relatives that no autopsy (and therefore no referral to the coroner) was necessary. Even in the two deaths which were examined by the coroner, there was an inadequate investigation which failed to uncover the truth. No death of a victim of Shipman was subject to an inquest until after his conviction. The present system therefore failed to protect the public.

The fourth report, which was published in July 2004, considered the regulation of controlled drugs in the community.

The fifth report was published in December 2004. It considers the handling of complaints against GPs, the raising of concerns about them, the procedures of the General Medical Council (GMC) and the revalidation of doctors. It makes significant recommendations for the more effective regulation of GPs. In March 2005, the Chief Medical Officer (CMO) announced that, in the light of the fifth report, a review of medical revalidation was being carried out, starting with a call for ideas. This has led to the postponement of the GMC's revalidation scheme. The review aims to give advice on further measures necessary to strengthen procedures for assuring the safety of patients in situations where a doctor's performance or conduct poses a risk to patients, to ensure the operation of an effective system of revalidation, and to modify the role, structure and functions of the GMC. Many of the detailed changes for GMC procedures recommended in the fifth report could also apply, where appropriate, to the Nursing and Midwifery Council (NMC) as could the results from the CMO's review.

The sixth and final Shipman report considered how many patients Shipman killed during his career as a junior doctor at Pontefract General Infirmary and in his time at Hyde.

Recommendations of the third report

This third report made extensive recommendations on many areas which are listed in *Box 14.2*. The Inquiry took into account feedback to a consultation paper published by the Fundamental Review of Death Certification and the Coroner Services in England, Wales and Northern Ireland chaired by Tom Luce and accepted the recommendations of the coroner's review on changes to scope and conduct of inquests.

The Inquiry recommended that a new coronial system should be established which would provide the following elements:

- An independent, cohesive system of death investigation and certification, readily accessible and understood by the public.

Box 14.2. Areas covered by the Shipman Inquiry into death and cremation certification and the role of the coroner

- Future of the coronial system
- Aim and purposes of the new coroner service
- Need for leadership, training and expertise in the coroner service
- Structure and organisation of the coroner service
- Death certification
- Registration
- Further investigation
- Pathology services
- Statutory duty to report concerns about a death
- Public education
- Audit and appeal
- Transitional arrangements
- The future

- It should establish the cause of every death.
- It should record the formal details accurately for the purposes of registration and the collection of mortality statistics.
- It should seek to meet the needs and expectations of the bereaved.
- Its procedures should be designed to detect cases of homicide, medical error and neglect.
- It should provide a thorough and open investigation of all deaths giving rise to public concern.
- It should ensure that the knowledge gained from death investigation is applied for the prevention of avoidable death and injury in the future.
- The legal and medical functions of the coroner's office should be carried out respectively by a medical and a judicial coroner who should be independent officer-holders under the Crown.
- The coroner service should have a corps of trained investigators, who would be the mainstays of the new system.
- The coroner service should be an Executive Non-Departmental Public Body (ENDPB), independent of the Department for Constitutional Affairs and the Department of Health.
- A board should govern the service and formulate policy, strategic direction and the promotion of public education of its work.
- Three members of the board would be the Chief Judicial Coroner, the Chief Medical Coroner and the Chief Coroner's Investigator.
- There should also be an advisory council to provide policy advice on all issues.
- The coroners' service should be administered through a regional and district structure with a regional medical coroner and at least one judicial coroner assigned to each region.
- Each region would be divided into between three and seven districts each with a population of about one million.
- Each district would have a medical coroner, a deputy, a team of coroner's investigators and a small administrative team.
- The coroner service would have jurisdiction over every death that occurs in England and Wales without the requirement for a report being made or the need for an inquest.

Recommendations for certification of death

Recommendations for death certification are that there should be one system for death certification for all deaths, whether death is to be followed by burial or cremation. Two forms would need to be completed:

- Form 1 would provide an official record of the facts and circumstances of death and be completed by a doctor, accredited nurse or paramedic or a trained and accredited coroner's investigator who confirmed that death had occurred.

- Form 2 would be completed by the doctor who had treated the deceased person during the last illness or if no doctor had treated the deceased person in the recent past, by the deceased's usual medical practitioner. Form 2 would contain a brief summary of the deceased person's recent medical history and the chain of events leading to death and the doctor could express an opinion as to the cause of death. There would be a statutory duty upon doctors to complete the death certificate and the General Medical Council should impose a professional duty for doctors to co-operate with the death certification system.

All deaths would be reported to the coroner service which would have responsibility for certification of death and decide if further investigation were necessary. Where form 2 stated the doctor's opinion as to the cause of death, the coroner's investigator would consult with the deceased's family and decide if certification could proceed. There should be random and targeted checks to consider whether fuller investigation was required. A new certificate of cause of death should be completed by the coroner's investigator or if an investigation has been undertaken by the medical coroner.

Registration

There should be a new certificate of cause of death for completion by a coroner's investigator or, where an investigation has been undertaken, by the medical coroner. In the future if it becomes possible to register a death on line, registration could on many occasions be effected by the informant (with assistance) direct from the district coroner's office.

Inquests

Under the proposals there should only be an inquest in a case in which the public interest requires a public investigation for reasons connected with the facts and circumstances of the individual case and decided by the judicial coroner. There would be a mandatory inquest in a few specified circumstances.

Where an inquest was not held, a report of further investigations would be prepared by the medical and/or judicial coroner, explaining how and why the deceased died. Any recommendation of the medical or judicial coroner should be submitted to the Chief Coroner, who should take it forward. Statutory powers including powers of entry, search and seizure of documents should be given to the coroner. The family should have the right to appeal against an autopsy being held or to make representations for one to be held.

Under the Amendments to the Coroners Rules 1984, which came into force on 1 June 2005, Rule 20 of the 1984 Rules, which sets out who is entitled to examine witnesses at an inquest, is amended by adding a partner of the deceased to the list of qualifying people. One effect of this amendment is that a partner is one of the persons who is entitled to be notified that material is being preserved and of the options for dealing with the material on the expiry of the retention period (see *Chapter 15*). Partner is defined as one of two persons (whether of different sexes or the same sex) who live as partners in an enduring family relationship.

Detailed proposals are made for the investigations by the medical and judicial coroners.

Deaths arising from medical error or neglect

The Shipman Inquiry report recommended that where deaths were or may have been caused by or contributed to by medical error or neglect they should be investigated by the coroner service. Initially the investigation would be by the medical coroner. If, following that investigation, it appeared to the coroner that the death might have been caused or contributed to by medical error or neglect, the case should be referred to the regional coroner's office for investigation by the regional medical coroner and judicial coroner. At regional office, the case would be investigated under the direction of a legally qualified person. The aim would be that at every regional office, there would be a small team of coroner's investigators who could develop expertise in medical cases.

The relationship between criminal proceedings relating to a death and investigations by the Health and Safety Executive and the medical and judicial coroners is also spelt out.

Statutory duty to report concerns

The recommended statutory duty to report concerns about a death should be placed upon any 'qualified' or 'responsible' person. Employers should encourage employees to report any concerns relating to the cause or circumstances of a death, and should pass on these reports to the appropriate quarter without delay and without any possibility of the reporter being subject to criticism or reprisal. The public should be educated about the functions of the coroners' service and should be encouraged to report any concerns about a death. The report also recommended that there should be a systematic audit of the coroner's service and rights of appeal.

Post mortems

It is recommended that all autopsies should be carried out to the standards recommended by the Royal College of Pathologists (2002) in its document *Guidelines on Autopsy Practice*. Pathologists should be free to carry out whatever special examinations they consider necessary for the completion of a thorough and accurate autopsy report, provided that there is proper medical justification for the conduct of an autopsy. Specific recommendations are made in relation to the use of toxicology in the investigation of deaths of which the cause is not immediately apparent. The report suggests that it should be the aim of medical coroners to move towards the use of toxicology in virtually all autopsies and in some cases where no autopsy is conducted. It should also be possible for a medical coroner to authorise a partial autopsy, with the proviso that if the pathologist considered that it was necessary to go beyond the authorised limitation, he or she should be free to do so. Guidance on the retention of organs and tissue would be provided by the coroner service, but families would have the right to object and appeal as they could in relation to the autopsies.

Reforming the coroner and death certification service

Following the third Shipman report a position paper was published by the Home Office in March 2004 and constituted the Government's response to the Fundamental Review of Death Certification and Coroner Services (Luce, 2003) and the Shipman Inquiry. This position paper set out the current system, a summary of the key proposals for change and explained the Government's approach. Appendix 3 provided a timetable for the implementation of the recommendations over the following three years. The key features it envisaged were for the new coronial service to be:

- Independent – free to judge the circumstances of a death without outside influence.
- Professional – its staff will be better regulated than at present and will benefit from continuous professional development, including training to high standards.
- Medically skilled – staffed with qualified medical practitioners, and with ready access to high level medical and public health advice.
- Modern – providing a high quality service to the public at large and particularly to the bereaved, recognising their special needs and the input they can make to the death investigation process.
- Consistent – a uniform service across England and Wales, and Northern Ireland, with unified high standards of performance.

- Robust – better able to prevent or detect foul play on the one hand and, on the other, itself subject to rigorous inspection and performance monitoring.
- Transparent – the public will understand the way it operates.

The key proposals put forward by the Government, as part of the reform of the coroner system and a complete overhaul of the death certification system include a reformed coroner system which would:

- Meet the needs of the bereaved and the public at large.
- Deal quickly with the majority of deaths.
- Identify more effectively those cases requiring investigation and target resources accordingly.
- Operate consistently across England and Wales and Northern Ireland.
- Have regional oversight of death trends through regional directors of public health.
- Be a better managed and more professional national service under a Chief Coroner, with around 40–60 coroners, and dedicated trained medical support.
- Be judicially independent.
- Have an advisory Coronial Council.
- Have direct links to public health.
- Incorporate a greater degree of medical expertise in scrutiny, training and accountability.
- Ensure there is a system of inspection and monitoring to attain high standards.
- Work within a new legislative framework for death investigation, with close links to other relevant professionals, for example registrars.

Death certification and the position paper

The proposals in the position paper provide for the verification of the fact of all deaths, for certification of the cause of death by the doctor, for scrutiny of all certificates by a medical examiner in the coroner's office and for referral to the coroner of all deaths, which cannot be certified or which are unnatural. Annex 1 provides an organisational chart for the proposed system.

Verification of the fact of death

Under the proposals the fact of death would be verified as a separate step from certification of the cause of death and could be undertaken by a doctor, a paramedic or senior nurse. This would enable the body to be removed more promptly from the scene of death.

Certificate of the medical cause of death

Doctors, who treated the deceased in the immediate past, would provide the first certificate of the cause of death and should specify when they last saw the deceased and why they are satisfied that they can certify death accurately. This certificate would be subjected to close subsequent scrutiny by a medical professional.

Medical examiner

The position paper proposed that after the first certification all deaths would then be referred to a different medical practitioner, to be known as the medical examiner. This would be a qualified doctor employed by the new coroner service and independent of the health service. The examiner would head a small team of staff, with a clinical background, to screen all cases under the examiner's close supervision. The medical examiner would have the power to authorise the burial or cremation in cases not reported to the coroner. Medical examiners could be responsible for keeping a database of deaths in their locality to help support public health initiatives as part of the need to strengthen understanding of the pattern of deaths that occur. Regional directors of public health could use this information to identify regional trends in deaths, monitor the effectiveness of current public health initiatives and inform future public health initiatives.

This system of certification would apply to all deaths.

Reports to coroners

The Position paper proposed that two types of death should be referred to the coroner:

- those from a list of reportable cases (eg. deaths in custody), and
- cases where the treating doctor is unable to certify the cause of death.

The coroner would have the responsibility of ascertaining who has died, and when, where and how the person died. The coroner would decide if:

- the medical cause of death can be determined on the information already available,
- any medical tests were required (including the need for a post mortem), or
- the case required an inquest.

The coroner could also have the power to conduct targeted further investigations as advised by the medical examiner (eg. deaths in a particular hospital or care home).

Work under way

The position paper identified the following areas as work under way:

- Providing higher quality and more consistent information for families.
- Supporting coroners in order to achieve greater consistency in decisions which related to the use of post mortem examinations.
- Developing coroners' procedures in relation to post mortem examinations.
- Identifying those resources currently in the system that might be used better or in different ways.
- Improving training for coroners, including work on communications and diversity; and working with the Coroners Officers Association to support its training programmes.
- Collecting examples of good practice and considering how to encourage their wider dissemination.
- Introducing appropriate performance management techniques for death certification.

Further suggestions contained in the position paper were taken up in the Briefing paper on Coroner service reform published in February 2006.

Coroners' service reform

In February 2006 the Minister of State for Constitutional Affairs announced the implementation of the first set of reforms: those relating to the coroners' service (Department for Constitutional Affairs, 2006a). The key reforms to be introduced were:

- Bereaved people will have a right to contribute to coroners' investigations. They will be able to bring their concerns to coroners even where a death certificate has been issued. A coroners' charter will set out the service bereaved people can expect.
- A Chief Coroner (accountable to the Government) and an advisory coronial council would be introduced to provide national leadership, guidance and support. Coroners would continue to be appointed and funded by their local councils and served by coroners' officers drawn from the local police or local authority.

The Chief Coroner will have the power to commission audits and inspections and will be responsible for monitoring the coroner's charter for bereaved people. The Chief Coroner will also have power to appoint judges in complex cases. The Coronial Council will include independent lay members and representatives of voluntary groups. It will act as a further check on standards and will advise the Chief Coroner on what service and strategic issues may need further scrutiny.

- A body of full-time coroners would be created and current boundaries would be reshaped to create a smaller number of coroner jurisdictions. The full-time coroners would be supported by a pool of assistant coroners to act in their absence. All new appointments to the service will be required to have a legal qualification.
- The investigation and inquest processes would be modernised and coroners would be given new powers to obtain information to help their investigations.
- In limited and specific cases such as some suicides and child deaths, coroners will have a new discretion to complete their investigations and decide on the facts without holding inquests, where no public interest is served by doing so.
- A chief medical adviser will be appointed to support the Chief Coroner to give advice on medical best practice and medical issues related to coroners' investigations.
- At local level funding will be provided to coroners to ensure appropriate local medical advice to support their investigation.
- Coroners will no longer have the task of determining whether a particular find should be classified as treasure. A new national coroner for treasure will be appointed to take on the work currently undertaken by coroners at local level.

A draft Coroners' Bill, together with a draft Charter for the Bereaved were published in June 2006 to enable pre-legislative scrutiny to be undertaken by the Select Committee for the Department for Constitutional Affairs. The Charter is considered first followed by the draft Bill.

Charter for the bereaved

Together with the Bill, a draft Charter for the Bereaved was published in 2006. Its stated objectives and values are that the coroner service will:

- Help bereaved people understand the cause of the death of the person who has died.

- Inform bereaved people about the roles of the coroner service and the powers of the coroner.
- Inform bereaved people of their rights and responsibilities if an investigation or inquest is conducted in relation to the death.
- Comply, where possible, with individual, family, and community wishes, feelings and expectations, including family and community preferences, traditions and religious requirements relating to mourning and to funerals, and respect for individual and family privacy.
- Enable bereaved people, including children and young people where appropriate, to be informed and consulted during the process of investigating violent, unnatural or unexplained deaths, or deaths of those in prison or other state custody, treating them with sensitivity and with dignity, and helping them to find further help where this is necessary.
- Answer bereaved people's questions as promptly and effectively as possible.
- Respond to concerns of bereaved people when they are not satisfied about the cause of death given on a death certificate.
- Provide information about how bereaved people may appeal against or complain about the service's decisions, and respond to appeals and complaints within the period specified by the Chief Coroner.

Standards of service

The standards stipulated in the Charter are as follows:

When deaths are reported to coroners, they or their staff will aim to contact the most appropriate next of kin, where known, within 24 hours to explain why the death has been reported and what steps are likely to follow.

Families will be given information, within 24 hours of confirmation of the identity of the person who has died, by coroners or their staff on where they can view the body if they wish to do so and on appropriate arrangements for viewing. They will be advised, as sensitively as possible, if the nature of the death may cause the viewing of the body to be particularly distressing. Wherever possible, the family may be offered a photograph of the body first.

Where a coroner orders a post mortem, families will be told by the coroner and the coroner's staff why it is necessary and when and where it will be performed, and what they should do if they would like to be represented by a doctor at the post mortem. These standards will also apply in the event of a second post mortem being commissioned by a coroner.

If the coroner decides not to hold a post mortem, the family can make representations and ask for the decision to be reconsidered.

Where there is an investigation but no inquest, coroners or their staff will, within 10 working days of its completion, offer the family a copy of the coroner's investigation report and will offer to explain any parts the family does not understand.

The family will be sent, by the coroner or staff and within two working days of its completion, a copy of the confirmation of the cause of death and the details of the person who has died. This will enable the family to bring any errors to the attention of the registrar or the coroner.

When there is to be a full inquest, information will be provided by coroners and their staff, of the timing, location, and facilities available at the place where the inquest will be held, wherever possible, four weeks before the date of the inquest.

Information will be provided by coroners and their staff about the purposes and processes involved at the inquest, who is likely to be present, what evidence is likely to be given and on the opportunities for the family to participate in proceedings, including the right to speak or the right to be represented. If the date and/or location of the inquest has to be changed, bereaved people will be informed within five working days.

Wherever possible, an appropriate private room will be provided for bereaved relatives when they attend an inquest.

Coroners or their staff will not release details, including photographs, of specific cases to the media without the consent of the family.

Participation of family

The Charter also sets out clear rights of the family to receive information from the coroner including the reports of any post mortems or other investigations and also ensuring that the family have the right to make suggestions over the timing of the inquest.

Availability of support and bereavement services

The Charter also states that coroners will maintain information on the main local and national voluntary bodies and support groups which offer help or support to people who have been bereaved, including bereavement as a result of particular types of incidents or circumstances. They will make this information available to family members or their representatives unless they request otherwise.

Deaths abroad

There are also undertakings in relation to deaths abroad when there is a connection between the death and circumstances arising in England and Wales (for example medical errors or malpractice, or an accident, in this country) or where action might reasonably be taken in England and Wales to avoid deaths in similar circumstances in future (for example, planning of overseas school trips) or where the coroner has reasonable cause to suspect that the death was caused as a result of a criminal act and if no equivalent of either a criminal investigation, a coroner's investigation or an inquiry is taking place, or has taken place, in the country in which the death occurred or where the person who has died was a member of the armed forces and died while on duty abroad. In addition, there may be special circumstances where a death overseas ought to be investigated even though none of the above criteria apply. The Lord Chancellor has power to require an investigation into a death which occurred abroad, where it appears to be in the public interest to do so. If the coroner decides that there will not be an investigation and the family disagree with this decision, they may appeal to the Chief Coroner or they may write to the Lord Chancellor to ask him to report the death to the Chief Coroner on the ground that it would be in the public interest to conduct an investigation into the death of the deceased. Coroners will also have power to report a death to the Chief Coroner if they believe the death should be investigated and they do not have power to do so.

Review and appeal rights of coroners' judicial decisions

The Charter clarifies the rights of interested parties to be consulted by coroners about the following decisions they take in individual cases (when they have indicated a wish to be consulted):

- Whether or not there will be a post mortem (this is subject to the identity of the dead person being known).
- When the body of the person who has died will be released (this is also subject to the identity of the dead person being known).
- Whether there will be an investigation by the coroner.
- Whether or not reporting restrictions should be imposed on inquest proceedings.
- The scope of an inquest.
- Whether there should be a jury.
- Which witnesses will be called at the inquest, including expert witnesses.

If family members are dissatisfied with how the coroner intends to proceed, they will be able to ask the coroner to review his or her decision.

In most cases, if there is disagreement between coroners and family membesr about any of the above, it will be resolved through discussion. If however, this is not possible, family members can appeal to the Chief

Coroner, setting out clearly their grounds for appealing the decision, wherever possible within a maximum of 15 working days (within two working days if it concerns a post mortem). In addition, appeals will also be possible against decisions in relation to:

- The cause of death given by the coroner following an investigation, but no inquest.
- The decision given at the end of an inquest.

Other complaints and comments

Bereaved people wishing to make a complaint about a failure to deliver other aspects of the service outlined in this Charter should do so in the first instance to the coroner. If they are not satisfied with the response they should address their complaint to the Chief Coroner.

The coroner system is committed to providing a service that meets the needs of bereaved people at a sensitive time, and welcomes comments from bereaved people about their experiences. They should be directed to the coroner who dealt with the case or the Chief Coroner.

Monitoring of the service

Monitoring of the service and therefore of the implementation of the charter will be the responsibility of the Chief Coroner who will require coroners to provide regular reports. The Chief Coroner will give the Lord Chancellor an annual report that will include an assessment of the consistency of standards between coroners' areas. The Lord Chancellor will publish any report given to him and lay a copy before Parliament.

Inspections of the service will be commissioned by the Secretary of State. This will involve consultation with bereaved people. In addition, the Chief Coroner will arrange surveys of service users from time to time.

Draft Coroners' Reform Bill

The draft bill was summarised as follows by the Government spokesman in June 2006:

> *The draft bill replaces the whole of the Coroners' Act 1988 although some of the clauses are a reworking of the 1988 Act using contemporary language. Most clauses are new, creating a governance structure and giving coroners powers aimed at improving*

the effectiveness of investigations, including removing boundary restrictions. Provision is also made to take treasure out of the mainstream workload of coroners.

Background

The policy in the Bill is underpinned by three main aims:

- An improved service for bereaved people and others who interact with the coroner system.
- The introduction of national leadership and improvements to enhance the local nature of the system.
- More effective coroners' investigations. The legislative changes proposed in the Bill are part of a package of reforms aimed at addressing some of the weaknesses in the present coroner system, identified in the reports of the *Fundamental Review of Death Certification and Investigation* and the Shipman Inquiry, both published in 2003.

Part 1. Investigations into deaths

Part 1 of the Bill contains measures relating to the appointment of coroners and investigations into deaths. Coroners will continue to be appointed and funded by their local authorities but new coroner area boundaries will be decided by the Lord Chancellor. There will be about half the number of coroners. Some coroners will be working for a cluster of local authorities and a lead local authority will be established which will have responsibility for making appointments, with the approval of the Lord Chancellor. Part-time assistant coroners will be appointed. The Bill distinguishes between the coroner's duty to investigate a death and the duty to hold an inquest. At the present time only about 10% of cases that coroners investigate conclude with an inquest. There are rules for inquests, such as the way in which the determination (or verdict) is delivered, and regulations governing other parts of the investigation, such as the commission and conduct of post mortem examinations.

Coroners will no longer be required to investigate certain categories of deaths such as deaths which occurred over 50 years ago and deaths abroad, except where it would be in the public interest to do so. There are new powers in respect of post mortem examinations and the coroner will be able to move bodies to any place for a post mortem in order to make better use of specialist pathology skills and specialist equipment where an investigation into a particular death requires it. The law on the suspension and resumption of inquests will be updated. These will cover circumstances where other inquiries or investigations are taking place, for example criminal investigations and inquiries under the Inquiries Act 2005, and will provide for coroners to be kept informed to enable them to make decisions about how to proceed.

The numbers of jurors for a coroner's jury is reduced and the circumstances in which a jury is required is changed.

Part 2. Investigations in relation to treasure

There will be one designated coroner, the 'Coroner for Treasure', who will deal with treasure across England and Wales. Hearings when necessary can be held in a range of locations around the country. The Treasure Act 1996 is amended to encourage reporting of treasure finds. Those who come into possession of treasure will have a responsibility to report it and not just the finders.

Part 3. Investigations and deaths

Part 3 of the Bill includes the following:

- Coroners to have increased power to require information to be provided to them and new powers to enter and search premises, and seize property.
- Provisions for the protection of children including a power to direct that a child gives evidence via live link or unsworn.
- Measures aimed at ensuring early release of bodies by requiring the consent of the Chief Coroner for retention for a prolonged period (designed, in particular, to prevent abuses by defendants in criminal cases who might insist that the body is retained on the remote possibility that it may be a significant source of evidence).

Part 4. Governance

Part 4 of the Bill includes the following:

- The appointment of a Chief Coroner:
    - to provide training for and guidance to coroners,
    - to receive complaints,
    - to hear appeals against coroners' decisions and determinations,
    - to provide an annual report and advice to the Lord Chancellor in respect of the coroner service.
- The Chief Coroner can sit as a coroner

  - has a power to invite the Lord Chief Justice to nominate a judge to preside over a particularly complex case
- The establishment of a national Coronial Advisory Council
- Appeal rights for interested persons against coroners' decisions to the Chief Coroner. Any further appeal is to the Court of Appeal on a point of law only.
- Powers for the Chief Coroner and Lord Chancellor in setting and reviewing standards.
- Deputy chief coroners to be appointed to support the Chief Coroner. One full-time deputy will be appointed with other deputies appointed as locums to hear appeals as required
- A new council, the Coronial Advisory Council, will be formed to provide advice and make recommendations to the Chief Coroner and Lord Chancellor on policy and operational matters relating to the coroners' service. It is intended that the Council will include members of the public who have had dealings with the service.
- The Lord Chancellor to issue guidance in the form of a Charter for Bereaved People setting out how bereaved people can participate in investigations and details of their rights.
- Coroners to provide regular information to the Chief Coroner, to enable him or her to monitor standards and to provide annual reports to the Lord Chancellor

Part 5. Supplementary

Part 5 of the Bill contains supplementary provisions, including the abolition of the office of coroner of the Queen's household. In future, any investigation which would have been carried out by the coroner of the Queen's household will be carried out by the coroner for the area where the death took place (unless, for example, the Chief Coroner directs another coroner to carry it out).

Department for Constitutional Affairs (DCA) Select Committee Report on the draft Bill

The draft Bill was scrutinised by the DCA Select Committee which made strong criticisms about some of the omissions in the Bill. In *Chapter 2* the failure to include changes to the death certification system is discussed. In addition the Select Committee noted that there was a failure to implement a national system for the office of coroner:

> *It is difficult to see how a Chief Coroner can function effectively as a force for standardisation without being part of a national*

> *service. A national service would almost certainly involve significant extra cost, but the failure to introduce one will mean that the current inequalities of resource will continue.*

To this recommendation the UK Government (2006) responded that:

> *The Government's aim is to have the best features of a national structure, headed by a Chief Coroner, with the best features of local service delivery. We believe we can successfully create a partnership between the police, local authorities, their local coroners and the Chief Coroner so that the service is embedded as an adequately funded local service, with national leadership and standards on key matters.*

The Select Committee's concerns that there was inadequate resourcing of the coronial service were rejected by the Government which considered that there is sufficient resource within local authorities' existing budgets to adequately fund the service.

The Government accepted recommendation 15 of the Select Committee that the class of 'interested persons' (with a right of appeal to the Chief Coroner from any decision) be substantially restricted and that limits be placed on the decisions of the coroner which are subject to appeal (paragraph 139). The Government stated that it intended to amend the bill accordingly before its introduction into Parliament. It intended to replicate the hierarchy of 'people in a qualifying relationship' which is listed in the Human Tissue Act 2004, and list the decisions made by coroners which will be subject to appeal.

The Government rejected the recommendation that medical support should be provided to coroners in accordance with the Home Office Position paper of 2004, since it considered that this was based on the rejected proposal that all deaths would be scrutinised by the coroner service. It considered that such a system would be overly bureaucratic and could lead to unnecessary delays for families in making funeral arrangements. It proposed to create the office of Chief Medical Adviser to support the new Chief Coroner. The Government agreed that too many post mortems were being carried out and that a strategy was needed to ensure that the right criteria and alternatives are in place so that, as far as possible, post mortems are carried out only when strictly necessary.

The Select Committee recommended that the Government took a bolder approach to reform of the coronial system, embodying in legislation an enhanced role in relation to public health and safety. This should be backed up with significant additional resources to produce a system which provides greater public benefit and value for money (paragraph 211). This recommendation was rejected by the Government which stated that it believed,

> *that the current proposals will give significant benefit and the best value for money and that the most vital role in relation to public health and safety will be provided by local coroners engaged in local partnerships and by the Chief Coroner taking a national view on these issues.*

Current situation

As a consequence of the Select Committee's recommendations and the Government response, changes will be required to the draft Bill before its introduction into Parliament and it does not feature in the Parliamentary timetable for 2008. The changes to the coroner's office are therefore unlikely to become law before 2009.

Conclusions

The current proposals for the reform of the coroner's office and death certification are less significant than those put forward in the Shipman reports and those accepted by the Home Office in its position paper in 2004. The third report of the Shipman Inquiry pointed out that very few of the proposals of the Brodrick Committee on the certification of death and coroner investigations in 1971 had been implemented, and even if they had been, it cannot be said that they would have prevented the Shipman tragedy. The hope of the Chairman Dame Janet Smith was that her Inquiry's proposals did not end in stalemate, like those of the Brodrick Committee. The draft Coroner's Bill implements some of the recommendations and other recommendations are to be brought in by secondary legislation. The timetable for both the final legislation and the dates of implementation are currently uncertain. Eventually however there will be significant changes in death certification and the office of the coroner which will have major implications for the health professional.

References

Coroners (Amendment) Rules 2005 SI 2005/420

Department for Constitutional Affairs (2006a) *Coroners' service Reform Briefing Note.* London: DCA

Department for Constitutional Affairs (2006b) *Select Committee Report on the Reform of the Coroners' System and Death Certification.* London: DCA

Home Office (1971) *Brodrick Committee Death and Cremation Certification and Coroner Investigations*. London: Stationery Office

Home Office (2004) *Reforming the Coroner and Death Certification Service. A Position Paper CM 6159*. London: Stationery Office

Luce T (2003) *Fundamental Review of Death Certification and the Coroner Services in England, Wales and Northern Ireland*. London: Home Office

Royal College of Pathologists (2002) *Guidelines on Autopsy Practice*. London: Royal College of Pathologists

Shipman Inquiry (2002) *First Report Death Disguised* published 19 July 2002. Available from: www.the-shipman-inquiry.org.uk/reports.asp

Shipman Inquiry (2003) *Second Report. The Police Investigation of March 1998* published 14 July 2003. Available from: www.the-shipman-inquiry.org.uk/reports.asp

Shipman Inquiry (2003) *Third Report. Death and Cremation Certification* published 14 July 2003. Available from: www.the-shipman-inquiry.org.uk/reports.asp

Shipman Inquiry (2004) *Fourth Report. The Regulation of Controlled Drugs in the Community* published 15 July 2004 Cm 6249. London: Stationery Office. Available from: www.the-shipman-inquiry.org.uk/reports.asp

Shipman Inquiry (2004) *Fifth Report. Safeguarding Patients: Lessons from the Past – Proposals for the Future*. Command Paper CM 6394 London: Stationery Office. Available from: www.the-shipman-inquiry.org.uk/reports.asp

Shipman Inquiry (2005) *Sixth Report: The Final Report*. London: Stationery Office. Available from: www.the-shipman-inquiry.org.uk/reports.asp

UK Government (2006) *Response to the Constitutional Affairs Select Committee's Report: Reform of the Coroners' System and Death Certification Cm 6943*. London: Stationery Office

CHAPTER 15

Post mortems

Box 15.1. An unwelcome request

Fred Harvey died three months after contracting a wasting disease which puzzled both his general practitioner and hospital doctor. The consultant physician wished to carry out a post mortem on Fred and asked his wife Muriel for permission. Muriel was a member of a religious sect of strict brethren who believed in the ultimate resurrection of the body. She therefore refused to allow Fred to be cut up. The consultant considered that he could not complete the death certificate until a post mortem had been carried out to ascertain exactly what was the cause of Fred's death. In addition, although he did not tell Muriel this, he wished to examine Fred for his own research and teaching purposes and in particular remove the liver and carry out research on it. What is the law?

The interim report on the Bristol paediatric heart surgery cases raised serious concerns about the lack of knowledge and consent given by parents to the removal, retention and storage of body parts taken from their children who had died. This was followed by the scandal at the Children's Hospital at Alder Hey Liverpool and the reports published following an inquiry. Subsequently the Department of Health (see Department of Health website) published a code of practice, forms and information leaflets about post mortem examinations. This was updated and replaced by a Code of Practice on Post Mortems published by the Human Tissue Authority (HTA) in 2006. This chapter considers the HTA guidance on hospital post mortems, the following chapters consider changes in relation to organ transplants and the removal, retention and storage of organs and tissue.

What is a post mortem examination?

The Department of Health (2003) has published a simple guide to what actually takes place at a post mortem. It defines a post mortem (autopsy) as an important medical examination that aims to find out more about a person's last illness and the cause of death. It will usually take place within two or three working days of the death. A full post mortem examination involves examination of each of the main body systems including the brain and all the contents of the chest and abdomen. It will normally include the removal and retention of small tissue samples for examination under a microscope. Sometimes whole organs may be retained for closer examination. A limited post mortem, if stipulated by the person giving consent, (unless the post mortem has been ordered by the coroner) can be agreed where the post mortem can be limited to one body cavity (for example the chest) or organ system (for example the lungs), but this may not provide all possible information about the disease or cause of death. The standards for undertaking post mortem examinations have been published by the Royal College of Pathologists (2002). After the post mortem the relatives are entitled to view the body before proceeding with funeral arrangements. Any organs or tissue which have been retained can be returned once they are no longer needed or they can be disposed of by the hospital, whatever is preferred. A copy of the report will be sent to the deceased's general practitioner and it should be possible for the person giving consent to the post mortem to make an appointment to discuss the results with the hospital consultant.

The present law

Human Tissue Act 2004

Following the publication of a consultation document *Human Bodies, Human Choices* by the Department of Health in July 2002, the Human Tissue Act 2004 was passed and has made significant changes to the law to protect the rights of relatives, including the creation of a criminal offence if the consent provisions to the removal, retention and storage of human tissue are not complied with. The law relating to organ donation is considered in *Chapter 16*. Failure to observe the statutory provisions relating to consent is a criminal offence under section 5 of the Human Tissue Act 2004.

Coroner requested post mortem

Where the coroner has requested a post mortem to be undertaken for the purposes of deciding whether an inquiry should be held into the death, no person, whatever their religious persuasion can refuse. Clearly the coroner would take into account any religious beliefs that the deceased or the relatives may have had and would only order a post mortem where this is considered essential. The HTA Code of Practice emphasises that although the consent of relatives is not required by the coroner, the reasons for the post mortem and the procedures to be followed should be explained sensitively to them. They should be given information about when and where the examination is to be performed and told of their right to be represented at the post mortem by a doctor, if they so wish.

The Coroner's powers derive from the Coroners Rules 1984 which were amended in 2005. The amendments came into force in 1 June 2005. The definition of partner is now one of two persons (whether of different sexes or the same sex) who live as partners in an enduring family relationship, and a relative as well as a partner.

Rule 5 of Coroners Rules 1984 states that where a coroner directs or requests that a post mortem examination shall be made, it shall be made as soon after the death of the deceased as is reasonably practicable. The rules also cover the medical practitioner who should undertake the examination. Where the deceased died in hospital the coroner should not ask a pathologist on the staff of the hospital to make the examination if he does not desire to do it, or if the conduct of a member of the staff of the hospital is likely to be called into question or any relative of the deceased requests a pathologist other than the hospital one. Under rule 7 the coroner is required to notify the following persons and organisations of the date, hour, and place at which the examination is to take place:

- Any relative (including partner) of the deceased who has notified the coroner of his or her desire to attend, or be represented at the post mortem examination.
- The deceased's regular medical attendant.
- If the deceased died in hospital, the hospital.
- The chief officer of police, if he or she has notified the coroner of a wish to be present.
- Other inspection agencies, etc., depending on the cause of death.

Under revisions to the Coroners' Rules made in 2005, a coroner who orders a post mortem examination and is notified about the retention of organs or tissue for examination has a duty to inform the relatives (including partner as defined above) or personal representative of the deceased person about the following before the post mortem is carried out:

- that the material is being kept,
- the period or periods for which it needs to be kept, and
- the options for dealing with the material once it is no longer required for the coroner's purposes.

These options are:

- lawful disposal of the material by burial, cremation or other lawful means

- return of the material to relatives to make their own arrangements, or
- storage of the material with appropriate consent for use for medical research or other purposes.

These options are discussed in the HTA's *Code of Practice on the Removal, Storage and Disposal of Human Organs and Tissue* which is considered in *Chapter 17*.

The HTA's *Code of Practice on Post Mortems* advises that there is legal provision for a copy of a coroner's post mortem report to be provided to relatives for a fee. They should be told about this and told when the report will be available, and how to obtain a copy. (No charge is payable for a hospital post mortem report.) Unless the coroner has reason to do otherwise, a copy of the post mortem report should in any case be provided to the deceased person's GP, and relatives may wish to discuss the findings with the GP.

Coroners have claimed that because of a shortage of pathologists children's bodies are taken miles away for a post mortem to be carried out, contrary to the rules which allow the removal of a body for post mortem only to an adjoining district. The Department of Health stated that there were intentions to amend the law to relax the boundary restrictions (Rose, 2008). (see *Chapter 14* on the Draft Coroner's Bill).

Purpose of coroner's post mortem

The Code of Practice advises that coroners' post mortem examinations are carried out to assist coroners in carrying out their functions. Although the consent of relatives is not required, the reasons for the post mortem and the procedures to be followed should be explained sensitively to them. They should be given information about when and where the examination is to be performed and told of their right to be represented at the post mortem by a doctor, if they so wish.

Retention of tissue following coroner's post mortem

The HFA *Code of Practice on the Removal, Retention and Storage of Tissue* states that consent is needed for the storage or use of material taken during a coroner's post mortem for scheduled purposes, once the material is no longer required for the coroner's purposes. The amendment to the Coroners' Rules provides a new Rule 9 which requires a pathologist to make provision, so far as possible, for the preservation of material which in his or her opinion bears upon the cause of death or the identification of the deceased. Where a pathologist preserves material under paragraph (1) he or she must notify the coroner of that fact forthwith in writing (which expression, for the avoidance of doubt, includes electronic communication). A notification under paragraph (2) must

- identify the material being preserved; and
  explain why the pathologist is of the opinion mentioned in paragraph (1).

The notification under paragraph (2) may

- specify the period for which he or she believes the material should be preserved, and
- specify different periods for different materials.

Where coroners receive a notification under paragraph (2) they must notify the pathologist of the period for which they require the material to be preserved, being such period as, in the coroners' opinion, the material needs to be preserved for the purpose of fulfilling their functions under the 1988 Act in relation to the deceased, and they may specify different periods for different material. Coroners must also notify

- one of the persons referred to in rule 20(2)(a), and
- any other relatives of the deceased who have notified the coroner of their desire to attend, or be represented at the post mortem examination.

In addition, the coronor must notify that the material is being preserved, the period or periods for which it is required to be preserved under paragraph (5), and the options for dealing with the material on expiry of a period notified under that paragraph. In the case of children who have identified themselves as such to the coroners, the coroners may, if they consider it more appropriate, notify a person who has parental responsibility for the child instead of notifying the child him or herself.

The options referred to in paragraph (6) are

- disposal of the material by burial, cremation or other lawful disposal by the pathologist,
- return of the material to a person referred to in that paragraph who requests that the material be returned, or
- retention of the material with the consent of a person referred to in paragraph (6) for medical research or other purposes.

If a period notified under paragraph (5) does not expire before the date on which the coroner's functions cease under the 1988 Act it shall expire on that date, and the coroner shall notify the persons referred to in paragraphs (5) and (6) accordingly.

The pathologist must, so far as possible, preserve material to which this rule applies until the expiry of the period notified to him or her in relation to it under paragraph (5).

In paragraph (7) 'child' means a person who has not attained the age of 18 years; and 'parental responsibility' has the same meaning as in the Children Act 1989.

Post mortem rules

Schedule 2 to the Coroners Rules 1984 sets out rules relating to the post mortem examination report. This was amended from 1 June 2005 so that it is now a requirement to declare whether any organs or tissue were removed from the body during the examination and retained and if so to specify who retains any such organs or tissue, and for what period or periods.

Preservation of material from special examination

A new Rule 12 is introduced by the Coroner's Amendment Rules on the preservation of material from special examination. As under the changes to Rule 9, pathologists are required to tell the coroner that they have preserved material from the special examination and the coroner must specify the period for which the material must be preserved. There is provision for the coroner to change that period should it be necessary, but it cannot extend beyond the date on which the coroner's functions cease. The coroner is also required to notify certain persons of the period for which the material is to be preserved, and the options for dealing with the material when that period expires. Once the date for preserving the material has passed the person preserving it must record what he or she has done with it. The rules also cover the preservation of material used for special examinations.

Local protocols

The Code of Practice on post mortems recommends local protocols between coroners and health organisations to ensure proper communication with the deceased person's relatives. Discussions about consent to store organs should ideally take place before the post mortem is carried out, and certainly before the coroner's time limit on storage expires. This not only avoids a second approach to relatives at a difficult time, but also ensures that material is not stored other than under the coroner's authority or with consent. If the deceased person's relatives indicate that they wish organs or tissue to be disposed of, this should be done as soon as possible and certainly within two weeks of the deadline on storage specified by the coroner. Where they have not expressed a preference by the time the coroner's time limit expires, the organs or tissue may be stored for up to six weeks. The relatives should then be advised that unless they specify otherwise, the organs or tissue will be disposed of in a further four weeks' time. The HTA Code of Practice also suggests that it should not be assumed that consent to a post mortem implies consent to removing and keeping blocks and slides.

Human Tissue Act 2004 and the coroner

Section 11 of the Act makes it clear that the consent provisions in Part 1 do not apply to anything done for purposes of functions of a coroner or under the authority of a coroner. Where people know, or have reason to believe, that the body of a deceased person, or relevant material which has come from the body of a deceased person, is, or may be, required for purposes of functions of a coroner, they shall not act on authority under section 1 in relation to the body, or material, except with the consent of the coroner.

Where no post mortem has been requested by the coroner

Where the hospital wishes to conduct a post mortem examination then it is essential that the legal requirements under the Human Tissue Act 2004 relating to consent are satisfied (see below). The deceased may have given consent to a post mortem and there is no statutory requirement that this should be recorded in writing, although clearly best practice would recommend a record of the deceased's wishes. Alternatively the deceased may have appointed a nominated representative who should be consulted. The Code of Practice published by the Human Tissue Authority should be followed.

Code of practice

A code of practice for families and post mortems was published by the Department of Health in the wake of the Alder Hey Inquiry to ensure that safe practices were in place. It had been recommended by the Chief Medical Officer for England in the *Removal, Retention and Use of Human Organs and Tissues from Post Mortem Examinations* in January 2001 (Department of Health, 2001) and was subject to consultation. It was updated and replaced by the *Code of Practice on Post Mortems* issued by the HTA and approved in 2006. The HTA's *Code of Practice on Post Mortems* covers the following topics:

- Introduction
- Scope of the code
- Patients who are dying
- Post mortem examination (autopsy)
    - Quality standards
    - Coroner's post mortem examination
    - Hospital post mortem
- Who can give consent?
    - Appropriate consent – adults
    - Appropriate consent – children
    - Nominated representatives
    - Qualifying relationships
- Discussing the post mortem with the family: who may seek consent?
    - What should the discussion cover?
    - Cultural traditions and language differences
- Information to be given to families after coroner's and hospital post mortem
    - Results of the post mortem investigation
    - Information about use of donated tissue and organs
- Maintaining proper documentation
- Disposal of tissue and organs
- Obtaining consent
- Training and support for staff
- Glossary

Who can give consent

Under the Human Tissue Act 2004 the appropriate consent is necessary to carry out a hospital post mortem (ie. one not ordered by the coroner).

Section 2 covers the appropriate consent for children and section 3 the appropriate consent for adults.

Consent for adults for hospital post mortem

The following are the appropriate consents:

- Consent by the deceased if the consent was in immediate force before death.
- If the above consent is absent, the consent of the deceased's

nominated representative. The Act makes certain stipulations about the appointment of nominated representatives.
- If the above two consents are absent, the consent of a person who stood in a qualifying relationship to the deceased immediately before he or she died. The Act sets out an order of priority of those in a qualifying relationship

The Code of Practice points out that:

Bereaved people should be treated with respect and sensitivity at all times, both to help them take important decisions at a difficult time and to ensure continuing improvements in care. The standards expected when seeking and obtaining consent are touched on in this document, but are set out in much greater detail in the HTA's Code of Practice on Consent.

The Code seeks to ensure that:

- Those close to the deceased person are given the opportunity to understand the reasons for hospital and coroners' post mortems, the processes involved, and their rights in the decision-making process.
- The wishes of the deceased person and those close to them are known and fully understood.
- Organs and tissue are only retained following post mortem with consent or other lawful authorisation (such as that of the coroner).
- General information about post mortem examinations is readily accessible.

The Code also emphasises that in any setting (NHS, academic or other), human tissue or organs may only be removed, stored, or used if appropriate consent has been obtained. Before the procedure starts, the person obtaining consent should, in collaboration with the pathologist, check that the post mortem examination and any removal, storage or use have been properly authorised. This authorisation will either come from a completed consent form, which must meet the standards required by this code, or from the coroner. (This does not imply that pathologists should necessarily be the ones to seek consent, but they should be involved in the process.)

Location of post mortems

The HTA in its *Code of Practice on Post Mortems* states that post mortems must be carried out in premises licensed by the HTA, in accordance with the conditions of the licence. The person to whom the licence applies (the 'designated individual') has a duty to ensure that others carrying out the licensed activity (in this case conducting a post mortem examination) on the premises are suitable persons to do so.

Responsibility of health professionals

The Code of Practice gives specific advice to health professionals who may be seeking the family's consent to a post mortem examination. It emphasises the need to give honest, clear and objective information, provide an opportunity for them to talk to someone they trust, provide reasonable time to reach decisions and provide support if they need and want it. Only then should they be asked to sign a consent form. Communication skills are essential and staff may need training to undertake these activities. The Code of Practice recommends that all NHS hospital trusts should have a designated, named individual who is available to provide support and information to families of the deceased where a post mortem examination may be required, whether this is requested by a hospital doctor or by the coroner. Privacy and comfort should be provided for the conduct of these meetings. The Code of Practice also lists the topics that should be covered in the discussions preceding consent being given for a post mortem.

Documentation

Different forms have been designed by the Department of Health (available on the website) for use in recording that consent has been given:

- When the coroner requests the post mortem examination of an adult, and the retention and use of tissue and organs (if appropriate).
- The hospital post mortem examination of an adult and the retention and use of tissue or organs, (if appropriate).
- When the coroner requests the post mortem examination of a baby or child and the retention and use of tissue and organs (if appropriate).
- The hospital post mortem examination of a baby or child and the retention and use of tissue or organs (if appropriate).

The Department of Health suggests that hospitals may wish to design their own forms for consent for fetal examination or for the examination of the products of conception. In order to explain to parents the benefits for paediatric pathology a video has been prepared (available from the NHS Response Line).

Application of the law to the situation in *Box 15.1*

If the doctor is unable to certify the cause of death, then this should be reported to the coroner, who would probably order a post mortem to take place. In this case, in spite of Muriel's religious objections, she cannot prevent the post mortem examination going ahead. In this situation, the examination is under the coroner's jurisdiction and the pathologist would only remove the liver if it is of relevance to the cause of death (and not because of the research interest of the consultant). If however the doctor knows the immediate cause of death and can complete the death certificate, he has no power to insist upon a post mortem without Muriel's consent nor is he able to remove the liver for his own research purposes. As a consequence of the Human Tissue Act 2004 the law has been tightened up to ensure compliance with public demands for openness, honesty and the rights of the relatives to give consent.

Future changes

The Government agreed with the recommendations of the Department for Constitutional Affairs Select Committee on the draft coroners bill that there should be fewer post mortems. The Select Committee had recommended that:

> *The Government adopt a strategy for reducing the number of post mortem examinations performed. This may include abolition of the '14-day rule'; provision of detailed information to the coroner and pathologist; adoption of written sudden death reports by the police; and consideration of a system similar to the Scottish 'view and grant' (paragraph 177).*
>
> Department for Constitutional Affairs (2006)

The UK Government (2006) partly accepted this recommendation:

> *We agree it is likely that too many unnecessary post mortems are being carried out. However the evidence is not conclusive enough at this stage to have an immediate explicit target for reduction. There is a need to have a strategy to ensure that the right criteria and alternatives are in place so that, as far as possible, post mortems are carried out only when strictly necessary. We will look further at ways of achieving this, including whether the extension of the '14 day' rule may be justified in light of current medical practice. We will prepare secondary legislation to deal with the detailed interaction between coroners, pathologists and the police. We do not think that the 'view and grant' system is the way forward – as the Scottish representative of the British Medical Association*

said in his evidence to the Committee, Scotland probably has too few post mortems – but we are watching developments in new technology carefully to assess whether pathologists may be recommended to make more use of non-invasive techniques.

At the time of writing a revised Coroner's Bill is awaited (see *Chapter 14*).

Conclusion

As the history of Bristol and Alder Hey shows, the conduct of hospital post mortems, and the removal, retention and storage of human tissue is a sensitive area. There are considerable benefits in clinical research and the understanding of diseases if relatives are prepared to give consent to the carrying out of post mortems to foster this knowledge. However it is essential that the request is handled sensitively and that all the relevant information is given to the relatives about the post mortem and about the possibility of any tissue being removed, retained and stored. Clearly the Department of Health would wish the scientific benefits that flow from analysis of tissue and organs after death and the conduct of post mortem examinations to continue and therefore it is essential that the general public is reassured that the correct procedures are in place, and are implemented and regularly monitored.

References

Coroners (Amendment) Rules 2005 SI 2005/420

Coroners Rules 1984 SI 1984/552 rule 5

Department for Constitutional Affairs (2006) *Select Committee's Report on the Reform of the Coroners' System and Death Certification*. London: Department for Constitutional Affairs

Department of Health (2001) *The Removal, Retention and Use of Human Organs and Tissue from Post-Mortem Examination. Advice from the Chief Medical Officer.* London: Department of Health

Department of Health (2002) *Human Bodies, Human Choices. A Consultation Document.* London: Department of Health

Department of Health (2003a) *Families and Post Mortems: A Code of Practice, Forms and Information Leaflets*. London: Department of Health

Department of Health (2003b) *A Simple Guide to Post Mortem Examination Procedure*. London: Department of Health

NHS Response Line: www.guide-information.org.uk/

Royal College of Pathologists (2002) *Guidelines on Autopsy Practice – Report of a Working Group of the Royal College of Pathologists*. London: Royal College of Pathologists

Rose D (2008) Children's bodies taken miles from families over shortage of pathologists.

The Times **4 January**

UK Government (2006) Response to the Constitutional Affairs Select Committee's Report: Reform of the Coroners' System and Death Certification Cm 6943. London: UK Government

Resources

www.opsi.gov.uk/si/si2005/20050420.htm

www.doh.gov.uk/tissue

CHAPTER 16

Organ transplants and dead donors

> **Box 16.1. Prior consent to organ donation**
>
> Mike, aged 18 years, was severely injured in a road accident. He was admitted to intensive care and placed on a ventilator. The consultant anaesthetist notified his parents that he was unlikely to survive and he would be tested to ascertain if he was brain dead. The parents were told that Mike was carrying a donor card and were asked about organ donation. They said that they did not agree with it, and were surprised that Mike was carrying a donor card. They did not wish the donation to proceed. What is the law?

The Human Tissue Act 2004 was passed following concerns resulting from the Alder Hey and other hospital scandals on organ removal, retention and storage and in the light of the feedback from the consultation document *Human Bodies Human Choices* which was published by the Department of Health and the Welsh Assembly in July 2002. Proposals for new legislation on human organs and tissue were published the Department of Health and the Welsh Assembly in September 2003. The basic provisions of the Human Tissue Act 2004 came into force in April 2006.

The Human Tissue Act 2004 has made considerable changes to the law on the donation of organs and tissue after death. It sets out a new legal framework for the storage and use of tissue from the living and for the removal, storage and use of tissue and organs from the dead. This includes 'residual' tissue following clinical and diagnostic procedures. The Human Tissue Act 2004 repeals and replaces the Human Tissue Act 1961, the Anatomy Act 1984 and the Human Organ Transplants Act 1989 as they relate to England and Wales. It also repeals and replaces the Human Tissue Act (Northern Ireland) 1962, the Human Organ Transplants (Northern Ireland) Order 1989 and the Anatomy (Northern Ireland) Order 1992.

The Human Tissue Act 2004

The Act makes provisions for the:

- Removal, storage and use of human organs and other tissue for scheduled purposes.
- Regulation of activities involving human tissue.
- Establishment of the Human Tissue Authority.
- Preservation for transplantation.
- Non-consensual analysis of DNA.
- Powers of inspection, entry, search and seizures.
- Offences by bodies corporate and prosecutions.

The Human Tissue Act established the Human Tissue Authority (HTA) as the regulatory body for all matters concerning the removal, storage, use and disposal of human tissue (excluding gametes and embryos) for scheduled purposes. This includes responsibility for living donor transplantation. The HTA has published five codes of practice including one on donation of organs, tissue and cells for transplantation (Human Tissue Authority, 2006a).

Consent

The Act makes consent the fundamental principle underpinning the lawful retention and use of body parts, organs and tissue from living or deceased

Box 16.2. Schedule 1 of the Human Tissue Act 2004

Part 1 Purposes requiring consent: General

- Anatomical examination (after the registration of death)
- Determining the cause of death
- Establishing after a person's death the efficacy of any drug or other treatment administered to him.
- Obtaining scientific or medical information about a living or deceased person which may be relevant to any other person (including a future person)
- Public display
- Transplantation

Part 2 Purposes requiring consent: Deceased persons

- Clinical audit
- Education in training relating to human health
- Performance assessment
- Public health monitoring
- Quality assurance

persons. Consent is required if the tissue, from a living or dead person, is to be used for one of the purposes listed in Schedule 1. These scheduled purposes are shown in *Box 16.2*.

Special provisions apply to the use of body material for research, where it must be ethically approved under regulations made by the Secretary of State.

The appropriate consent must be obtained before body parts can be removed. Appropriate consent for adults means either the consent of individuals, or their consent in writing before their death. This must have been signed by individuals in the presence of at least one witness or signed at the direction of the individuals concerned, in their presence and in the presence of at least one witness or have been contained in a will. For purposes other than public display or anatomical examination (of non-excepted material, see below) appropriate consent means consent before death, consent by a person appointed (under section 4) or the consent of a person who stood in a qualifying relationship to that individual immediately before he or she died. Section 4 enables people to appoint one or more persons to represent them after their death in relation to consent for the purposes of section 1.

The HTA has published its *Code of Practice on Consent* (2002b). This provides overall guidance on the provisions and implications of the Human Tissue Act 2004 and should be read in conjunction with the other four codes of practice published by the HTA, ie:

- Donation of organs, tissue and cells for transplantation.
- Post mortem examination.
- Anatomical examination.
- Removal, storage and disposal of human organs and tissue.

The *Code of Practice on Consent* covers the topics shown in *Box 16.3*.

Application of the law to the situation in *Box 16.1*

Mike was carrying a donor card and if there is no evidence that he has withdrawn his consent to organ donation then that would count as an appropriate consent for the purposes of the Human Tissue Act 2004. Under section 3(6) where people concerned have died 'appropriate consent' means their consent if a decision of theirs was in force immediately before they died. Unless they have evidence that Mike withdrew his consent to organ donation before his death, his relatives would have no right to prevent the organ donation. The Act does not require Mike's consent to be in writing, but clearly there are advantages if it is. However the donor card would be the equivalent of a written request.

Box 16.3. Contents of the HTA *Code of Practice on Consent*

Introduction
The scope of the Human Tissue Act
The question of consent
Statutory requirements for consent
- The living
- The deceased
- Exceptions for research in specific circumstances

Who can give consent?
- Tissue from the living – competent adults
- Tissue from the living – adults who lack capacity
- Tissue from the living – children
- Tissue from the deceased – adults
- Tissue from the deceased – nominated representatives
- Tissue from the deceased – qualifying relationships
- Tissue from the deceased – children
- Fetal tissue

The process of consent
- When to seek consent
- Who should seek consent?
- Religion, culture and languages
- What information should be given?
  Tissue storage and use from the living
  Tissue storage and use from the deceased
- Use of documentation
- Form of consent
- Written consent
- Multiple consents (eg. post mortem examination/research)
- Nature and duration of consent
- Withdrawal of consent

Existing holdings
Consent and the use of DNA
Powers of the court/the HTA to dispense with the need for consent
Glossary

Prior consent by donor by word of mouth

Section 1(1) of the Human Tissue Act 2004 lists activities that are lawful if done with the appropriate consent and subsection (c) in that list is:

the removal from the body of a deceased person, for use for a purpose specified in Schedule 1, of any relevant material of which the body consists or which it contains.

As can be seen from *Box 16.2* Schedule 1 includes, as a specified purpose, transplantation.

As noted above, the Act does not require the consent to be in writing. The HTA Code of Practice states that the Human Tissue Act makes clear that where adults have, while alive and competent, consented to one or more of the scheduled purposes taking place after their death, then that consent is sufficient for the activity to be lawful. It recommends that:

In cases of potential donation, trained staff should determine whether the deceased person had given consent for organ, tissue or cell donation by checking with the NHS Organ Donor Register or any other source, such as a will. If consent is established, the deceased person's relatives or those close to them should be told.

If no records are held, an approach should be made to the deceased person's relatives or close friends by a transplant coordinator or a member of the team who cared for the patient, or both together, to establish any known wishes of the deceased person.

If the family or those close to the deceased person object to the donation, for whatever purpose, when the deceased person (or their nominated representative) has explicitly consented, clinicians should seek to discuss the matter sensitively with them. They should be encouraged to accept the deceased person's wishes and it should be made clear that they do not have the legal right to veto or overrule those wishes. There may nevertheless be cases in which donation is inappropriate and each case should be considered individually.

From the 1 September 2006 the presumption is that if donors are on the Organ Donor Register, they want their organs to be used and the next of kin do not have a right in law to overrule those wishes. The family should still be consulted and should be encouraged to allow the deceased's wishes to prevail.

Box 16.4. Donation of organs where the deceased has consented.

Bob, aged 23 years, was severely wounded in a road traffic accident and realised that he was dying. He told the nurse that if possible he would like his organs to be used for transplantation. The nurse recorded this in his notes and told her colleagues. Following Bob's death his body was preserved for the purposes of organ donation, but his girlfriend and parents were opposed to the use of his body for such purposes. What is the law?

Application of the law to scenario in *Box 16.4*

Turning back to *Box 16.4* it follows that if the nurse can give evidence that Bob was mentally competent when he gave consent to the use of his organs then this consent will override the refusal by his girlfriend or his parents. Since Bob died following a road accident, his death would be reported to the coroner who should be notified of Bob's consent to organ donation. It is likely that the coroner would give approval to the organ removal and donation. Clearly if Bob were to be carrying a donor card, there would be less room for dispute with the relatives.

Nominated person

Section 4 of the Human Tissue Act 2004 enables adults to appoint one or more persons to represent them after their death in relation to consent for the purposes of section 1, ie. giving an appropriate consent for the purposes listed in Schedule 1. The appointment can be made orally or in writing and can be general or limited to consent in relation to such one or more activities as may be specified in the appointment. An oral appointment under this section is only valid if made in the presence of at least two witnesses present at the same time. A written appointment under this section is only valid if:

- It is signed by the person making it in the presence of at least one witness who attests the signature.
- It is signed at the direction of the person making it, in his presence and in the presence of at least one witness who attests the signature, or
- It is contained in a will of the person making it, being a will which is made in accordance with the requirements of
  - Section 9 of the Wills Act 1837 (c. 26), or
  - Article 5 of the Wills and Administration Proceedings (Northern Ireland) Order 1994 (S.I. 1994/1899 (N.I. 13)).

Where a person appoints two or more persons under this section in relation to the same activity, they shall be regarded as appointed to act jointly and severally unless the appointment provides that they are appointed to act jointly.

An appointment under this section may be revoked at any time. The same provisions about oral or written consent apply to the revocation. A person appointed under this section may at any time renounce his or her appointment. To act as a nominated representative an appointee must be an adult and not excluded by regulations to be drawn up by the Secretary of State.

The Code of Practice suggests that trained healthcare professionals should make reasonable enquiries at the hospital, the prospective donor's GP or with the deceased person's relatives to establish if a representative has been nominated.

Communication between health professionals where deceased has given a prior consent

The Code of Practice states that the Human Tissue Act makes it clear that where adults, while alive and competent, consented to donation after their death, then that consent is sufficient for human tissue donation to be lawfully carried out. It recommends that in cases of potential deceased donation, the transplant coordinator or delegated person should be approached at an early stage and asked to determine whether the deceased person had indicated a wish to donate his or her organs and/or tissue after death, carried a signed organ donor card or had registered on the Organ Donor Register. This should be done before the relatives are approached.

It suggests that once it is known that the deceased person consented to donation, the matter should be discussed sensitively with the deceased's relatives. They should be encouraged to recognise the wishes of their relative and it should be made clear, if necessary, that they do not have the legal right to veto or overrule the deceased person's wishes.

Removal of organs for transplantation where there is no prior consent by the deceased

Qualifying relationship

Where there is no prior consent from the deceased, nor a nominated person to give consent then section 3 enables consent to be obtained from the person who stood in a qualifying relationship to the deceased immediately before he or she died.

Under Section 27 of the Human Tissue Act the HTA has the duty to lay down the standards expected in relation to the obtaining of consent where consent is obtained from a person in a qualifying relationship.

Box 16.5. Absence of prior consent by the deceased

Bob was severely injured in a road accident and close to death. Health professionals were wondering as to whether his organs could be taken for transplantation. There is no evidence that he has ever given consent, nor has he appointed a nominated representative for such purposes

Section 27(4) states that the qualifying relationships for the purpose of giving consent should be ranked in the following order:

- spouse or partner,
- parent or child,
- brother or sister,
- grandparent or grandchild;
- child of a brother or sister,
- stepfather or stepmother,
- half-brother or half-sister,
- friend of longstanding.

Relationships in the same paragraph of subsection (4) should be accorded equal ranking. So if there are several siblings, neither take precedence over the other, for example on grounds of age or gender.

Consent should be obtained from the person whose relationship to the person concerned is accorded the highest ranking in accordance with subsections (4) and (5).

If the relationship of each of two or more persons to the person concerned is accorded equal highest ranking in accordance with subsections (4) and (5), it is sufficient to obtain the consent of any of them.

In applying the principles set out above, a person's relationship shall be left out of account if:

- he or she does not wish to deal with the issue of consent,
- he or she is not able to deal with that issue, or
- having regard to the activity in relation to which consent is sought, it is not reasonably practicable to communicate with him or her within the time available if consent in relation to the activity is to be acted on.

The Secretary of State may by order amend subsection (4).

To be classified as a partner there is no requirement that the couple should have entered into a civil partnership under the legislation. Section 54 (9) states that for these purposes a person is another person's partner if the two of them (whether of different sexes or the same sex) live as partners in an enduring family relationship.

Disputes between those in a qualifying relationship

The Code of Practice suggests that where there are differences of opinion between people in qualifying relationships, decisions will need to be made on a case-by-case basis, taking into account:

- the views of the deceased person, which are paramount,
- the view of the highest-ranking person – if a spouse or partner refuses consent, then that must take precedence even if other family members would be willing to give consent, and
- the views of other qualifying persons. If, for example, a spouse consents to donation, but other family members object strongly, the benefits of carrying out the transplantation should be weighed against the distress and resentment that would be caused by proceeding in the face of strong opposition. This will be especially sensitive where people in equally ranked qualifying relationships disagree.

Application of the law to the scenario in *Box 16.5*

Having excluded the possibility of Bob having given consent, and the absence of any nomination by Bob of a representative, the hospital manager can turn to the person in a qualifying relationship with Bob using the list shown previously to determine who is the highest ranking such person. If Bob is unmarried and has no clear partner, then it will be his parents who are able to give consent. If the parents make it clear that they do not wish to deal with the issue of consent, or they are unable to do so, then the next person in the ranking can be approached. The HTA Code of Practice states that it is advisable to record this in the case notes and this should also be done if the activity for which consent is sought is such that it would not be practical to communicate with the highest ranking person within the time available.

The Code of Practice also points out that obtaining appropriate consent only makes the activity lawful if it goes ahead – it does not mean that it is obligatory.

The Code of Practice suggests that an agreed position should be reached by inclusive discussion, where possible. This will need careful explanation of the options and the potential benefits of donation. The 'ranking' provision in the Human Tissue Act should not be used to impose one family member's wishes over others where there are strongly held objections that might outweigh any benefit. Great care should be taken to assess whether ignoring the family's strongly held objections might outweigh the benefits of proceeding.

Children

Section 2 of the Human Tissue Act 2004 defines what is the appropriate consent in relation to a child. The appropriate consent is the consent of the child. Competent children could give consent to the use of their organs after their death. If the child has died and there is a pre-existing consent to organ donation, then that would be valid. Alternatively if there is decision of the child not to consent to organ donation, then that will be decisive. However in the absence of any decision by a competent child, if a child has died, then the appropriate consent can be taken from a person who had parental responsibility for him or her immediately before death, or where no person had parental responsibility immediately before he or she died, the consent of a person who stood in a qualifying relationship at that time. Qualifying relationship has the same meaning as that given above.

Special provisions apply when the body is to be used for public display or anatomical examination.

Competence of the child

The test used in the Gillick case (*Gillick v. West Norfolk an Wisbech Area Health Authority*) as to whether a child is competent would be used to determine if a child is capable of giving an appropriate consent. Children are competent if they have sufficient intelligence and understanding to enable them fully to understand what is involved. Children would clearly have to be given full information about the nature of the decision which is to be made and all its implications.

The HTA Code of Practice notes that:

> *Clearly, in any case where a child has given consent to donation, especially if the child has self-registered on the Organ Donor Register, it is essential to discuss this with the child's parents or someone with parental responsibility and take their views and wishes into account before deciding how to proceed.*
>
> *In cases where the deceased child's wishes are not known, every effort should be made when the child dies to establish the parents' wishes. In those very rare situations where the parents cannot be contacted, the consent of the person who was in the closest qualifying relationship to the child at the time of death can be sought.*
>
> *Where a child is the prospective donor, special efforts should be made to obtain parental consent to use the child's organs for transplantation. If, in very rare situations this is or proves impossible (eg. the parents died at the same time as the child), the consent of the person who was in the closest qualifying relationship with the child at the time of death should be sought.*

Box 16.6. Organ donation and children

Jacob, aged 9 died when he fell off a shed roof. He is placed on a ventilator and nursing staff ask his parents if they would agree to his organs being donated. What is the law?

Application of the law to the scenario in *Box 16.6*

There appears to have been no opportunity to have asked Jacob if he would have been prepared to have been a donor, which would have been possible had he been competent. Nor does it appear that he has made any decision earlier. In the absence of consent from Jacob, those in a qualifying relationship with him would make the decision. His parents would come first in the priority list given above. If there are problems over contacting them, the appropriate consent would be sought from the person next in the list of those in a qualifying relationship.

Working party on brainstem death and guidelines for the identification and management of potential organ and tissue donors

In March 1998 a working party established through the Royal Colleges of Physicians (Department of Health, 1998) prepared the *Code of Practice for the Diagnosis of Brain Stem Death*. The working party also provided guidelines for the identification and management of potential organ and tissue donors. These guidelines consider the role of the transplant co-ordinator, contact with relatives, partner and carers of the patient, the retrieval of organs and tissue, transplant arrangements and tissue banking. An appendix sets out a flow chart for the management of potential organ and tissue donors.

Preservation of body for purposes of donation

Section 47 of the Human Tissue Act 2004 states that where part of a body (ie. of a deceased person) lying in a hospital, nursing home or other institution is or may be suitable for use for transplantation, it shall be lawful for the person having the control and management of the institution

- to take steps for the purpose of preserving the part for use for transplantation, and
- to retain the body for that purpose.

However the authority given under this section only extends to the taking of the minimum steps necessary for the purpose mentioned in that provision, and to the use of the least invasive procedure.

Once it has been established that consent making removal of the part for transplantation lawful has not been, and will not be, given, then the authority under this section ceases to apply.

Guidance on the process for preservation is provided in the British

Transplantation Society's guidelines relating to solid organ transplants from non-heart beating donors which are available on its website.

Future changes

The Human Tissue Act 2004 retained the previous law on 'opting in' or the consent of the relatives to organ donation. There has been a recent debate over the need to increase the number of organs available for transplant. In 2003 about 6000 persons were awaiting an organ transplant and many would die before one became available. There are about 11 million people on the Organ Donor Register.

One suggestion is that there should be an opting-out system, rather than an opting-in one, ie. you carry a card if you do not want your body used for transplant purposes, and the absence of a card implies an agreement to the organs being transplanted. This suggestion has not met with wide acceptance, although an Organ Donation (Presumed Consent and Safeguards) Bill was introduced into Parliament in 2004 and would have had the effect of an opting out system.

An alternative suggestion is that there should be a legal duty for the professionals to request an organ transplant from the relatives of the deceased or prospective deceased. This is described as the required request system. It has the advantage of removing some of the embarrassment that professionals feel when they have to broach the matter with relatives. They are able to say, 'I hate having to ask you this, but I have no option as it is my legal duty to do so; would you agree to the possibility of X's organs being used for transplant?' It is thought that such a statutory request would lead to more organs being forthcoming without the necessity for a change in the Human Tissue Act itself. The relatives would still have the freedom to refuse, but they would also have the opportunity to agree. An initiative supported by actors and actresses in the TV soap Coronation Street was designed to increase the number of organ donors. Information for potential donors is given on a Department of Health website. It was followed by a scheme whereby credit card companies will ask customers applying for a card to sign up on the organ donor register.

In 2007 the Chief Medical Officer raised the issue of having an opting out system where there would be a presumption in favour of donation unless the deceased had made a clear decision against any organ donation after death. A UK-wide Organ Donation task force appointed by the Department of Health to investigate improvements to the transplant services reported in January 2008. It made recommendations on increasing the number of transplant co-ordinators, strengthening the network of retrieval teams, identifying potential donors sooner and mandatory training of critical care staff. It set up a sub-committee to look at the issue of presumed consent which will report in the summer of 2008. The implementation of its recommendations may lead to an increase in the numbers of donors and possibly to the conclusion that no change in the law on consent is required.

Conclusions

The principle of consent underpins the philosophy of the Human Tissue Act 2004. It is essential that NHS trusts review their procedures to ensure that the provisions of the Act are implemented and that there is regular monitoring and staff training on the implications of the new legislation. This also applies to the removal, storage and retention of tissue which is considered in *Chapter 17*.

References

Department of Health (1998) *A Code of Practice for the Diagnosis of Brain Stem Death*. London: Department of Health

Department of Health (2000) Credit cards to promote organ donation. London: Department of Health

Department of Health and Welsh Assembly (2002) *Government Human Bodies, Human Choices A Consultation Report*. London: Department of Health

Department of Health and Welsh Assembly (2003) *Government Proposals for New Legislation on Human Organs and Tissue*. London: Department of Health. Available from: www.doh.gov.uk/tissue

Gillick v West Norfolk and Wisbech Area Health Authority [1985] 3 All ER 402 (HL)

Human Tissue Authority (2006a) *Code of Practice No 1 Consent*. London: Human Tissue Authority

Human Tissue Authority (2006b) *Code of Practice No 2 Donation of Organs, Tissue and Cells for Transplantation*. London: Human Tissue Authority

Resources

www.bts.org.uk/standards.htm

www.nhs.uk/organdonor

CHAPTER 17

Removal, retention and storage of organs and tissue

> **Box 17.1. Unwanted removal**
>
> Diane's daughter, aged six months, died in hospital following heart surgery. It had been explained to her that there was only a tiny chance of the operation succeeding. She opted for burial of the baby. She subsequently discovered that the heart had been removed without her consent and her child had been buried without her heart. She is very upset and is considering suing the trust for compensation. Is she likely to succeed?

Considerable public concern was raised when it was learnt that human organs from children who had died had been retained at Bristol Royal Infirmary. New guidance was considered necessary when, during the inquiry into allegations of professional misconduct in carrying out paediatric heart surgery, it was learnt that more than 11 000 children who had died in the past 40 years had had their organs used for research in British hospitals without the explicit consent of their parents. At the same time, concerns were raised about the retention of human brains and spinal cords at the Walton Centre, Liverpool and of children's organs at Alder Hey Hospital. The Report of the Royal Liverpool's Children's Inquiry (chaired by Michael Redfern QC) on the retention of organs and body parts was published on the 30 January 2001 (Department of Health, 2001a). Its publication coincided with three other publications:

- A report of a *Census of Organs and Tissues Retained by Pathology Services in England* carried out by the Chief Medical Officer (Department of Health, 2001b).
- *The Removal, Retention and Use of Human Organs and Tissue from Post-Mortem Examination,* advice from the Chief Medical Officer (Department of Health, 2001c).
- *Consent to Organ and Tissue Retention at Post-Mortem Examination and Disposal of Human Materials* (Department of Health, 2001d).

The Inquiry found that thousands of children's body parts had been collected at the hospital, some going back to before 1973. Most, however, were retained after 1988 when Professor Richard Van Velzen was appointed to the Department of Pathology and there was a huge increase in the number of organs removed and retained.

In response to the Redfern Report, the Secretary of State set up a Retained Organs Commission under the Chairmanship of Professor Margaret Brazier. It was a special health authority with the following functions:

- Oversee the return of tissues and organs from collections around the country.
- Ensure that collections are accurately catalogued.
- Provide information on collections throughout the country.
- Ensure that suitable counselling is available.
- Act as an advocate for parents if problems arise.
- Advise on good practice in this area.
- Handle inquiries from families and the public.

Its work was ended and it ceased to exist in March 2004.

Legal action by parents who had suffered as a result of the removal and retention of organs from their dead children in a group litigation action was initiated and the court agreed that the legal costs would be capped at £506500 (*AB and others v. Leeds Teaching Hospitals NHS Trust and in the Matter of the Nationwide Organ Group Litigation*). On 26 March 2004 the High Court ruled, in respect of three test cases, that where hospitals had illegally removed the organs in post mortem examinations without the parents' consent, parents could claim damages if they had suffered psychological injury (*AB and others v. Leeds Teaching Hospitals NHS Trust and another*). Damages of £2750 were awarded in one of the test cases, the other two lost.

In October 2000, the British Medical Association issued advice to its members that relatives should give informed consent to the retention of organs. It should also be made clear that relatives can refuse consent to a post mortem examination, unless it has been ordered by a coroner.

As a consequence of these developments the Human Tissue Act 1961 was replaced by the Human Tissue Act 2004 which makes it an explicit requirement that the informed consent of the parents or relatives must be obtained for the post mortem to be carried out, and for the removal and retention of organs or tissues and the introduction of criminal offences for failure to obey the laws.

The Human Tissue Act 2004

The Human Tissue Act 2004 repeals and replaces the Human Tissue Act 1961, the Anatomy Act 1984 and the Human Organ Transplants Act 1989 as they relate to England and Wales. It also repeals and replaces the Human Tissue Act (Northern Ireland) 1962, the Human Organ Transplants (Northern Ireland) Order 1989 and the Anatomy (Northern Ireland) Order 1992.

Human Tissue Authority

The Human Tissue Act also establishes the Human Tissue Authority (HTA) as the regulatory body for all matters concerning the removal, storage, use and disposal of human tissue (excluding gametes and embryos) for scheduled purposes. This includes responsibility for living donor transplantation. The HTA is also responsible for giving advice and guidance on the Human Tissue Act and for licensing establishments that carry out particular activities under the Human Tissue Act. One of the HTA's statutory functions is to issue codes of practice. The following codes were issued:

- Consent.
- Donation of organs, tissue and cells for transplantation.
- Post mortem examination.
- Anatomical examination.
- Removal, storage and disposal of human organs and tissue.

These codes give practical guidance for carrying out activities that lie within the HTA's remit and lay down the standards expected. The HTA (2006) Code of Practice Number 5 is on the removal, storage and disposal of human organs and tissue retention and covers the topics shown in *Box 17.2*.

Consent

The appropriate consent must be obtained to remove relevant material from a dead body. Further discussion on the appropriate consent can be found in *Chapter 16*.

It is an offence under the Human Tissue Act to remove relevant material from a dead body for any scheduled purposes without obtaining consent other than under the coroner's authority or under proper authority for criminal justice purposes. The HTA's *Code of Practice on Consent* (see *Chapter 16*) and *Code of Practice on Post Mortems* (see *Chapter 15*) provide further information on the relevant consent.

Use of fetal tissue

The use of fetal tissue comes under the provisions of the Human Tissue Act and the appropriate consent must be obtained to its retention, storage and use.

Box 17.2. Code of Practice 5 on Removal, Storage and Disposal of Human Tissue

Introduction

Scope of the Code

Removal

- Consent
  - Organs/tissue removed from the living
  - Organs/tissue removed after death
  - Coroner's post mortems
  - Storing tissue, including blocks and slides, for scheduled purposes
- Principles of acquisition
- Record keeping
- Cultural/religious considerations
- Preservation for transplantation

Storage

- Storage of whole bodies
- Existing holdings
- Storage of relevant material taken from the living
- Storage of relevant material taken after death
- Non-consensual analysis of DNA
- Methods of storage
- Appropriate storage period

Disposal

- Policy on disposal
- Organs/tissue removed from the living
  - The patients' wishes
- Organs/tissue removed after death
- Surplus material from tissue samples
- Existing holdings of unidentifiable and identifiable but unclaimed, human tissue and organs
- Fetal tissue

Appendix A: The disposal of existing holdings of unidentifiable and identifiable but unclaimed human tissue and organs

Appendix B: Disposal following pregnancy loss before 24 weeks' gestation

The term 'fetal tissue' covers any pregnancy loss before 24 weeks and includes a great variety of stages of development. Guidance on the use of fetal tissue is given in Appendix B of the HTA's Code of Practice on Removal, Storage and Disposal of Human Organs and Tissue Retention. Its stated aim is to help healthcare professionals to develop or modify their hospital's policy on disposal following pregnancy loss before 24 weeks' gestation. It refers to advice previously given in HSG(91)1916 and replaces the advice given in EL(91)144,17 which is hereby revoked. The issues covered in this advice were consulted on by the Department of Health in the 2002 consultation *Human Bodies, Human Choices.*

Fetal tissue can be disposed of by burial, cremation or incineration but it is vital to obtain the consent of the mother or couple to the chosen method of disposal. Incineration should be carried out in accordance with previous Department of Health (1991) guidance. The maceration and sluicing method of disposal is not permitted for fetal tissue.

Any use of fetal tissue for research or clinical purposes must also be approved by the mother or couple.

Application of the law to the situation in *Box 17.1*

The principle has been established by the High Court that where hospitals had illegally removed the organs in post mortem examinations without the parents' consent, parents could claim damages if they had suffered psychological injury. Many hospitals have however offered ex gratia payments to families who have suffered in this way, without requiring the family to go to court. Diane would be advised to seek assistance from her Patient Advocacy and Liaison Services who could put her in touch with any local group and ensure that her complaint was fully investigated. It may not be necessary to take legal action in order to have her situation recognised and compensated.

Long-term storage

In its *Code of Practice on Removal, Retention and Storage of Human Tissue*, the HTA suggests that long-term storage in tissue banks for future research may be acceptable to many donors or their relatives who have given their consent for such storage. But, it should not be forgotten that one of the most consistent complaints of relatives distressed by organ storage was that tissue and organs had, in fact, simply sat on a shelf for years with no prospect of ever being used. The Code of Practice suggests that NHS trusts and other organisations should therefore develop local policies for reviewing holdings. These should lay down:

- the frequency of review, and
- the criteria for disposal/further storage.

These local policies should take account of the duty to the donors to make use of their donations wherever possible and therefore the prospects of the material being put to good use.

Documentation

The *Code of Practice on Removal, Retention and Storage* states that

> *NHS Trusts and other establishments should ensure they have systems in place to maintain proper records and documentation for all tissue and organs they acquire and/or pass on to others.*
>
> *The Designated Individual (the person responsible for activities carried out under the licence and for compliance with the licence. Under the EU Tissue and Cells Directive, Article 17, the Designated Individual (DI) is equivalent to the 'Responsible Person') named in licences issued by the HTA should ensure that such systems are in place. It is important to be able to track what happens to organs and tissue for health and safety reasons – for example, should an infection occur, resulting in the need to trace people who came into contact with the material. Keeping proper records of donated material also demonstrates respect for the donation.*
>
> *The duty to create and maintain proper records starts with the establishment where the material is removed from the body, or where the material is identified as surplus to requirements for healthcare purposes and is set aside for a scheduled purpose. Such initial records should include:*
>
> - *details of who gave consent*
> - *exactly what the consent related to, and any restrictions on use stipulated during the consent process*
> - *what processes are applied to the tissue*
> - *if tissue is transferred, when and to whom and, if relevant, when and how disposal is undertaken.*

Tissue may be transferred from one place to another many times. So that an audit trail can be maintained, each establishment that handles human organs or tissue must have systems that can record:

- when the material was acquired, and from where,
- what has been consented to,
- the uses to which the material is put while in the establishment's care and any processes applied to it, and
- when the material is transferred elsewhere, and to whom.

The Code of Practice points out that European Directive 2004/23/EC requires that adequate systems be set up to ensure the traceability of human tissue and cells intended for human applications. It is implemented through European Directive 2006/86 in October 2006 which covers traceability requirements, notification of serious adverse reactions and events and certain technical requirements for the coding, processing, preservation, storage and distribution of human tissues and cells (2006 OHL 294/32).

Conclusions

It is hoped that the clarity provided by the new legislation and in the codes of practice published by the Human Tissue Authority will prevent any repeat of the organs scandals in Bristol, Alder Hey and elsewhere. The intention is that the consent provisions will be easily understood and implemented, so that parents and others will be prepared for the tissue and organs of their dead relatives to be examined and used for research purposes in the knowledge that their stipulations will be respected. In this way the development of medical knowledge together with respect for the rights and sensitivities of those bereaved will be facilitated.

References

AB and others v. Leeds Teaching Hospitals NHS Trust and in the Matter of the Nationwide Organ Group Litigation Lloyd's Rep Med 7[2003] 355

AB and others v Leeds Teaching Hospitals NHS Trust and another The Times Law Report 12 April 2004

British Medical Association (2000) *Consent to Organ Retention.* London: British Medical Association

Department of Health (1991) *Health Service guidelines (91)19 – Disposal of Fetal Tissue.* London: Department of Health

Department of Health (2001a) *The Royal Liverpool's Children's Inquiry Report.* London: Department of Health

Department of Health (2001b) *Chief Medical Officer's Report of a Census of Organs and Tissues Retained by Pathology Services in England.* London: Department of Health

Department of Health (2001c) *The Removal, Retention and Use of Human Organs and Tissue from Post-Mortem Examination. Advice from the Chief Medical Officer.* London: Department of Health

Department of Health (2001d) *Consent to Organ and Tissue Retention at Post-Mortem Examination and Disposal of Human Materials.* London: Department of Health

European Directive [2006] OHL294/32

Human Tissue Authority (2006) *Code of Practice 5 Removal, Storage and Disposal of Human Organs and Tissue Retention.* London: Human Tissue Authority

CHAPTER 18

Wills: Making and execution

> **Box 18.1. Execution of a will at night**
>
> Bill Murphy was involved in a head on collision when driving his motor bike on a motorway at 3.00 a.m. He was brought into accident and emergency barely conscious with serious internal injuries and coughing up blood. He knew that he was extremely ill and could die. He had not made a will, and was anxious to record his wishes. He asked the nursing staff if they would write down for him his wishes and sign it on his behalf with witnesses. The accident and emergency staff knew that they should not get involved in writing or witnessing a will but doubted if they could get a solicitor or manager to the department in time before Bill died. Because Bill was so agitated, they wrote down on a piece of paper what Bill said. Two staff then signed the will and another signed it on behalf of Bill who was too weak to sign it. Later that night Bill died.
>
> A few weeks later the accident and emergency department were notified that Bill's sister was disputing the will which left everything to his two brothers and nothing to her. She said that the formalities were not complied with and that it was not a proper will.

There are extremely strict rigid legal rules that apply to the making and execution (which is the signing and witnessing) of a will. This contrasts with the informality of the making of a 'living will' (except in a life-sustaining situation), which was considered in *Chapter 11*. If these rules are not complied with, then the will is invalid and the property will pass according to the rules of intestacy (ie. without a will) unless an earlier will, which would have been overruled by a later valid will, is in existence. (There is a rule that a subsequent will will repeal an earlier will unless it is the intention that it should be read in conjunction with that earlier document.)

Health professionals and wills

The best advice to nursing staff in relation to the drawing up or signing of wills for patients is 'do not get involved'. Ideally, if a patient makes it known that he wishes to make his will (the person making a will is known as the testator), the unit manager should be advised and the patient's solicitor called. The nurse should not be involved. The validity of a will can be challenged on several grounds:

- The testator was not mentally competent.
- The will was not executed according to legal requirements.
- The mind of the testator was under the influence of another person.

It is therefore wise to ensure that hospital staff are not involved in the execution of a will, since they could be drawn into protracted, time-consuming and costly disputes between relatives claiming the estate. A person under 18 years cannot make a valid will (unless on active duty in the armed forces, see below).

Mental competence

Since one of the reasons for challenging a will is that the testator was not mentally competent at the time of its execution, it is advisable to record the mental competence of the patient in the documentation and the fact that a solicitor has come to assist a patient in the making, signing or witnessing of the will.

Medical opinion should be obtained to confirm that the patient is mentally competent. To be mentally competent for the purposes of making a valid will, testators must be aware of the significance of their acts and be of sound mind, memory and understanding. If there is a statement in the medical records that the patient signed the will on such and such a day and that his or her state of mind was rational, clear and unconfused, while that is not in itself evidence of the truth of what is stated, it should at least contain sufficient information to assist professionals in the recall of events, should they be subjected to cross-examination on the patient's mental competence.

In a case heard in April 2006 the Court of Appeal ruled that a racehorse trainer who left his two employees a £2 million stud farm was so stricken with multiple sclerosis that he lacked the necessary capacity to make a valid will (Horsnell, 2006). As a consequence the will he made in June 2001 was held to be invalid and the farm was to go to his daughters under a will that he made in 1997. The Court of Appeal held that the question was whether the testator's mental state had crossed an imprecise divide beyond which he lost the testamentary capacity to make a valid will. It dismissed the employee's appeal against an earlier court and ruled that the will was invalid.

Undue influence

Another ground on which provisions of a will can be challenged is that the patient was subjected to undue influence at the time of signing it so that its provisions do not represent his or her real intent. Nursing and medical evidence thus may become crucial in any such legal dispute on the possible independent state of mind of the patient at this time.

In several cases both lack of testamentary capacity and the undue influence of another person have been argued to challenge the validity of a will. For example in one case (*Wilkes, in the estate of*) a brother, FW, applied for the revocation of probate on the grounds that at the time his mother executed a will in favour of his brother, GW, she was not of sound mind so that she was unaware of its contents, and the execution of the will had been brought about by the undue influence of his brother. The court held that GW had produced evidence of the testamentary capacity of the mother, and although GW was capable of being aggressive and difficult with others, there was no evidence that he was ever aggressive towards his mother. The application was refused.

Lack of testamentary capacity and undue influence were argued unsuccessfully in a case (*Allen v. Emery*) where the beneficiary of an earlier will (under which the beneficiary, a relative of C, the testatrix, was given her house) sought to challenge the validity of a later will, made two years later, under which the house was bequeathed to a friend of C. C died 9 days after the later will was executed. The court held that the defendant had discharged the burden of showing that C had testamentary capacity to make the later will and also the burden of proving that C knew and approved the contents of the later will and there was no undue influence.

In a contrasting case (*Vaughan v. Vaughan*), a new will was drawn up by G replacing one which divided the residue of a mother's estate equally between her four children. The new will left the bulk of her estate to her fourth son J and G died four days later. The siblings challenged the validity of the new will and the court held that while in the absence of actual coercion, undue influence could not be proved from the fact that a testator had been persuaded to make a will in favour of a particular legatee. There were a number of factors which gave rise to a suspicion that the will did not accord with G's intentions and J had been unable to remove them. Nor had J been able to discharge the burden of proof as to G's testamentary capacity when the disputed will was drawn up and executed.

Execution of a will

The actual signing and witnessing of the will is known as the execution of the will and strict rules are in force in relation to the validity of the process.

Box 18.2. Requirements of a valid will

Section 17 Administration of Justice Act 1982 amending Section 9 of the Wills Act 1837

No will shall be valid unless

- it is in writing and signed by the testator, or by some other person in his presence and by his direction; and
- it appears that the testator intended by his signature to give effect to the will; and
- the signature is made or acknowledged by the testator in the presence of two or more witnesses present at the same time; and
- each witness either
  - attests and signs the will; or
  - acknowledges his signature,
  - in the presence of the testator (but not necessarily in the presence of any other witness), but no form of attestation shall be necessary.

Additional requirements:

- the testator must be over 18 (unless in the armed forces or the merchant navy);
- the testator must have the required mental competence at the time he signs the will.

These have been eased slightly since 1982, but the revised procedures must be strictly followed. Any irregularity in the execution of the will may lead to the will being declared invalid. There are no special forms to be used although these are available. The legal requirements are set out in *Box 18.2*.

There is no requirement that the will is dated. However there are clear advantages in so doing if there are other wills and it is necessary to ascertain which is the latest. The testator can place a mark or initials to represent a signature and can have his or her hand guided to do so. Such help would not invalidate the will. A will could be signed on behalf of testator but the signature must be made in his or her presence and under the testator's direction.

Exemptions from statutory requirements

Certain wills are seen as privileged from these statutory requirements, ie. are not covered by them. For example, the wills of soldiers, sailors and airmen on actual military service do not have to comply with the strict requirements set out in *Box 18.2* and in addition can be made by a person aged under 18 years. Any form of words, whether written or spoken by the testator in the presence of a credible witness is sufficient to establish a valid will.

Other rules relating to wills

Any person who signs a will as a witness is prevented from being a beneficiary under the will and this applies to the spouse as well. (In one case where the solicitor allowed the beneficiary's spouse to sign the will, the solicitor was liable for the lost inheritance.) If the testator intends leaving a gift to the NHS trust or its staff, then no one from the NHS trust should be involved in the drawing up or signing of the will, otherwise the gift could be invalidated on the grounds of undue influence. If a patient or relative makes it clear that they wish to make a gift to the hospital in a will, then they should be thanked and advised to seek independent advice on the drawing up and execution of the will. The court has made it clear that solicitors have a duty to beneficiaries to ensure that a will is properly drawn up and executed.

In a recent case (*Humbleton v. Martin Tolhurst Partnership*) the court held that where a firm of solicitors were instructed to draft a will but did not supervise its execution, they had a duty to check that it had been properly executed when it was returned to them for safekeeping. In this case the solicitors failed to notice that the will had not been signed by the testator and the claimant succeeded in her claim against the solicitors for her loss of entitlement under the will.

Testators can dispose by will of any property or interest to which they were entitled. However testators cannot make a binding disposition of their own dead body, which would overrule the executor's right and duty to dispose of it according to law. This is however subject to individuals' rights under the Human Tissue Act 2004 to donate their body or parts for transplant medical education or research. (This is considered in *Chapters 16* and *17*.)

One of the effects of the Civil Partnership Act 2004 is that the Wills Act is amended so that any provisions relating to a married person now include a person in a civil partnership as defined by the 2004 Act.

Costs in probate cases

Who pays the costs of any legal dispute is extremely important as in a lengthy dispute, these could exceed the amount to be won. The usual rule is that the person who has lost the case pays the costs of the other side (ie. the costs follow the event). However in probate cases there are two exceptions to this rule (*Kostic v. Chaplin and others*):

- Where a testator had been the cause of the litigation, costs should come out of the estate and
- Where the circumstances led reasonably to an investigation of the matter, costs should be borne by both sides.

Application of law to the situation in *Box 18.1*

In the situation of Bill Murphy described above, Bill's sister may well allege that the will is invalid on the grounds of its actual execution. It may be for example that she could challenge the fact that Bill did not actually sign it (although as has been seen it is possible for a person to sign it on his behalf) or that it was not properly witnessed because the witnesses were not present at the same time. In addition Bill's sister may also challenge the will on other grounds: for example that he lacked the necessary mental competence (having just been involved in a hideous motor bike accident) or that her brothers had exercised undue influence upon him. (The staff may not be aware of these facts.) The fact that the staff were involved in the execution of the will, which is now alleged to be invalid by Bill's sister, means that they could be called upon to give evidence to the court about what happened that night in the accident and emergency department: Bill's mental state, how the details on the will were recorded, and how the signing and witnessing took place.

Conclusion

The possibility that staff may be called to give evidence in litigation over the validity of a will illustrates the advantages of nursing staff ensuring that, where possible, experts are involved in the execution of wills for patients and they are not involved in the witnessing of the will. Hospitals should provide advice on what staff should do where patients ask for help in drawing up a will. Hospital managers may provide on call assistance on a 24-hour basis and it may be possible to access a duty solicitor. Clearly there are advantages in setting up in advance a clear procedure, so that nursing and other health professionals are not involved.

References

Allen v Emery sub nom Cooer (Deceased) Re [2005] EWHC 2389, (2005-6) 8 I.T.E.L.R.358 Chancery Division

Horsnell M (2006) Workers lose £2m court fight over stud farm will. *The Times* **April 29**: 34

Humbelstone v. Martin Tolhurst Partnership (a Firm) The Times 27 February 2004 Chancery Division

Kostic v. Chaplin and Others The Times Law Report 11 January 2008

Vaughan v Vaughan [2002] EWHC 699 [2005] WTLR 401 BID check on the 2002

Wilkes, in the estate of [2006] W.T.L.R. 1097 Chancery Division

CHAPTER 19

Property and procedures following death

Box 19.1. Property of the deceased

A patient was brought into hospital following a heart attack at a garden centre and was found to be dead on arrival. His widow realised that he was carrying the house keys in his pocket and asked for them so that she could return home. The sister stated that the keys had to be left in the safe until after the post mortem, even though the widow told her that she would not be able to get into her house without them. She returned to the house with her daughter, but was unable to get in and had to hire a locksmith the next day (Wright, 2000).

When a patient has died, there is an obligation on the staff to ensure that the property is listed and accounted for. Usually the personal representative will arrange for clothes and small personal items to be taken away. However it is advisable that any property that looks as though it might be of some value is handed over to the executor or personal representative only on production of the grant of probate or letters of administration relating to the estate. A form of indemnity may be required to protect the NHS trust. This is the only way in which the NHS trust can defend itself if it is challenged for handing the property over to the wrong person.

The Department of Health's (1992) guidance on patients who die in hospital was replaced in 2005. This states that:

> *The care with which these possessions are treated by the hospital staff will be seen as a reflection of the level of respect and dignity with which the deceased is cared for.*

The guidance points out that the return of property can be a cause of complaint from the next of kin and may require sensitive handling by bereavement services staff. It gives the advice shown in *Box 19.2*.

Listing the property

As can be seen from *Box 19.2* there should be an agreed procedure for

Box 19.2. Department of Health guidance on deceased patients' property

- Washing and folding all clothing before it is returned
- Guidance to all ward staff about the care and presentation of the deceased's possessions
- Acquisition of special bags for the return of property
- The return of damp and dry possessions in different bags
- Policy of automatically disposing of soiled clothing rather than giving it to the next of kin
- Policy of accepting unwanted clothing and possessions from the next of kin, storing them for a period of time in case they change their minds and then passing them on or disposing of them as appropriate
- A safe in the bereavement service office for the secure storage of valuables due to be returned that day
- Provision of sufficient secure storage facilities within the bereavement service office
- Detailed documentation of personal possessions (especially those of potential financial or emotional value with the deceased's medical records
- The use of terms to describe jewellry and watches that do not make assumptions about what they are made of, eg. white metal or yellow metal rather than silver or gold
- A procedure to enable the timely collection of all possessions into one place so they can all be returned together to the next of kin
- Policy that all rings will be removed by the mortuary staff or funeral director in case they have to be cut off
- Documenting in detail the return of possessions, including a description of each item and a note about its condition, to be signed by the person who receives them

listing the property of patients following the admission of unconscious patients not capable of looking after their own property or on the death of a patient. The person drawing up the list should have a colleague present who could act as a witness, in case there was a subsequent claim that the individual checking the property had stolen something. No assumptions should be made about the quality of the possessions, hence the term 'yellow coloured' or 'silver coloured' would be used to describe a ring or bracelet rather than gold or silver, respectively. Notes of money should be carefully counted and valuable possessions should be placed with a copy of the list in the ward safe or handed over to the general office (or if one exists, the bereavement services office) for safe keeping. Relatives should be given a copy of the list with details over how the valuables can be retrieved from the management. Clothes should be bagged and listed and can be given to any relatives prepared to take them. Where clothes have been badly soiled or damaged as a result of the incident which led to the death, pockets should be checked for contents, and put into a bag marked for destruction and the relatives notified that this is the intention, although the relatives could have the option of taking them away (subject of course to any public health precautions). Further suggestions about clothing can be seen in *Box 19.2*.

Liability for property belonging to another

Voluntary bailment

In general, people do not become liable for other people's property unless they can be shown to have assumed some responsibility for it. The person who undertakes to look after the property of another person is known as a bailee. The person whose property it is, is known as the bailor. Thus, if a patient were to give a gold watch to the ward sister, the sister on behalf of the NHS trust acts as bailee of that property entrusted to it by the patient, the bailor. It is the duty of the bailee to carry out the instructions of the bailor and to surrender the property of the bailor when requested to do so or as previously agreed. In most circumstances, the relationship of bailor/bailee is a voluntary one and one person cannot force another into being the bailee of his or her property. When the person agrees to act as bailee (and there may be no reward for doing so), a transfer of possession takes place so that the bailee then becomes liable. In contrast with the usual principles of negligence, once the existence of the bailment is established, it is not for the bailor to establish negligence by the bailee, but for the bailee to show that he or she exercised all reasonable care for the goods and was not negligent. This is a reversal of the usual burdens of proof.

Involuntary bailment

Another duty of care could arise in relation to property under the law of negligence. If an unconscious patient is brought into the accident and emergency department, the NHS trust and the professionals have a duty to care for that patient and this would include caring for his or her property if the patient is unable to look after it. This is known as involuntary bailment. Involuntary bailment would also arise on the death of a patient in hospital. The hospital has a duty to take care of the property until such time as it can be handed over to the appropriate person.

Indemnity

Where it would seem reasonable to release property to a person who appears to be the next of kin or entitled to have its use, health staff can protect themselves by asking the relative (or other person) to sign a form of indemnity. This requires the individual taking the property to agree that in the event of a dispute arising, where another person claims that the property should have been given to him or her, the person who received the property from the hospital, will reimburse the hospital for any claims that the rightful owner might have.

The Department of Health guidance

The Department of Health (1992) recommends that units should try to confirm that any claimant who comes forward is in fact entitled to administer the estate. It advises that:

> *Units need not insist on Probate or Letters of Administration before handing over property to a suitable person administering the estate where the value of the property held by the hospital does not exceed £5000. They should obtain a receipt for the property which contains an undertaking to indemnify the unit against all possible claims.*

The supplementary advice (1997) advises that the local authority should be asked to arrange burial or cremation where the trust believes the relatives have the means to pay but are refusing.

Application of the law to the situation in *Box 19.1*

Had the hospital been more reasonable in dealing with the widow in this situation, they could have agreed that she would be allowed to take the house keys home that night, but sign an indemnity form whereby if someone claimed that she was not entitled to have those keys and was prepared to sue the hospital for having given them to the widow, the widow would reimburse the hospital for any costs incurred by it in such a case. Clearly on the facts it is unlikely that the widow is not entitled to stay in the house after the death of the husband, but there may be a dispute over the property of the deceased which involves ownership of the house. In the vast majority of cases there would be no repercussions following from the hospital giving the widow the keys, and the indemnity form should protect the trust in those extremely rare situations where this did not apply.

Box 19.3. A dispute over property

Following the death of Jim, a widower, his brother and his sister, who had not spoken to each other for over 20 years, claimed that they were entitled to take away his property from the hospital. This consisted of his clothes, a yellow wedding ring (which may have been gold), a watch (which looked valuable) and cash of £250. The ward manager was not aware of the dispute between the relatives and since his brother had been a frequent visitor to the hospital she gave the property to him. Jim's sister then arrived and claimed that she was entitled to the property and the ward manager should not have passed it to the brother. What is the situation in law of the ward manager?

Personal representative

The person who deals with everything owned by the person who has died is known as the personal representative. Where the deceased left a will, then the personal representative would be the executor who is named in the will. Where there is no will, the personal representative is known as the administrator and would be the next of kin. The personal representative has the responsibility of paying all the deceased's debts, taxes and expenses and making payments from the estate. When all these payments are made, the rest of the deceased's estate can be paid out according to the wishes of the deceased as recorded in his or her will, or according to the rules on intestacy. The personal representative has to apply to the probate office for a grant of probate to deal with the deceased's estate.

Next of kin

Who is the next of kin? Often this question is posed to a patient when a person is admitted to hospital and the answer may be 'my wife, my daughter or similar relative' and this is then written on the admission documentation. Patients may nominate a friend as their next of kin, indicating that they would wish that person to be the main point of contact. The law interestingly does not use the term 'next of kin'. Where a person has made a will then those entitled to inherit the estate are identified in the will subject to the rights of certain dependants to claim under the Inheritance (Provision for Family and Dependants) Act 1975 for financial provision out of the deceased's estate.

Where the person has not made a will then the personal representative of the deceased will arrange for probate and the distribution of the assets according to the hierarchy set by the Law Reform (Succession) Act 1995 (see below). There would appear to be no legal reason why patients cannot identify who they would wish as the main contact but this person may not be the lawful owner of the patient's possessions should the patient die. However the hospital can protect itself by use of the indemnity forms described above.

Under Section 71 and Schedule 4 of the Civil Partnership Act 2004 (see below), enactments relating to wills, administration of estates and family provision are amended so that they apply in relation to civil partnerships as they apply in relation to marriage.

Intestate succession

The order for distribution varies as to whether deceased individuals were married or not and whether they had children.

The situation for a married person (or person in a civil partnership) with children is as follows:

- The spouse gets everything up to £125 000 and personal possessions.
- Anything remaining is divided into two:
  - half goes to the children at 18 or younger if married,
  - half in trust during the spouse's lifetime during which time she/he takes the income; on the death of the spouse this goes to the children.

Married person (or person in a civil partnership) with no children:

- If there are parents, brothers or sisters of the whole blood, nephew or nieces.
  - The spouse gets everything up to £200 000 and personal possessions.
  - Anything remaining is divided into two with half going to the spouse and the other half to parents (or to brothers or sisters or their children)
- If there are no parents, brothers or sisters of the whole blood, nephews or nieces
  - Spouse takes the whole estate.

Unmarried person (or person not in a civil partnership) with children:

- Estate goes to children at 18 or younger if married.
- If a child predeceases, leaving children, they inherit.

The order for an unmarried person (or person not in a civil partnership) with no children:

- Parents.
- Siblings of the whole blood or their children.
- Siblings of the half blood or their children.
- Grandparents.
- Uncles, aunts of the whole blood or their children.
- Uncles, aunts of the half blood or their children.
- The Crown (or the Duchy of Lancaster or Duke of Cornwall).

Estate belonging to the Crown

Where the deceased died intestate and is not survived by any relatives, then the estate belongs to the Crown and, if over £250, should be reported to the Treasury Solicitor. If the patient was domiciled in Cornwall or Lancaster at the date of this death, then it should be referred to the Duchy of Cornwall or the Duchy of Lancaster, respectively. The Treasury Solicitor will require thc following information of the deceased:

- Full name
- Permanent address
- Address at which death occurred
- Date of death
- Marital status and if widowed, name and date of death of husband/wife
- Certificate of birth, marriage and death
- Details of relatives
- Details of inquiries to find relatives
- Age at death
- Place and date of birth
- Occupation and last employer
- Any knowledge of life history or visitors
- Any other identifiable property
- Details of social security benefits

The local authority has a statutory duty under Section 48 of the National Assistance Act 1948 to safeguard the moveable property of hospital patients if no other suitable arrangements have been made to do so.

Civil Partnership Act 2004

The purpose of the Act is to enable same-sex couples to obtain legal recognition of their relationship by forming a civil partnership. They may do so by registering as civil partners of each other provided:

- They are of the same sex.
- They are not already in a civil partnership or lawfully married.
- They are not within the prohibited degrees of relationship.
- They are both aged 16 or over (if either is under 18 and the registration is to take place in England, Wales or Northern Ireland, then that person must have parental consent).

Application of the law to situation in *Box 19.3*

It is understandable that a ward manager would give the property of the deceased to a person who had regularly visited the deceased in ignorance of a claim by another relative. The ward manager could have protected herself by giving the clothes and non-valuable items to the person who regularly visited the patient, but retained the possibly valuable property until such time as the letters of probate had been produced and they could then be handed over to the authorised persons. A letter of indemnity could have been requested, but where the property could have a significant value the preferable procedure would probably be to retain the property, since it may well be that a person who took property away when not entitled to it, would not be able to reimburse the hospital if the rightful owner were subsequently to sue the hospital.

Conclusion

There have been many disputes over entitlements to property of the deceased and there are clear advantages if health professionals follow the set procedure (with sensitivity that was lacking in the situation in *Box 19.1*) in order that they can avoid being embroiled in the legal wranglings of relatives. This means that staff must have a clear understanding of the legal position and make it clear to relatives why the rules must be followed at a time when the relatives may be extremely distressed. It is an obvious advantage to staff if there is a hospital booklet explaining the legal position and the procedures which are followed by the staff, which can be handed out to relatives and friends. It is also important for staff to ascertain if the patient is a partner in a civil partnership which will give rights as next of kin to his or her partner after death.

References

Department of Health (1992) *Patients Who Die in Hospital.* HSG(92)8 supplemented by HSG(97)43. London: Department of Health. Available from: www.dh.gov.uk/PolicyAnd Guidance/Organisation

Department of Health (2005) *When a Patient Dies: Advice on Developing Bereavement Services in the NHS.* London: Department of Health

Wright O (2000) Widow forced to break in to home. *The Times* **28 August**: 5

CHAPTER 20

Legal action following a death

Box 20.1. Untimely death

Diane was a staff nurse working in an accident and emergency department. One Saturday night several drunken men came in with one suffering from a head injury with blood pouring down his face. Diane asked him to come to a single cubicle, but against her wishes the others insisted on accompanying him. In the jostle, Diane was pushed to the floor and struck her head on the edge of a stainless steel trolley. Staff came to her aid and she was admitted as an inpatient and died shortly afterwards. Her family wish to pursue her legal rights after her death. What is the law?

The fact that a potential claimant has died does not mean that any claim that they may have dies with that person, whether or not the claim relates to the death. Some claims may arise with the death of an individual, others which existed before death, may continue afterwards. This chapter examines the laws which apply.

Law Reform Miscellaneous Provisions Act 1934

Under this legislation the estate of the dead person is able to continue certain legal actions as though the person were still alive. The personal representative acts on behalf of the estate and can continue actions which have already commenced or begin those that the deceased was entitled to bring but died before being able to do so. This includes the right to sue those responsible for bringing about the death of the deceased. The only exception to this rule about the continuation of actions brought in the name of the deceased or against the estate of the deceased is an action for defamation. In defamation the cause of action dies with either the injured person or the wrongdoer.

Fatal Accidents Act

Any person who was dependent upon the deceased is entitled to sue a person(s) responsible for causing or contributing to the death of the deceased, as a consequence of which they have lost their income and support that the deceased provided. The amount of compensation payable is dependent upon the earnings of the deceased and the amount which he or she spent on the dependants. The Civil Partnership Act 2004 amends the Fatal Accidents Act 1976 so that, for the purpose of having a right of action for wrongful act causing death, a dependant includes the civil partner or former civil partner of the deceased (S.83 Civil Partnership Act 2004).

In February 2004 it was reported in *The Times* that the husband of a woman, Lorraine Blatt, who died after an operation on a caesarean scar won a High Court case against her plastic surgeon, Winston Shaer, who was ordered to pay £261 938 to her family.

If the mother of young children were to die in a car accident where another driver was to blame, the children could claim under the Fatal Accidents Act for the loss of dependency on the deceased. This would include the cost of a nanny to replace the mother's services and the loss of the mother's pastoral care. The fact that these services may be provided for free by relatives would probably be disregarded. In addition, if the children were involved in the accident and suffered post-traumatic stress as a consequence, there could be a claim in respect of their psychological injury.

Where personal injuries or death occurs following a road accident when the driver was uninsured, then the Motor Insurers' Bureau will pay compensation. This applies even where the victim knew that the negligent driver was uninsured. The Court of Appeal held that a widow was entitled to recover compensation under the Fatal Accidents Act 1976 from the Motor Insurers' Bureau even though her husband, the deceased, knew that the driver was uninsured (*Phillips v. Rafiq and another*).

Criminal Injury Compensation Authority (CICA)

Compensation may also be payable to the relatives of those killed as a result of criminal actions. Further information may be obtained from the Criminal Injury Compensation Authority (CICA) which administers the compensation scheme. As an example of an award by the CICA, the father of the young person who died at a party held by Barrymore was paid £6800 in compensation by the CICA (*The Times*, 2007).

Criminal prosecution

An inquest will be held to determine the identity of the deceased and where, when and how the deceased died. The purpose of the proceedings cannot include the finding of any person guilty of murder, manslaughter or infanticide (Coroners Act 1988 S11(6)). At any time the inquest can be adjourned to enable criminal proceedings to take place. The police will investigate the death, passing papers to the Crown Prosecution Service who may prosecute those concerned. If the deceased was able to make a statement prior to death about the circumstances of his or her death then this can be taken and admitted in evidence even though there is no opportunity for the statement maker to be cross-examined upon the statement.

Accountability of health professionals responsible for death: Gross negligence

The House of Lords has recognised the principle that a health professional could be found guilty of manslaughter if the deceased died as a result of gross negligence on the part of a health professional (*R v. Adomako*) (see *Chapter 8*). The Corporate Manslaughter and Corporate Homicide Act 2007 which came into force on 6 April 2008 enables an organisation to be sued where a person to whom it owed a duty of care is killed by its negligence.

Continuation of legal action after death: Time limits

Where a criminal offence has occurred, in the case of serious crimes there is no time limit to bringing a prosecution against the accused. There used to be a time limit in a prosecution for murder, where the death had to result within a year and a day of the infliction of the injury. However this time limit was removed in 1996 and there is no longer any time limit between the injury inflicted by the accused and the death arising.

In civil cases there are fixed times within which a civil action can be brought. Under the Limitation Act 1980 in a case of negligence where a claim for personal injuries is being made, the action must be brought within three years from the cause of action arising or the date of the knowledge of the cause of action arising. However where people are of unsound mind or incapable of managing their own affairs (ie. under a mental disability) and the disorder prevents them from bringing an action within the appropriate time limits, the time limits do not commence until the disability ceases, which in most cases will be at death. Therefore if a baby is born with severe brain damage, the time limit for bringing an action for compensation in respect of alleged negligence which caused the harm, will not arise until the person dies. There is then a period of three years within which the personal representatives can bring the action (or longer if they lacked the requisite knowledge). In a significant decision the House of Lords ruled in January 2008 that claims could be brought by the victims of rape and sexual assault outside the time limit, if the judge ruled that the personal characteristics of the claimant might have prevented him or her acting as a reasonable person (*A v. Hoare; X and*

Another v. Wandsworth LBC; C v. Middlesborough Council; H v. Suffolk CC; Young v. Catholic Care (Diocese of Leeds) and Another).

Death of a claimant

What happens if the injured person dies before the limitation period? Section 11(5) of the Limitation Act 1980 states that if the injured person dies before the expiration of the limitation period (ie. three years from the action arising or the date of knowledge) then the time within which the action should be brought is three years from the date of death or the date of the personal representative's knowledge, whichever is the later.

Defamation and the deceased

As noted above there is no right of action for the relatives of a deceased person who is being defamed to sue in respect of that defamation. This is because defamation protects the reputation of a person: it makes actionable an untrue statement which would lower the reputation of a person in the eyes of right thinking people. Presumably the law considers that once a person has died, his or her reputation is of no account. The reverse is also true: if a person who is accused of defamation dies, then the action cannot be continued. Most health professional registration bodies, such as the General Medical Council and the Nursing and Midwifery Council, would require their registered practitioners to respect the confidentiality of the deceased and not disclose information given to them in confidence unless one of the legally recognised exceptions applied (eg. being questioned in court).

Human rights and death

The articles of the European Convention for the Protection of Human Rights, which were incorporated into the law of the United Kingdom by the Human Rights Act 1998 came into force on 2 October 2000. Article 2 recognises the right to respect for life and states that:

> *Everyone's right to life shall be protected by law. No one shall be deprived of his life intentionally.*

This article has been interpreted by the courts as placing a duty upon the State to ensure that there was a procedural mechanism whereby the cause of death might be investigated, and responsibility for the death ascertained, through an investigation held in public which must be both judicial and effective.

In one case (*R (Khan) v. Secretary of State for Health*) a child was admitted to St. James Hospital, Leeds and diagnosed as suffering from B cell lymphoma. She was given haemodialysis which included an infusion of potassium chloride. It was vital that the amount of potassium chloride being administered was regularly and routinely checked. She was given a grossly excessive dose of potassium. She suffered a heart attack and died. The hospital did not inform the coroner of the excessive potassium level and the body was released for burial within 24 hours in accordance with Muslim law. The police investigated, successfully applied for an exhumation order, but concluded that the precise cause of death could not be determined with certainty and the father was informed that no criminal proceedings would be instituted. The father's solicitor unsuccessfully sought funding to allow the father to be represented at the inquest, which was opened and then adjourned while the issue of funding was pursued. The NHS litigation authority admitted liability for the death. The father applied to the Secretary of State for funding for a public non-statutory inquiry. He was suffering from a psychiatric illness which affected his ability to deal with his own affairs and other people. The Secretary of State decided that there was no power to provide funding, and he was not prepared to hold a separate inquiry, the trust having conducted investigations of its own. The father applied for judicial review of the Secretary of State's decision. The High Court refused the application so he appealed to the Court of Appeal. The Court of Appeal held that the State's duty under article 2 had not yet been discharged; the family had played no part in the investigations by the police or the trust; the latter lacked independence and the blanket admission of civil liability in such a complex case was not informative.

While in most cases the coroner's inquest would meet the article 2 requirements, in this particular case, which was very complex, the father would not be able to explore the prospects of a verdict of neglect and/or a report by the coroner without legal representation. If the Secretary of State provided funding for the father or set up an inquiry the requirements under article 2 would be satisfied. A further hearing would be necessary to consider the funding possibility.

Application of the law to the situation in *Box 20.1*

Diane's right to obtain compensation for the civil wrong which led to her death will survive her death and her personal representative, who takes responsibility for her estate, can bring an action on behalf of the estate. The Law Reform (Miscellaneous Provisions) Act 1934 enables the estate to seek compensation for the death. The amount payable is regulated by statute and currently about £10 000 is awarded. This enables the funeral costs to be met. In addition, any person who was a dependent upon Diane (eg. her children) can bring an action under the Fatal Accidents Act to claim the loss which they have suffered from the civil wrong that has taken place. They would have to establish what proportion of her earnings they received (as opposed to what she spent entirely on herself) and claim for the loss that they have suffered. In addition in theory the estate could bring a private prosecution against those who caused her death, but it would be preferable (from the point of view of costs and administrative resources) for the Crown Prosecution service to bring a public prosecution for murder, manslaughter or grievous bodily harm. As far as her claim for criminal injury compensation, Diane's relatives have the right to make a claim in respect of her death to the Criminal Injury Compensation Authority.

Conclusion

The right of the estate of a person who has died to sue in respect of that death is important. However, under the Law Reform Miscellaneous Provisions Act the estate is usually only able to receive about £10 000, roughly the cost of the burial and funeral expenses. Where however there were dependants upon the deceased person, then considerably larger sums of compensation can be obtained, depending on the level of the resources provided by the deceased.

References

A v. Hoare The Times Law Report 31 January 2008

C v. Middlesborough Council The Times Law Report 31 January 2008

Coroners Act 1988 Section 11(6)

H v. Suffolk CC The Times Law Report 31 January 2008

Phillips v Rafiq and another The Times Law Report 21 February 2007

R v. Adomako [1995] 1 AC 171; [1994] 3 All ER 79

R (Khan) v Secretary of State for Health [2003] EWCA Civ 1129; [2004] Lloyds's Law Rep Med 159

The Times (2004) News item: Death payout. *The Times* 24 February

The Times (2007) Payout over Barrymore party death. *The Times* **5 December**

X and Another v. Wandsworth LBC The Times Law Report 31 January 2008

Young v. Catholic Care (Diocese of Leeds) and Another The Times Law Report 31 January 2008

Resources

Criminal Injuries Compensation Authority (CICA) London (headquarters) CICA Morley House, 26–30 Holborn Viaduct, London EC1A 2JQ; Tel: 020 7842 6800; Fax: 020 7436 0804

CHAPTER 21

Financial provisions following death

> **Box 21.1. No money for a funeral**
>
> Arthur Jones is terminally ill with cancer and his wife, Joan, who visits every day is overcome with grief. The staff nurse takes her aside to offer support and counselling and discovers that her main anxiety is that she has no money to pay for a funeral. Arthur was a gambler and Joan was unable to save any of their social security income for the future. She says that she would not want him to have a pauper's funeral, and she clearly does not know what that is or what help is available. What is the situation?

There are a bewildering array of benefits available from NHS trusts (for example, travelling expenses to hospital), from social security, thc Department for Work and Pensions (in which there is a business unit known as the Disability and Carers Directorate) the local authority and the Department for Trade and Industry. Each benefit has its own conditions of entitlement; some are backdated and some only payable from the date a claim has been made. Information on the rights and responsibilities of what to do when someone dies can be obtained from the Direct Government website. Any person who gives advice in this area must ensure that it is up to date. It is preferable to give individuals the source of where advice can be obtained rather than pretend to have full comprehensive up-to-date knowledge.

The following information is only a brief outline of the benefits currently available and further details should be obtained from the relevant departments. A new system for bereavement benefits was introduced in April 2001.

Benefits fall into one of three categories

- Benefits available as of right.
- Benefits available on a means-tested basis either through social security or the local authority.
- Benefits which are work related and eligibility depends upon meeting

certain criteria relating to length of continuous service and other conditions laid down in the legislation.

Bereavement payment

This payment is based on the deceased's National Insurance contributions and is a one off payment to the widow if she is under 60 or widower if he is under 65 or a person is over State pension age. Alternatively it is paid if the widower is over State pension age and the deceased was not entitled to a retirement pension based on her own contributions when she died.

Bereavement allowance

This is an allowance paid for 52 weeks from the date of bereavement. It is based on the deceased's National Insurance contributions and payable to a widow or widower who was aged 45 or over at the date of death and is not bringing up children.

Widowed parent's allowance

This is also based on the deceased's National Insurance contributions and provides regular payments for widows or widowers who are bringing up children. The person must be bringing up at least one child, or expected the deceased's baby, or expected a baby as a result of artificial insemination or in vitro fertilisation.

The Social Fund: Payment for funeral costs

Help towards the costs of a funeral is available from the Social Fund administered by the Department for Works and Pensions (DWP). The payment depends upon the financial circumstances of the person paying for the funeral, not the financial circumstances of the deceased. It is a one off payment which can be claimed any time after the date the person died and up to three months after the date of the funeral. It must have been reasonable for the person to take responsibility for the costs and the funeral must usually have been in the United Kingdom. If the dead person had assets, then the money can be claimed back from the deceased's estate. People eligible to claim this funeral payment are those who are in receipt of one of the following:

- income support,
- income-based jobseeker's allowance,
- housing benefit,

- council tax benefit,
- working tax credit where a disabled worker is included in the assessment,
- child tax credit at a rate higher than the family element, or
- pension credit.

The claim can be made to the Jobcentre Plus. An application form must be completed. Proof of identity may be requested by the office. The funeral payment will usually cover the costs of a simple, respectful low cost funeral, normally within the UK and covers the charges of the burial authority or crematorium, certain necessary travel expenses and up to £700 for other funeral expenses. The claim form may be downloaded from the Department for Work and Pensions website. However the grant may be reduced where a lump sum is due on the death of the deceased for funeral costs, and any contribution from a charity or relative and other financial support.

The Social Fund may also assist in providing community care grants, budgeting loans, crisis loans, sure start maternity grants and cold weather payments. More information is available from the Department for Works and Pensions website.

Other benefits

Other benefits are available, depending upon the circumstances of the widow or widower at the death (Department for Works and Pensions, 2003a). These include: jobseeker's allowance; child benefit; child tax credit and working tax credit; winter fuel payments; income support (minimum income guarantee); housing benefit and council tax benefit; and children with special needs (disability living allowance or severe disablement allowance). Information about help with health costs is available on an advice line. If the deceased died as a result of pneumoconiosis, byssinosis or other specified disease, the widow or widower may be able to get specific benefits. Further information is available from the Department for Works and Pensions (2004, 2005). Additional help is available for lone parents.

Remarriage

Remarriage by the widow or widower would lead to a cessation of bereavement benefits or widow's benefits.

Employment-related benefits

Some widows or widowers may find that they are entitled to receive a lump sum payment and/or regular income from their deceased spouse's employer. The employer would normally notify the widow or widower of this entitlement on being informed of the death, but a check with the former employer may be justified.

Probate

The personal representative of the deceased (the executor named in the will, or the administrator if there is no will) has the responsibility of applying for probate which gives him or her the authority to manage the deceased's estate. This may involve claiming from social security any arrears of benefits which are payable. The social security office should be shown form BD8 (the form of certification of registration of death) obtained from the Registrar and a form of application to claim the arrears should be completed.

Taxation

The Inland Revenue (2001) has published a booklet, *What To Do About Tax When Someone Dies*. This gives the basic details of the role of the personal representative, a trustee or beneficiary and sources of further information. It explains that further income tax on behalf of the deceased may be payable (eg. tax on property rents which were received gross), or tax may be repaid, capital gains tax may be payable (if capital gains exceeding the annual allowance were made by the deceased prior to his or her death) and inheritance tax rules. (Transfers between husband and wife and civil partners following death are not at present subject to inheritance tax.)

Application of law to the situation in *Box 21.1*

The staff nurse should reassure Joan and direct her to the social work department or other appropriate persons within or outside the organisation who can give her further information. The information should cover both the benefits which she would receive on Arthur's death and also any benefits to which Arthur is entitled. There is a scheme for rapid payment of benefits if someone is terminally ill. It would appear from the few facts given here that Joan is in receipt of income support and therefore she would be able to apply for a funeral grant. Should it turn out that Arthur did have some assets, obviously unknown to Joan, then the payment could be recovered from his estate. A check should be made to see if Arthur had been paying into a scheme to pay for the funeral or had a life insurance policy. If however he dies penniless, then Joan does not have to repay the sum. The funeral directors should be notified that the costs will be paid for from the Social Fund, and they will have experience in ensuring that the costs are within the amounts usually regarded as acceptable to the Social Fund managers. Joan may also be entitled to other benefits discussed here and should be given advice on where to seek full information of her entitlements.

Conclusion

Nurses and other health professionals cannot be expected to know the details of the current social security provisions and other allowances on death and for the bereaved. However since many relatives may worry (perhaps unnecessarily) about the consequences for them financially of the death, it is important that there are sources of advice and information available and nurses should ensure that they know to whom the relatives should be referred. The available benefits and the terms on which they are offered frequently change, so it is important that any information in the ward is regularly updated. There could be liability for negligent advice, if as a result of a nurse giving the incorrect information, a person loses entitlement to a benefit, because the individual is out of time in applying for it. The Department for Works and Pensions (2003b) has also published a general guide on what to do after a death in England and Wales.

References

Department for Works and Pensions (2003a) *Leaflet GL*. London: Department for Works and Pensions

Department for Works and Pensions (2003b) *What to Do After a Death in England and Wales Leaflet D49*. London: Department for Work and Pensions

Department for Works and Pensions (2005) *Leaflet DB1 A Guide to Industrial Injuries Scheme Benefits*. London: Department for Works and Pensions

Department for Works and Pensions (2004) *Leaflet SD6 Ill Disabled Because of Disease or Deafness Caused by Work*. London: Department for Works and Pensions

Inland Revenue (2001) *What to Do About Tax When Someone Dies. Personal Taxpayers Series IR 45*. London: Inland Revenue

Resources

www.dwp.gov.uk

Benefits advice line 0800 91 77 711

www.direct.gov.uk/en/RightsAndResponsibilities/Death

CHAPTER 22

Access to records of deceased

> **Box 22.1. Accessing records after death**
>
> Following the death in hospital of John, a dispute has arisen over his will and the allocation of his property. He married twice and had a son from each marriage, who have never got on well. In his will he left his terraced house to the son, Bruce, who most frequently visited him at home and in hospital. The other son, Ben, however, feels that Bruce exerted undue influence upon the father and that the property should have been equally divided between the two of them in the absence of any other relatives. Ben also believes that his father lacked the necessary mental capacity when he made his will and therefore the will is invalid on those grounds as well. Ben is seeking to access his father's health records to try and establish the mental state of his father at the time he made the will. He has applied to see the records. Will he be able to access them?

In *Chapter 20* we considered the rules relating to bringing actions in the name of the deceased after death and the relevant time limits. In this chapter we consider rights of access to the records of the deceased and rules relating to storage and retention times and the duty of confidentiality to matters relating to the deceased.

Access to Health Records Act 1990

The only provisions remaining from the 1990 Act are those that relate to the records of a person who has died. All the other provisions have been repealed by the Data Protection Act 1998 which covers personal records whether held in computerised or manual form.

Under Section 3(1)(f) of the Access to Health Records Act 1990 where a person has died, the patient's personal representative and any person who may have a claim arising out of the patient's death may apply for access to the deceased patient's health records. Where such an application is made, access shall not be given if the record includes a note, made at the patient's request, that he or she did not wish access to be given on such an application. Nor will access be given by record holders to any part of the record, if they are of the opinion that it would disclose information which was not relevant to any claim that may arise out of the patient's death.

A life insurance company may seek information in order to decide whether to make a payment under a life assurance policy and may require doctors to give information about the cause of death. Doctors can release information in accordance with the Access to Health Records Act 1990.

Confidentiality

The General Medical Council in its 2004 guidance to doctors advises that doctors still have an obligation to keep personal information confidential after a patient dies. Whether or not disclosure is justified will depend upon any directions from the patient; the nature of the information; whether it is already public knowledge or can be anonymised; the intended use to which the information would be put; and the effect upon relatives of the disclosure of that information.

Death certificates as public documents

The death certificate is a public document and can be accessed and the cause of death therefore made known.

Secrecy and AIDS

The Terrence Higgins Trust has published an information sheet on the disclosure of HIV on death. It reiterates the General Medical Council advice on doctors certifying the cause of death that doctors should identify a communicable disease, where this has contributed to the cause of death, rather than write in the immediate cause of death such as bronchopneumonia and also tick Box B indicating that they could provide further information. The leaflet states that the Office of National Statistics has confirmed that HIV/AIDS should ordinarily be regarded as a natural cause of death.

Post mortem report

While the findings of post mortems are not made public, the report could be accessed through the courts if relevant to an issue arising in litigation. If there is no court order, the relatives could give consent to the disclosure of the post mortem report.

The courts and anonymity after death

Several cases have been concerned with issues of privacy after death. Thus in the case of *Re X (a minor)* the court held that the interests of those who have been bereaved should be balanced against the freedom to publish. The facts of the case were that X was a young girl whose father died when she was seven. She was described as psychologically fragile and highly strung. A friend of the father wrote a book, the first chapter of which described the father's private life as being utterly depraved. The girl's stepfather saw a copy of the book pre-publication and was afraid that the account would be gravely damaging to a sensitive child. He asked the publishers to revise the first chapter. They refused and he applied for an order making X a ward of court and for an injunction restraining publication of the book so long as it contained the offending passages. The judge made an order making X a ward of court and issued an injunction restraining publication of the book until the first chapter had been rewritten in a form acceptable to the stepfather or the court. The defendant's appeal to the Court of Appeal succeeded on the grounds that rights of freedom of speech and free publication were at least as important as the rights of individuals, whether adults or minors. The interests of X could not be allowed to prevail on the wider interest in the freedom of publication.

The court has also imposed anonymity after the person's death in cases involving declarations about the withdrawal of treatment from a mentally incapacitated person (*Re C*). In this case the patient has suffered brain damage and entered into a persistent vegetative state. In 1995 the court made a declaration that life-sustaining treatment could be discontinued. The judge also restricted publicity regarding the patient, his family and the hospital to prevent identification of them. The Official Solicitor applied to the court for guidance as to the continuing validity and effect of the order restricting publicity. The President of the Family Division Sir Stephen Brown held that the restrictions on publicity had been made without a time-limit. There was a potential effect on medical and other staff's care of a patient if they knew that, on the death of the patient, their anonymity would be lost. That consideration also applied to parents and members of the family of the patient. The death of the patient had not brought to an end the need for the restrictions in the order and the order remained in full. There was no application to discharge (ie. end) or vary the order, but if and when such an application was made the position might be different.

Application of the law to the scenario in *Box 22.1*

An application for access to the health records of John could be made under the provisions of the Access to Health Records Act 1990. The holder of the records would have to check whether there was any note from John about withholding of access. In addition the court has the power to require the disclosure of records which were relevant to an issue arising in the dispute.

Conclusions

The death of the patient does not release registered health professionals from their obligation to respect the confidentiality of the deceased. Access can be obtained to health records of the deceased, but there are clear statutory controls over such rights.

References

General Medical Council (2004) Confidentiality: Protcting and Providing Information. London: General Medical Council

Re C (Adult patient; publicity) [1996] 2 FLR 251 Terence Higgins Trust Information Sheet Disclosure of HIV on death February 2003

Re X (a minor)(wardship: restriction on publication) [1975] Fam 47 [1975] 1 All ER 697

Further reading

Atkinson J (2007) *Advance Directives in Mental Health – Theory, Practice and Ethics.* London: Jessica Kingsley Publications

Bielanska C, Terrell M (eds) (2004) *Elderly Client Handbook.* 3rd edn. London: The Law Society

Brazier M (2007) *Medicine, Patients and the Law.* 4th edn. Harmondsworth: Penguin

Carey P (2004) *Data Protection – A Practical Guide to UK and EU Law.* 2nd edn. Oxford: Oxford University Press

Committee of Experts Advisory Group on AIDS (1994) *Guidance for Health Care Workers' Protection Against Infection with HIV and Hepatitis.* London: HMSO

Deakin S, Johnston A. Markensinis B (2007) *Markensinis and Deakin's Tort Law.* 6th edn. London: Clarendon Press

Denis IH (1999) *The Law of Evidence.* Andover: Sweet & Maxwell

Department of Health (1993) *AIDS/HIV Infected Health Care Workers.* London: Department of Health

Dimond BC (1998) *Legal Aspects of Complementary Therapy Practice.* Edinburgh: Churchill Livingstone

Dimond BC (1999) *Patients' Rights, Responsibilities and the Nurse.* 2nd edn. Dinton: Central Health Studies, Quay Publications

Dimond BC (2002) *Legal Aspects of Pain Management.* Dinton: Quay Publications/Mark Allen

Dimond BC (2002) *Legal Aspects of Patient Confidentiality.* Dinton: Quay Publications/ Mark Allen,

Dimond BC (2003) *Legal Aspects of Consent.* Dinton: Quay Publications/Mark Allen

Dimond BC (2005) *Legal Aspects of Midwifery.* 3rd edn. Hale: Books for Midwives Press

Dimond BC (2008) *Legal Aspects of Nursing.* 5th edn. Harlow: Pearson Education

Eliot C (2007) *The English Legal System.* 8th edn. Harlow: Pearson Education

Glynn J, Gomez D (2005) *Fitness to Practise: Healthcare Regulatory Law, Principles and Process.* Andover: Sweet and Maxwell

Grainger I, Fealy M, Spencer M (2000) *Civil Procedure Rules in Action.* 2nd edn. London: Cavendish

Harris DJ (2005) *Cases and Materials on the European Convention on Human Rights.* 2nd rev ed. London: Butterworth

Harris P (2007) *An Introduction to Law.* 7th edn. London: Butterworth

Health and Safety Commission (1999) *Management of Health and Safety at Work Regulations: Approved Code of Practice.* London: HMSO

Hendrick J (2006) *Law and Ethics in Nursing and Healthcare.* 2nd edn. Cheltenham: Nelson Thornes Publishers

Herring J (2006) *Medical Law and Ethics.* Oxford: Oxford University Press

Ingman T (2006) *The English Legal Process*. 11th edn. Oxford: Blackstone Press

Jay R (2007) *Data Protection Law and Practice*. 3rd rev. Andover: Sweet & Maxwell

Jones MA (2003) *Medical Negligence*. 3rd edn. Andover: Sweet & Maxwell

Jones MA (2007) *Textbook on Torts*. 9th edn. Oxford: Oxford University Press

Jones MA, Morris AE (2005) *Blackstone's Statutes on Medical Law*. 4th edn. Oxford: Oxford University Press

Keenan D (2004) *Smith and Keenan's English Law*. 14th edn. Harlow: Longman

Kennedy I, Grubb A (2000) *Medical Law*. 3rd edn. London: Butterworth

Leach P (2005) *Taking a Case to the European Court of Human Rights*. 2nd edn. Oxford: Blackstone Press

Lee R (2007) *Tolley's Health and Safety at Work Handbook*. 19th edn. London: Tolley

Mason JK, McCall-Smith RA, Laurie GT (2002) *Law and Medical Ethics*. 6th edn. London: Butterworth

McHale J, Fox M (2007) *Health Care Law*. 2nd edn. Andover: Sweet & Maxwell

McHale J, Tingle J (2007) *Law and Nursing*. 2nd edn. London: Elsevier Health Sciences

McLean S (2007) *Impairment and Disability: Law and Ethics at the Beginning and End of Life*. London: Routledge-Cavendish

Metzer A, Weinberg J (1999) *Criminal Litigation*. London: Legal Action Group

Miers D, Page A (1990) *Legislation*. 2nd edn. Andover: Sweet & Maxwell

Montgomery J (2003) *Health Care Law*. 2nd edn. Oxford: Oxford University Press

Murphy J (2006) *Street on Torts*. 12th edn. London: Butterworths

Richardson PJ (ed) (2007) *Archbold Criminal Pleadings, Evidence and Practice*. 55th rev edn. Andover: Sweet and Maxwell

Rowson R (2006) *Working Ethics – How to be Fair in a Culturally Complex World*. London: Jessica Kingsley

Stauch M (2005) *Text and Materials on Medical Law*. 3rd edn. London: Cavendish

Steiner J (2006) *Textbook on EC Law*. 9th edn. Oxfrod: Oxford University Press

Tingle J, Cribb A (2007) *Nursing Law and Ethics*. 3rd edn. Oxford: Blackwell Publishers

Tingle J, Foster C (2002) *Clinical Guidelines: Law, Policy and Practice*. London: Cavendish

Tschudin V (2002) *Ethics in Nursing: The Caring Relationship*. 3rd edn. London: Butterworth-Heinemann

Vincent C (ed) (1995) *Clinical Risk Management*. London: BMJ Publishing

Wheeler J (2006) *The English Legal System*. 2nd edn. London: Pearson Education

Wilkinson R, Caulfield H (2000) *The Human Rights Act: A Practical Guide for Nurses*. London: Whurr Publishers

Index of cases

Index of statutory instruments and statutes

General index

D

R

S

T